KITCHENS

THE BEST OF
Fine Homebuilding

KITCHENS

THE BEST OF
Fine Homebuilding

The Taunton Press

Cover photo: Kevin Ireton

Back cover photos: Roe A. Osborn (left and center)
Kevin Ireton (right)

Taunton
BOOKS & VIDEOS
for fellow enthusiasts

Printed in the United States of America
10 9 8 7 6 5 4 3

For Pros / By Pros™: Kitchens (The Best of Fine Homebuilding)
was originally published in 1997 by The Taunton Press, Inc.

For Pros / By Pros™ is a trademark of The Taunton Press, Inc.,
registered in the U.S. Patent and Trademark Office.

The Taunton Press, Inc.
63 South Main Street
P.O. Box 5506
Newtown, Connecticut 06470-5506
e-mail: tp@taunton.com

Library of Congress Cataloging-in-Publication Data

For Pros / By Pros™: Kitchens (The best of Fine homebuilding).
   p. cm.
   Includes index.
   ISBN 1-56158-329-4
   1. Kitchens — Remodeling.   I. Taunton Press.
II. Fine homebuilding.
TH4816.3.K58K585   1998
643'.4 — dc21   96-52597
                                    CIP

CONTENTS

INTRODUCTION

I NEARLY SET a kitchen on fire once. My friend John and I were remodeling the place. We had to start by removing the old cabinets. The gas stove was staying, though, and we were able to scoot it out of the way just enough so that we didn't have to deal with disconnecting the gas line.

On a job site, every horizontal surface becomes a workbench, so I threw a drop cloth over the stove to protect it from tools and hardware. While I turned to do something else, John swung on his tool apron, and in doing so, bumped one of the controls on the stove. A front burner came to life and instantly ignited the drop cloth.

John quickly pulled the drop cloth into the backyard, leaving behind an 8-in. ring of burning canvas, which I beat on like a conga drum until the flames subsided. In the end, there was no damage done, and I learned a good lesson about gas stoves. But I remember being glad the homeowner hadn't walked into the room just then.

You won't find that remodeled kitchen in this book, which is a collection of articles from past issues of *Fine Homebuilding* magazine. Instead, you'll find some much more interesting kitchens, along with articles about making countertops, choosing sinks, installing dishwashers, and other topics related to designing and building kitchens. Because they were written by builders and architects, discussing their own work, these articles amount to expert advice about the priciest real estate in any house: the kitchen.

—Kevin Ireton, editor

Designing a Functional Kitchen

Planning around your family's lifestyle and work habits will get you beyond standard solutions

by Sam Clark

The key to kitchen design is movement—how people move through the house; how supplies, tools and foods are moved in the kitchen itself; and how people use their arms, legs, eyes and hands as they prepare meals and clean up afterwards. A small, simple kitchen designed in harmony with this movement will be a more inviting and efficient place to work in than the most lavishly equipped showplace laid out with standard formulas and stock cabinets.

Siting—Begin with how the cooking area will fit into the house. Siting the kitchen in the house is as important as siting a house on the land. No interior design can compensate for a lack of light and air; so the first step is often to take down walls, add windows or move the kitchen to a brighter part of the house.

Remodeling a kitchen often means reorganizing the house plan (drawing facing page, bottom). Consider the chief activities of your home, such as cooking, eating, visiting, entertaining, sleeping, studying, playing, listening to music, cleaning, reading, coming in and going out. Your kitchen design to a large extent will determine how these activities mesh.

In some cases the best relationship between two activities or spaces is the same for most households. A kitchen entry near the garage, for example, is always ideal. Indoors, the dining table should be near the cooking area.

But on many questions, family needs will differ. The dining area is a good example. If your entertaining tends to be informal, you might want the dining table to be in the kitchen or open to it. Guests can help cook, and the cleanup crew need not be excluded from after-dinner conversation. On the other hand, you may prefer a separate and more formal dining room. It isolates the cook, but it also isolates kitchen mess. The same considerations apply when you decide whether to include a conversational sitting area in the kitchen.

Decorating magazines often recommend a kitchen play area for families with small children, but segregating the play area would be much better for many families. Similarly, the stereo, the laundry, a homework and hobby area, or a TV might either fit well in your kitchen or disrupt it. In general, a more open and inclusive layout works best when the family is small or relatively well disciplined, and when there is a quiet den to retreat to.

Siting and layout have a more telling effect on how pleasant and functional the kitchen will be than any decorating you might do. If your funds are short, spend first on the layout, and be stingy with the cabinets, appliances and fixtures. You can always upgrade the equipment later.

Three principles regulate the internal design of the kitchen work area, or indeed any work place: storage at the point of first use, grouping counter space and equipment into work centers, and ordering these centers according to work sequences.

Storage—Most people store things by category. The beans are stored with the flour because both go in canisters. Corned-beef hash and chicken noodle soup go together in a larder because they come in cans. In an efficient plan, though, foods and equipment should be stored where they will be used first. You rinse dried beans and dilute canned soup, so both should be stored near the sink. Flour is usually scooped dry right into a large mixing bowl, so it should be kept near the bowls. The canned hash goes straight into a skillet—store it at the stove. Think the same way about utensils. Saucepans are usually filled with water first, so they might well be stored at the sink. Griddles belong near the stove.

Many items, such as knives, can openers, mixing bowls, cooking oil, and salt and pepper, are used at two or three different stations. It makes sense to store them in several small stashes rather than in one central spot.

Work centers—Since different kinds of kitchen work call for different tools, supplies and work surfaces, the kitchen should be divided into distinct work centers, set up to make the basic jobs as convenient as possible. Though the centers have been defined many ways, I find it most useful to picture three basic centers: the *cleanup center* at the sink, the *mix center,* and the *cooking center* at the stove.

The *cleanup center* (**A**) is for dishwashing and for cooking tasks that require water. Its focus is the sink, which should have about 2 ft. of counter on the dirty-dish side (a good place for this is an inside corner where two counters meet) and at least 20 in. of counter on the clean-dish side. It also needs either a built-in dishwasher (24 in. wide and 34½ in. high) under the counter, or a large dish drainer, which can be built in above the sink. A trash can should be nearby. All the soaps,

pot-scrubbers and sponges you use for washing dishes are kept here. A set of drawers or wire bins for potatoes, onions and other non-refrigerated produce is nice if there's room.

Though tableware is often stored in a separate serving center, dishes you use every day really belong near the sink. The chore of putting clean dishes and pots away in cupboards and drawers all over the kitchen is archaic and unnecessary. If you have a dishwasher, build racks or shelves for clean dishes within arm's reach. If you wash by hand, a draining dishrack built above or to one side of the sink can be designed to hold most of the daily dishes and basic bowls and saucepans. This will give you a place to put rinsed dishes away wet, eliminating the need to dry or drain them first. Given this arrangement, washing dishes by hand will take about the same effort as loading and unloading the dishwasher, so you may decide to do without a dishwasher and use its space beneath for storage.

The *mix center* (**B**) is the place where ingredients are combined. Think of the mix center as your main work surface. It should be roughly 3 ft. to 5 ft. long. Bowls, whips and whisks, electric mixers and blenders, measuring tools, baking dishes, spices, shortening, oil, baking powder and grains are among the items properly stored here.

The *cooking center* (**C**) is the third major work area. It encompasses the stove, and attendent utensils—griddles, skillets, spatulas, hot pads. The cooking center also needs a work surface and a heatproof area to set down hot dishes. It's the place to store oil, some spices and the foods that go straight onto the burners or into the oven. You will probably need additional counter space here, either all on one side of the stove or in sections on each side. Often the cooking center is expanded to create a second large work area for preparing big meals and to make space for a second cook to work. I like a large butcher block here, and perhaps a compost drawer (photo p. 11, top) for easy cleanup.

Sometimes a large counter between the sink and stove, equipped with portable trivets and cutting boards, can serve as a combined mix and cooking center. This is an excellent plan for one orderly cook or for tight layouts, as long as a kitchen table or sink counter can be requisitioned when you need extra space.

Many books and magazine articles assign the refrigerator to the mix center. This gives

Three work centers.

The cleanup center (A) is at the sink. It includes either a dishwasher or a large dish drainer over the sink, as shown. Foods and tools used first at the sink are stored in the cleanup center. The mix center (B) is a counter where recipes are usually put together. Often it is next to the refrigerator. Mixing utensils and staple ingredients belong here. Open shelving makes it easy to locate what you need. The mainstay of the cooking center (C) is the stove. Frying pans are kept here, along with the food that goes directly into them. In the photo below, the pots and pans hang from an overhead rack. All of the kitchen centers have accessible storage areas.

A

C

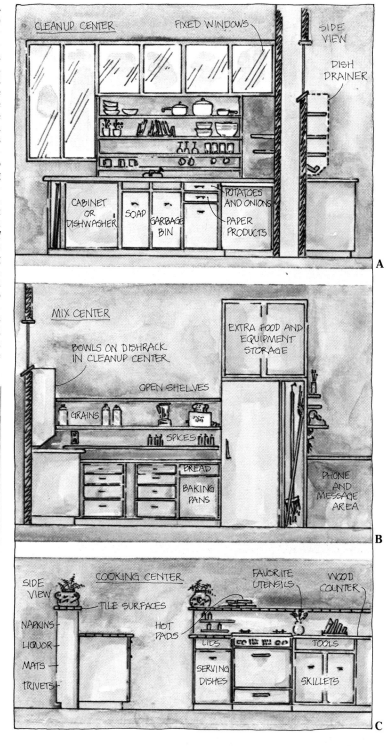

A

B

C

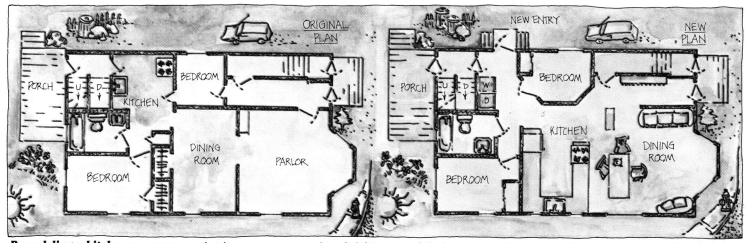

Remodeling a kitchen may mean moving it to a more convenient, brighter part of the house, out of the main traffic flow, yet close to the living and dining areas. In the original plan, left, the kitchen is far from the dining room, in a dark, cramped corridor between the entry and the rest of the house. In the new plan, right, a well-lit kitchen with ample counters is open to the dining and living spaces; and a new entry simplifies the path in and out.

the kitchen layout a nice symmetry: three centers, each with its own major appliance. But functionally, the refrigerator—along with a 12-in. or 18-in. counter on its handle side to make loading and unloading convenient—can be separate as long as it is not too far from the work stations. Treating the refrigerator as a fourth layout component gives you much greater flexibility because it multiplies the possible configurations.

If space allows, two small additional centers may be useful. A *serving center*, located on the table side of the stove, can hold serving bowls and spoons, napkins, tablecloths, or placemats, trivets and the like. Heatproof counters are handy here. Mounted on casters, a serving center can double as a serving cart. A *planning center* with a desk, cookbooks, a phone, a message board, pencils and mail slots is also nice to have if a small spot at the edge of the work area is available.

You'll also need spaces at the work centers for small appliances, bread, snacks, a radio, coffee and tea, and liquor. Sometimes subcategories of this kind are elaborated into additional centers such as a bar, a hobby center, a canning center, a recycling center, a snack center and so on, making the kitchen needlessly large and destroying its efficiency. I think it's best to keep things simple. Stick with the basic centers, and use special drawers, shelves or racks as subcenters.

Work sequences—When possible, arrange the work centers to correspond to logical work sequences. The drawings below show the travel path for preparing a cooked vegetable in two different layouts. In the one on the left, the path is short and logical from the back door to the table. In the one on the right, it is not. No sequence will work perfectly for all types of kitchen work, but a good order to strive for might go thus: from back door to refrigerator to sink center to mix center to cooking center to table.

Layout methods—Many books and articles on kitchen planning suggest arriving at a design by collecting "kitchen ideas" the way kids collect baseball cards; eventually you have a complete set. I like a different approach. Get a notebook, put a comfortable chair in a corner of your current kitchen, and watch what happens. Observe who does which jobs. Identify which tasks seem simple and straightforward, and which clumsy and time-consuming. Notice when people rub their backs in pain, when they reach comfortably, where collisions occur. Determine which jobs now require extra steps, and which can be completed with just a few. Kitchen researchers used to compare layouts by listing or photographing every reach, bend, search and step. Without going to the lengths they did, you can use careful observation to evolve your new or improved kitchen.

Based on these observations and your other ideas, write a program—a list of your design goals. It should include the ways you want your new kitchen to be different from your present one. Here's an example.

Cooking area: more storage; space for two cooks at once; space for freezer; direct access to yard and car.

Desired special features: very sunny; spacious feeling; family encouraged to help out; guest and cooks not isolated—guests help out.

Activities to be included in kitchen: phone; meal planning; laundry; canning; desk.

Things to be excluded: street noise; TV noise; formal visiting (separate parlor desired); older children's noisy play.

Dining: all meals in kitchen; seating for five daily, up to ten maximum with guests; dine on south wall, overlooking garden; no view of street from table.

Cost: money, $6,500 max.; time, ten weekends at ten hours of work each, or 100 hours.

Disruption: No more than a month of living in dust, but up to three months with some details incomplete.

Next, begin drawing possible layouts, locating the kitchen within the home, and the work centers within the kitchen. Include all areas inside and out that may be involved or related to the design. Beware of the standard U, L, galley, island, and peninsular layouts you see in all the kitchen books and decorating magazines. These conventions were devised over 30 years ago as guidelines for evaluating kitchens in mass-produced housing. They usually result in decent, general-purpose designs, and you can learn from them. Just don't be bound by them. In remodeling, for ex-

ample, trying to achieve a standard U or L could force you to move walls, stairs, doorways or plumbing that could just as well stay in place.

Beware also of the well-known triangle rule. The work triangle was developed around 1950 at the U iversity of Illinois as a test for layouts in tract housing. According to the studies done there, the distances between the three

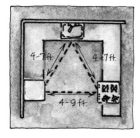

major appliances (the sink, stove and refrigerator) should be within the limits shown at left. If they are longer, the cook will take unnecessary steps. If they are shorter, the kitchen will be congested, and the work areas too small. Many people base their kitchen layout entirely on this idea. I think that intelligent storage and well-thought-out work centers are much more important.

Although standard design conventions are helpful rules of thumb, they shouldn't be followed slavishly. Draw your possible layouts as freely, playfully and loosely as you can.

Evaluating layouts—Evaluate your plans by comparing each with your design program and with the notes you made during observation. Fasten push-pins at the main stations of your plans, then wind yarn from point to point as you imagine performing various cooking and cleanup sequences. The length of yarn you use gives you a scaled measurement of the hypothetical distances traveled, so you can check the efficiency of each design for a given task.

Designing work centers—Design the work centers by making a series of elevation drawings in the same scale you used for the plans. Refer again to your initial program and to the notes you made during your observations. This is where the principle of storage at the point of first use comes into play. The design of the centers should reflect the specific ways in which each will be used. First plan the work surface itself. Most kitchen designs force us to work standing up, assembly-line style. If there's room, plan one or two places where a tired or meditative cook can work sitting down. An old-fashioned kitchen table, for example, isn't just a spot for informal meals. It also lets two or three people work sitting down and facing each other instead of staring at the wall.

In each area, find the counter height that leaves your back straight and your arms comfortable while you work. Have someone measure from your elbow to the floor while you stand straight with your upper arm vertical and forearm horizontal. For most people, a counter two or three inches below this point will be just about right for washing dishes, making sandwiches, and for most cooking activities. For kneading bread, rolling out dough, mixing heavy batters, or working with

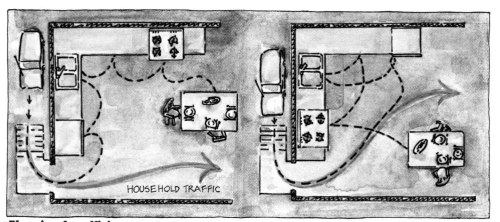

Planning for efficiency. Both of these layouts look fine until you trace the travel paths for a typical kitchen task. Then the superiority of the arrangement on the left becomes evident.

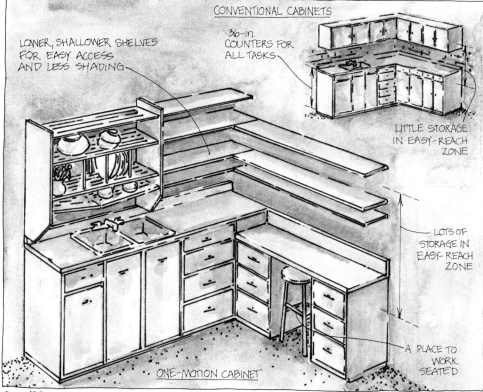

LOWER, SHALLOWER SHELVES FOR EASY ACCESS AND LESS SHADING

36-in. COUNTERS FOR ALL TASKS

LITTLE STORAGE IN EASY-REACH ZONE

LOTS OF STORAGE IN EASY-REACH ZONE

A PLACE TO WORK SEATED

ONE-MOTION CABINET

Sensible counters and cabinets are built for convenience. Storage is designed for specific contents, counter height is tailored to the task, and drawers make it easy to retrieve things. Most of the storage space in standard cabinets is hard to reach. All counters are the same height, and there are no special accessories like the composting drawer and the knife slot in the photos at left.

long-handled tools, the counter should probably be 6 in. to 7 in. below the elbow, especially if you bake regularly. This will leave the stove and sink counters a few inches higher than the mix-center counter.

Consider your counter surfaces carefully. Raw or oiled wood is good for chopping vegetables, but not for chopping raw meats (because of potential bacterial contamination). Tile will resist heat at the stove. Plastic laminate, polyurethaned wood and other non-porous surfaces are convenient at the mix and sink centers. Remember that you can always use trivets or cutting boards on top of a counter that won't stand up to heat or chopping. Just make sure that the sink counter won't be damaged by water.

Next, plan storage. If the first rule of work-center design is storage at the point of first use, the second is to give prime locations to items used most often. While it's nice to have all your bowls handy, it is essential to have your favorite one or two immediately at hand. Arrange things so that these everyday items can be put away and retrieved without wasted movement. Items you use constantly should be available with a single motion if possible.

A knife slot at the back of the counter (photo above left) is a good example of one-motion storage. The reach is short, there are no doors or drawers to open, and the knives, at hand height, are accessible without your having to stoop or stretch. The rack is fully visible, and selection is easy. The knives are handle up, so that you can grasp the one you want with the grip required for its use.

Remember that all storage isn't equal. Some spots are harder to get at than others. Any-

thing above 20 in. and below 60 in. (roughly between the knees and the shoulders) can be reached comfortably. The drainer, the knife rack, open shelves at or a little below eye level, and other racks just above counter height are one-motion locations. The bottom shelves of enclosed overhead cabinets and the top one or two drawers below the counter are almost as handy. You have to open something, but there's no bending or stretching. Lower drawers and higher shelves are accessible, but you have to stoop or reach to get at them. The top shelf and bottom drawers, which are outside the 20-in. to 60-in. field, are quite inconvenient. The worst spot of all is on fixed shelves behind doors in base cabinets, because finding something there inevitably requires a lot of shifting of the stored items and fumbling in the dark.

The drawing above contrasts standard and functional kitchen storage. In conventional kitchens, the best storage spot—the back of the counter—is the one place no storage is provided. Overhead cabinets usually start about 54 in. above the floor, which is at the top of the area easily reached by the average person. A typical base cabinet has one good storage spot, the top drawer. Most of its contents are buried in the deep fixed shelves.

A more functional model might look something like the one-motion cabinet in the drawing above. It would have narrow open shelves at the back of the counter, perhaps up to head height, or racks designed for specific contents. Almost everything below counter height would be in drawers, on rolling shelves, or on racks mounted to the inside of cabinet doors. This was the model developed by the Cornell

Kitchen, the most advanced and also the most ignored of the 1950s research kitchens.

Locate the most used items first. Then find storage for the items used regularly but not constantly. Finally, deal with the turkey pan, waffle iron and other infrequently used items.

A good test of the designs you draw in elevation is to imagine performing work sequences, movement by movement. Picture each reach, step or grasp, each opening or closing of a door or drawer. Think where your hand will be at the exact moment you need a tool—this is the ideal storage location. These imaginary movies are analogous to the string diagrams you performed on your layouts.

A kitchen designed in this way does not just save time; it changes what it feels like to work in the kitchen. Your movements as you cook become more economical, deft and sure. Work bounces and jerks less, and flows more. Because cooking becomes more artful and graceful, the work becomes a pleasure in itself.

The kitchen you design this way may look odd. It will probably have fewer doors than other kitchens, and more drawers. It will have more racks, bins, and other special storage setups. The various counter heights may give it a less streamlined look. However, it will cost less, because it will have been designed for function, not show. Perhaps most important, it will have been designed for the way people move through your house, and the way you and your family cook and clean up, so it will work better for you. □

Sam Clark is a carpenter and author. His book, Rethinking the Kitchen, *will be published in the fall of 1983 by Houghton Mifflin.*

Opening Kitchens to Everyone

Careful layout and varied counter heights make kitchens more accessible to people of different physical conditions

by Sam Clark

Can you spot the differences? Kitchens can be accessible without looking unusual. The cabinets to the right of the stove can be removed and the countertop lowered to create a workspace for someone in a wheelchair. For the same reason, the doors and toe-kick below the sink are removable. Cabinets are lower than normal, and an easy-to-reach dish-draining rack hangs above the sink. There's also room for a wheelchair to move freely.

Accessible kitchens don't have to be more complicated or expensive than conventional kitchens. The main component in accessible design costs nothing: It's called awareness. With small adjustments to details and dimensions, the kitchen can be convenient for people of any age, height, strength or physical characteristic. If done well, the accessible kitchen won't call attention to itself (photo above).

This approach can strengthen all kitchen designs, not just those for disabled clients. All cooks appreciate features that make it easier to store tools and supplies and more comfortable to cook (sidebar p. 14) and to move about the kitchen. I include such features in all of the kitchens I design.

A basic layout includes the proper amount of turning space—An adequate layout for mobility-impaired users is a nearly invisible element of accessible design. I make sure kitchens will work for those in wheelchairs. Although wheelchairs can negotiate openings 32 in. wide, passages, halls and entries should be at least 36 in. wide or wider where possible. A turning circle, an open area 5 ft. in diameter, allows a person in a wheelchair to change directions easily. I provide turning circles at strategic locations, particularly in the middle of work areas (top drawing, facing page). Most U- or L-shaped kitchens will have open areas larger than 5 ft. in diameter.

The turning circle can extend under cabinets to some extent. Making the toe-kick space 12 in. high and 6 in. deep allows a wheelchair user's feet to move under cabinets. A large knee space under a work top can accomplish the same thing. If an open work top is 48 in. wide, up to 19 in. of a turning circle could extend below it. The narrower the work top, the less a circle can overlap the counter. In the bottom drawing, the counters are only 4 ft. 3 in. apart, but the high toe-kick space and knee space combine to provide a nearly complete turning circle.

When a full 5 ft. of space is unavailable, as is often the case with galley or island layouts, an alternative to the 5-ft. turning circle, called the T-turn, can be used. A 36-in. wide knee space under a counter allows a wheelchair user simply to turn into the knee space and back out the other way to change directions (bottom drawing). When the obstruction is an island, eating counter or other built-in, it's usually easy to detail for modification later, if needed, particularly if flooring goes all of the way under the piece.

The American National Standards Institute (ANSI) A117.1 standards (Council of American Building Officials, 5203 Leesburg Pike #708, Falls Church, Va. 22041; 703-931-4533) give a more detailed summary of various clearances needed for full wheelchair mobility.

Drawers work better than cabinets and doors—The standard base cabinet has two or three shelves behind a door and perhaps a single shallow drawer at the top. It's hard to see things in the cabinet and difficult to get them out, and items in front obstruct items at the back. Many people find this design inconvenient, but to people who use wheelchairs, who have trouble seeing or who have any kind of difficulty grasping things or leaning over, the design is unworkable.

Drawers or rollout shelves are a better idea (photo p. 14). They bring contents forward into the light, and items can be easily retrieved. With full-extension hardware, the total depth of the cabinet is available for storage. When drawer heights are matched to contents, drawer bases will usually hold at least 50% more than door cabinets. Where the kitchen design requires doors, at least use rollout shelves.

In my designs, most base cabinets are drawer bases except where there's a specific reason for another configuration, such as tray slots. Because drawers are expensive, I make them wide, which doesn't cost much more than making narrow ones. A few huge, deep drawers can make sense, but five or six shallow ones sometimes are better.

The right door and drawer handles can make a big difference in any kitchen. D-shaped pulls are easy to grasp even for people with severe arthritis in their hands. These pulls are available in wood, plastic and metal, and in many styles and colors.

Lowering upper cabinets helps everybody—Standard upper cabinets are 54 in. to 56 in. above the floor, and even the first shelf is beyond the reach of many wheelchair users. The second shelf is just barely reachable by a short, standing person. The top shelf is available only to those taller than about 5 ft. 7 in. For wheelchair accessibility, codes require that the bottom shelf be no higher than 48 in. The simplest adjustment is to lower upper cabinets until they're 14 in. or 15 in. above the counter, which puts them within reach for many wheelchair users.

The area between the counter and the upper cabinets also is often ignored by kitchen designers. Shallow shelves or racks can make good use

Both floor plans allow 5-ft. turning areas

Turning circles are used where space allows. *Turning circles provide maneuvering room for wheelchair users and can be designed into a floor plan in various ways. One turning circle in this L-shaped kitchen floor plan extends partially under the breakfast table while another 5-ft. turning circle is available within the open area of the floor plan.*

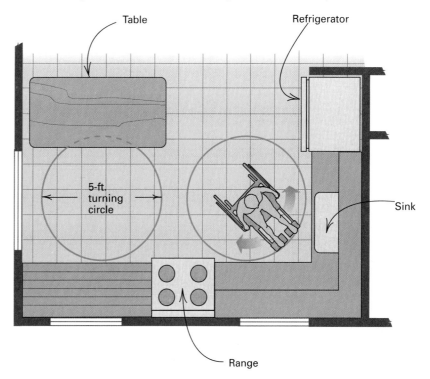

In smaller kitchens, T-turns work best. *A wheelchair user can make a T-turn by pulling beneath the accessible sink, backing out either way and pulling forward. The turning circle also includes the high toe-kick spaces beneath the countertops on both sides of the sink.*

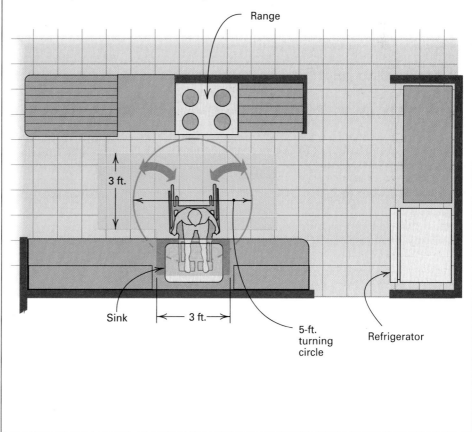

Choose appliances for ease of access and control

There are key points to remember in selecting appliances, although it can take some looking to find appliances that work well for accessibility. Knobs, switches and other controls of many appliances are small, are hard to grasp or require more force than the 5 lb. allowed in the codes. If knobs can't be operated with a closed fist, a lot of people might have trouble with the controls.

• Accessibility codes allow a maximum of 6½ in. for the depth of a kitchen sink. Anything deeper, positioned at maximum height, fails to leave the required 27 in. of knee room below. Most good-quality sinks are 7 in. to 8 in. deep, but major makers also offer special models, at a premium price, that are shallow enough. However, a little research at home centers has shown that many manufacturers make low-end single and double sinks that sell for $50 to $75 and that are around 5½ in. deep.

• Paddle-shaped or lever handles are easier to operate than round knobs. Large touch pads or push plates work well. Controls should be located where they're easy to see and to use.

• Faucets with levers or paddle handles are easiest to operate.

• Domestic dishwashers are designed to be installed under standard 36-in. counters. Adjusting levelers on the bottom allows about 1 in. of travel, although it's hard to fit the dishwashers under a lowered counter and still have them be removable when service is necessary. The Swedish company ASKO (P. O. Box 851805, Richardson, Texas 75085-1805; 214-644-8595), which markets its dishwashers in the United States, has some full-size models that fit neatly under 34-in. counters.

• Side-by-side refrigerators are the most accessible because both freezer and refrigerator compartments are within reach. Codes also permit single-door models in which half of the freezer compartment is below 54 in.

• At 36 in., the standard stove is too high for some users. The stove can be made easier to use if a knee space is provided next to it. Separate cooktops and ovens allow even greater flexibility. For example, a cooktop can be mounted in an adjustable counter with knee space below. A conventional wall oven can be mounted so that one oven rack aligns with the counter to make transferring dishes easier. With careful planning, side-hinged ovens of various types can be installed so that a pot can be transferred directly from the oven to the counter. Stoves also should have easy-to-operate controls located where the user doesn't have to reach across burners.—S. C.

Alternatives to fixed shelves. A person in a wheelchair could easily reach things stored in the large drawers on the left or in the slide-out shelves. This whole cabinet base also is removable to allow the countertop to be lowered.

of this space for storing frequently used items such as spices or utensils. I often build simple, open shelves, sometimes only 4 in. to 8 in. deep, that start close to the backsplash. Another convenient alternative to standard uppers is a pantry unit that contains many relatively shallow shelves, closely spaced and dimensioned to match contents.

There are no standard customers, counters and counter heights—Every customer is different, so every kitchen is different. The standard 36-in. counter is relatively convenient for most people who work standing. In custom-kitchen work, it's not uncommon to raise counters 2 in. to 3 in. for taller clients or to lower them for shorter clients. Sometimes sink counters are raised because people work down in the sink, not up at its rim. Baking counters are sometimes lowered to make kneading easier.

Counters set up for seated work are essential for wheelchair users. They're also desirable in any kitchen for cooks who get tired and want to sit down. Usually, this type of counter will be 30 in. to 32 in. high, and no higher than 34 in. It will be at least 30 in. wide, with a knee space at least 27 in. high. If the knee space is 36 in. wide, it can double as part of a T-turn space.

Cabinet manufacturers make a standard accessible cabinet for a 34-in. high counter, which is near the upper limit for the seated user and near the lower limit for standing workers. However, the evolving practice is to provide a variety of counter options—including seated work areas—and sometimes to make counter heights adjustable.

One way to offer choices is to build in a variety of permanent counter options. For example, the counters at the sink and stove can be the standard 36-in. height because of nearby appliances. A segment on each side can be lowered to 32 in. Also, a small, built-in table at one end can provide a handy additional counter with knee space and a place to eat.

Quick conversion to a barrier-free sink

Good design allows easy modification for wheelchair use. The author lifts the sink-cabinet doors off their hinges, raises the bottom shelf out of the cabinet and removes the toe-kick board, which had been screwed into place. The whole process of transforming the sink into an accessible kitchen work area takes less than five minutes.

Changing counter heights is easiest if two counters are separated by space or by an appliance. A change of counter material at an inside corner provides another natural place to change counter heights. I like to make kitchens easy to modify later as needs change, particularly if the current client doesn't want or need accessible features. Some modifications are very easy. In the photo on p. 12, an ordinary table can make an excellent open work area that can be repositioned easily. Work islands can be moved as long as the finish flooring runs under them. Changes to the cabinets themselves can be relatively simple if you plan.

In the kitchen shown on p. 12, the two cabinets to the right of the stove can be pulled out to create a wide, comfortable counter with knee space. The continuous kick space was precut to make removal easy. The finish flooring runs under the removable cabinet, just in case.

To lower this counter, I take out a removable 2-in. high section of the 6-in. high kick space. I se-cure such cabinets with a minimum of fasteners to make removal as easy as possible.

Sink cabinets present special challenges— Ideally, the kitchen configuration should be adjustable for different users. I've found various simple ways to do this. The sink counter can be reinforced at the front with an apron so that it spans adjacent cabinets and is supported by simple cleats at each end. The counter height can then be changed by repositioning the cleats. If the water-supply lines are flexible and the drain telescopes, no replumbing is needed. To maximize knee space, I like to have the drains swing straight back to the wall and to have the trap mounted on the wall instead of right below the sink bowl. It's also good if a removable panel covers the pipes to avoid contact with a hot pipe. A cabinet to the left or right of the sink slides out to make an area for working seated. I don't mind how this looks, but most clients want a more standard appearance, which includes doors un-der the sink. I've found a couple of ways to provide conventional doors and make the cabinet removable, if necessary.

In the kitchen on p. 12, European hinges can be unscrewed, and the doors removed. The kick space and bottom shelf have been precut at each side of the sink cab, which makes it possible for a carpenter to open the area under the sink with two or three hours of work. At a Friends Meeting House in Plainfield, Vermont, I did this more neatly on some custom cabinets (photos above). The doors are on lift-off hinges and can be re-moved in seconds. The cabinet shelf rests on the kick space and lifts out. The 3-ft. section of kick space is held in place with two screws, which, once removed, creates an accessible sink.   □

Sam Clark, a designer/builder in Plainfield, Vermont, specializes in accessible design. He is coauthor of Building For A Lifetime, *a book on accessible design and construction published in 1994 by The Taunton Press. Photos by Steve Culpepper.*

Custom Kitchen Planning

A designer's thoughts on renovating the home's most complex room

by Matthew Kaplan

The kitchen is the most difficult room to design. No other area contains such a crush of objects—from cereal boxes to sinks—and such a stew of human activities. Deciding which objects must be accommodated is one of the first steps in kitchen planning. At the same time, refrigerators, ovens and other mechanical helpers should not encroach on the largest and most important spaces, which belong to the people who cook, work and dine there. Planning a kitchen renovation to meet their needs means that both construction options and personal preferences must be recorded, organized and integrated.

Before I begin designing a kitchen, I interview the owners to find out what they will need. Their old kitchen is thoroughly analyzed and often reveals characteristics that can be useful in the new design, such as hobbies, collections of plants, or small dining areas. The most important element in developing a custom-tailored room is a detailed, written description of the owner's ideal kitchen. Obviously, later on compromises will be made for lack of money or lack of space, but I have found it better to modify, revise or even eliminate features than to add on in the latter stages of planning.

The kitchen form—As an aid in developing a written description, I ask my clients to fill out a kitchen form similar to the one shown on the right. It is organized from the general to the par-

---

THE KITCHEN FORM

Use of space—Describe in detail all functions.

Sewing/ironing/	*Desk*
laundry	*Play area*
Bar/dining-room	*Other*

Major appliances—Makes and models to be chosen during preliminary design phase. Underline those you would include.

Range	*Dishwasher*
commercial-features	*trim panel*
residential-features	*Sink*
Ovens	*number of*
double or single	*compartments*
gas or electric	*faucet action*
venting required	*spray, pop-up drain*
self-cleaning	*soap dispenser*
color, size	*chopping board*
doors - glass vs. solid	*garbage disposal*
Cooktop	*Grill*
gas	*Freezer*
electric	*Compactor*
commercial	*Washing machine*
residential	*location*
Refrigerator/freezer	*front or top loading*
ice maker	*Dryer*
color, size	*gas*
side by side	*electric*
top or bottom freezer	
trim kit	

Small appliances—Those you own or plan to purchase. Will they be displayed or concealed?

Toaster	*Electric knife*
built-in	*chargeable*
portable	*nonchargeable*
Toaster oven	*Can opener*
Coffee maker	*electric*
Coffee grinder	*manual*
Mixer	*drawer-mounted*
Food grinder	*wall-mounted*
Blender	*T.V.*
Ice crusher	*Radio*
Yogurt maker	*In-counter motor for*
Scale	*combination*
Ice-cream maker	*appliances*
Deep fryer	*Other*

Storage types—Concealed or displayed.

Foods	*Canisters for staples*
stored in quantity	*Spices*
and used daily	*location*
packaged, canned,	*Paper goods*
jars, bottles	*Tea, coffee*
Bread	*Wine, liquor, aperitif*
storage location-	*Pots, pans*
special drawer	*Fondue set*
Potatoes and onions	*Glassware and dishes*
type of storage	

Decorative

Wall	*Stained glass*
applied fabric	*Plants*
graphics	

Other considerations

Intercom	*New doors and*
Smoke detector	*windows*
Burglar alarm	*Air conditioning*
Fire extinguisher	*Lighting*

---

ticular, from the description of functions to the housing of kitchen equipment and supplies.

Use of space. If the kitchen is complex, it is also the most versatile space in the house, and you can't spend too much time discussing use. It is used for cooking and dining in traditional ways, for kibitzing over coffee with neighbors, and even for paying bills and doing homework. If there are young children, incidentally, now is the time to take their presence into account so that you can design tamper-proof storage areas and safe play areas.

Major appliances. Consider large appliances next because, after spaces for people, these take up the most room. Many people decide to buy new appliances when renovating kitchens. Although the information about types, sizes and special features is not crucial in the early stages of planning, it's important to order appliances as soon as possible. By setting up delivery dates about two months before the anticipated completion of the project, you may avoid price increases and you'll expedite construction. If an incorrect model is sent, it can be returned at once and little harm will be done. If you are planning to include custom cabinet work, the cabinetmaker can ascertain exact sizes and note the location of appliance seams that might affect cabinet detailing. Electricians and plumbers can determine in advance what connections will be necessary. The disadvantages of ordering appli-

Within this 15-ft. by 15-ft. kitchen there is an informal dining area, an island counter, the usual battery of appliances, a pastry counter and a wine vault housing 1,000 bottles.

This kitchen was designed so that two cooks could work there simultaneously. All the details—from appliance choices to activities—were discussed before plans were drawn.

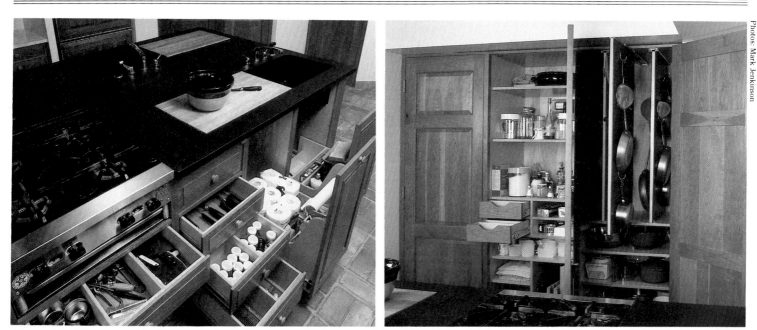

Photos: Mark Jenkinson

Above, cleft slate was used for the countertop (left) because of its beauty and durability. Although it is expensive and heavy, hot pots cannot damage it. Two maple cutting boards were recessed in the slate. Under-counter drawer space was designed to accommodate the owners' needs. Floor-to-ceiling pantry and cabinet (right) was designed to accommodate all sizes of pots and pans.

Cabinets and Countertops—

Cabinet design requires a bit of head-scratching. For the kitchen shown on these pages the clients wanted a tone of warmth and elegance. The cherry gave the warmth; the molding, the elegance.

Once we had decided upon the molding profile shown below, I thought about joinery. I had intended to mill the profile into the rails and stiles, joining the corners with a mortise-and-tenon joint and coping the ends of the rails to the profile of the stiles, giving a good fit with lots of gluing surface. But a molding so ornate made coping impossible. I decided to join the stile and rail with a spline joint, and add the door molding afterwards.

After several hundred feet of cherry molding

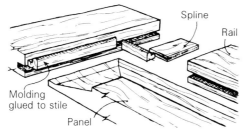

Spline
Rail
Molding glued to stile
Panel

had been milled to my specifications, I realized that it would dwarf the panels. After many experiments, I decided to cut down the molding, using just the curl. I think it works—a little spicy, but light-handed.

The slate countertops are held in place by gravity. I ran a bead of silicone on the top of the ¾-in. plywood frame and used black silicone between slate edges, but otherwise used no hardware—no L-braces or joining plates—to attach slate to wood. Although the top of the slate is cleft and quite irregular, the bottom is finely cut and perfectly flat.

Cooking surfaces built into wooden cabinets can be problematic and dangerous because extreme changes in temperature or moisture are hard on wood. To isolate the cooktop's intense heat, I lined its opening in the cabinet with Transite insulation board and then fitted a specially fabricated stainless-steel liner. Because this insulation board has asbestos fibers, cutting it with a saw will put these fibers into the air and your lungs. Instead of cutting, I suggest wetting and scoring it repeatedly with a utility knife until you can snap it easily.   □

—Peter Dechar, a cabinetmaker in Brooklyn, N.Y.

ances early are the possibility of theft if no one lives in the building, or that they'll be in the way during construction.

Selections of major appliances are influenced by how the owner will use the appliance, performance of the appliance, size and capacities needed, gas or electric hookups, optional accessories wanted and durability. The choices are narrowed down until they coincide with the space available, the location of utility lines and the kinds of finished surfaces planned for the completed kitchen. Here are some points to consider in deciding on appliances:

Commercial ranges are expensive and take up too much space; their purchase is unjustified for most households. Domestic ranges are the best bet, especially easy-to-clean models with trim that overlaps the countertop.

Double ovens allow for simultaneous preparation of dishes that require different cooking temperatures. The height of the double ovens is flexible; I like to position the top one so that its open door will align with the countertop. This allows for the easy transfer of hot dishes.

Cooktops are often used in conjunction with double ovens. I recommend cooktops 30 in. long because they consume little counter space and their shallow depth allows more drawer space underneath. The standard height of cooktops is about 36 in., but I place them slightly lower, from 32 in. to 34 in. This height allows easier stirring and a better view into deep pots. Because many cooktop dishes need short cooking times and high temperatures, I favor gas cooktops over electric. Either type should have removable trays under each burner and removable tops for easier cleaning.

A dishwasher with the fewest buttons is the best choice. Not only will it be less expensive, but most of the buttons on complex models are seldom used anyway.

Sink styles are nearly infinite, and selection depends upon the cook's preferences. Heavy-duty sinks are worth the extra money. Stainless-steel sinks pair nicely with plastic laminate counters, and synthetic stone sinks work well with slate, granite or marble counters. Sink height depends on the height of the principal cook; best in general is the 32-in. to 34-in. height I recommend for cooktops. A lever-type faucet is

handy because you can turn it with your wrist if your hands are dirty. Pop-up drains obviate having to fish in hot, greasy water for drain plugs.

Washers and dryers stacked vertically conserve space, an advantage in small rooms; side-by-side machines under counters also create unobtrusive laundry areas.

Small appliances and storage. After locating major appliances and cabinets, think about any special equipment you'd like to have close at hand. It's useful to know if an extensive collection of small appliances will require additional outlets or if a blender needs an in-counter motor. Some people are crazy about their spices and like to display them in special racks. Others want to have such staples as potatoes and onions close at hand. These specifics are important once work begins on preliminary drawings, because the counter space must accommodate all the equipment and supplies that will be used there.

Lighting. Make sure that working surfaces are broadly illuminated. Although I prefer the warm light of incandescent bulbs, newly developed warm-white fluorescent tubes are worth considering. They use less electricity, burn cooler and

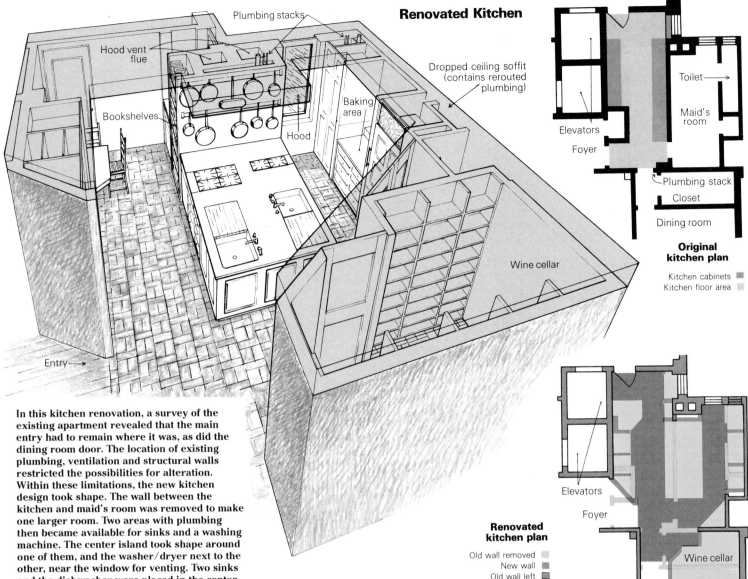

Renovated Kitchen

Plumbing stacks

Hood vent flue

Bookshelves

Hood

Baking area

Dropped ceiling soffit (contains rerouted plumbing)

Entry →

Wine cellar

Original kitchen plan

Toilet →

Maid's room

Elevators

Foyer

Plumbing stack

Closet

Dining room

Kitchen cabinets ▨
Kitchen floor area ▨

Renovated kitchen plan

Old wall removed ▨
New wall ▨
Old wall left ▨
New kitchen cabinets and closets ▨
New kitchen floor area ▨

Elevators

Foyer

Wine cellar

Dining room

In this kitchen renovation, a survey of the existing apartment revealed that the main entry had to remain where it was, as did the dining room door. The location of existing plumbing, ventilation and structural walls restricted the possibilities for alteration. Within these limitations, the new kitchen design took shape. The wall between the kitchen and maid's room was removed to make one larger room. Two areas with plumbing then became available for sinks and a washing machine. The center island took shape around one of them, and the washer/dryer next to the other, near the window for venting. Two sinks and the dishwasher were placed in the center island. Gas cooktops are near the existing chimney flue for venting.

provide more diffuse light. If you want light fixtures inside vent hoods, use commercial housings to seal out moisture and to contain the glass bulb should it break.

Surveying the space—Photos of the existing kitchen layout are helpful during schematic drawing stages, so take them as early as possible. Photos record stylistic elements such as intricate plaster work, wood moldings or paneling that may affect the final design, if you are trying to preserve the style.

After measuring the kitchen, document the composition and condition of existing surfaces and the locations of existing mechanicals, such as plumbing, electrical wiring and vents. Information about these systems is easy to get: Where were the old appliances, fixtures and the lines that served them? To be sure I remember the location of mechanicals, I'll often sketch in the systems on Polaroid photos while I'm on the site. But to know for sure what is behind the walls, it's sometimes necessary to cut into them. By determining the routes of mechanical systems early, you know the parameters of dif-

ferent design solutions. For example, you may not want to move sinks and dishwashers across a room if it means installing a new system of drain pipes to accommodate them. Although pipes and wiring are flexible to a degree, some choices are prohibitively expensive. Cutting into walls for a look can be crucial, for surprises uncovered after construction begins can make meticulously drawn plans useless.

Schematic drawings—From the filled-in kitchen forms and the survey you'll have enough information to begin drawing a number of kitchen schematics. There are as many methods of depicting kitchen space as there are books on the subject, but I prefer to draw a basic floor plan from the survey and to sketch various alternatives on tissue-paper overlays. I prefer a scale of ½ in. to 1 ft. Any larger size requires an inordinate amount of drawing, and anything smaller produces drawings without much detail.

The order of allocating space roughly follows that of the kitchen form, beginning with the movement of people. Main corridors must always be wide—3 ft. to 3½ ft. is minimum—so

that people returning home with groceries or passing while cooking have enough room. If several cooks will be working together, all the corridors should be at least 3 ft. wide.

Venting and waste line requirements have a lot to do with appliance location. Sinks, washing machines, gas cooktops and electric ovens require venting to the outside and should be placed as close as possible to a wall or a chimney vent (shown in the drawing above). Gas ovens and refrigerators are the most flexible to place.

Counter space is always a battle at the end, for each major appliance must have a counter next to it. Calculate drawer and shelf space when you sketch what each wall of cabinets and appliances will look like. Pantries and floor-to-ceiling storage cabinets save space and are more convenient to use than conventional cabinets.

Where confusion about the drawings persists, chalk final plans on walls or floors. This way you can walk around in the space and live with it awhile before beginning construction. □

Mathew Kaplan is an architect who practices in Brooklyn, N.Y.

Expanding a Kitchen, Step by Step

In renovation, one thing always leads to another

by Eric K. Rekdahl

Renovation work is full of surprises. Even in simple-looking jobs, digging into one area will invariably expose unanticipated problems in another, which in turn will force you to rearrange something else. Good renovators are clever enough both to anticipate some of the trouble they're likely to run into and to know that lots more will show up. They are flexible enough to improvise when plans go awry, and imaginative enough to take advantage of situations as they arise. Technical skills are also important to minimize tedium and frustration.

When Dick and Renie Riemann acquired their 1928 Tudor Revival house, designed by the architect John Hudson Thomas, they also inherited a kitchen with 48 sq. ft. of floor space and 5½ ft. of countertop, separated from the dining room by two doors and a pantry (drawing, below). The refrigerator was in the laundry, a sagging foundation was causing the floor to droop, and inadequate framing had cracked the plaster.

The Riemanns wanted a modern, functional kitchen with a family eating area and a desk for planning. They wanted an open, informal space, with enough room for guests to chat with the cook. The obvious solution was to eliminate as many walls as possible, streamlining the maze-like circulation created by the pantry, kitchen and laundry room. They also wanted to enlarge the kitchen by enclosing an area north of the laundry wall that was covered by an overhanging second-story bedroom floor.

Laundry wall—The area was broken up into so many small rooms that we hardly had space to set up our equipment and move around. By removing the non load-bearing walls (D, G and E in the drawing), we created a good-sized working area. This was straightforward work, except for a problem we had anticipated: The cast-iron drain from an upstairs toilet ran through wall D. We disconnected the plumbing and removed the pipe. It would have to be relocated later.

Then we tackled wall B, the laundry's north wall. It was framed with a 2x4 stud wall, which carried 4x6 floor joists for the bedroom above. Instead of removing the wall and replacing the top plate with an 8x10, we kept the double 2x4 top plate and sandwiched it between two rough-

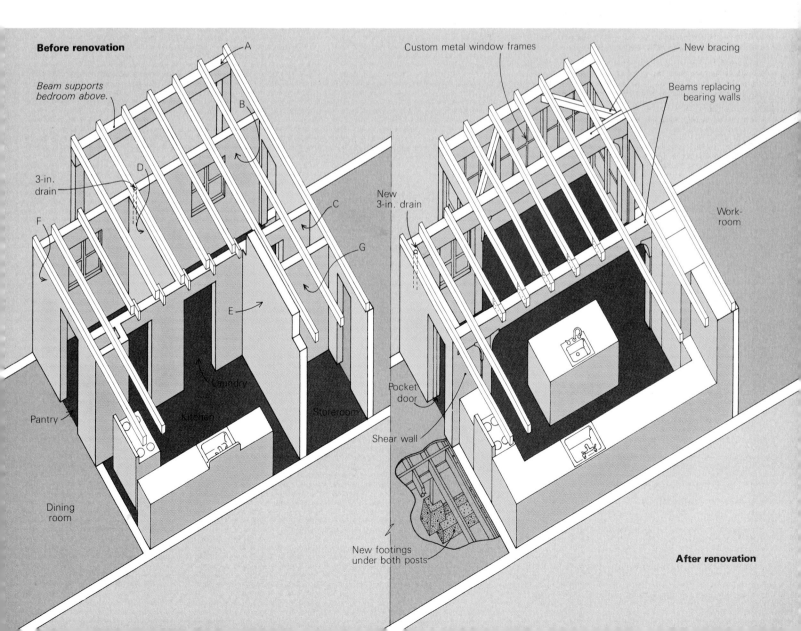

Before renovation

Beam supports bedroom above.

3-in. drain

Pantry

Dining room

Laundry

Kitchen

Custom metal window frames

New bracing

Beams replacing bearing walls

New 3-in. drain

Work-room

Pocket door

Shear wall

Storeroom

New footings under both posts

After renovation

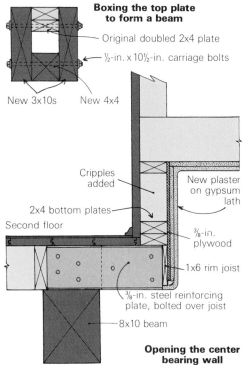

Boxing the top plate to form a beam

— Original doubled 2x4 plate

— ½-in. x 10½-in. carriage bolts

New 3x10s   New 4x4

Cripples added

2x4 bottom plates

Second floor

New plaster on gypsum lath

⅜-in. plywood

1x6 rim joist

⅜-in. steel reinforcing plate, bolted over joist

8x10 beam

Opening the center bearing wall

Opening up the north wall of the kitchen revealed 10-in. long 2x6s supporting an upstairs wall (below). These were replaced with steel plates and 4x6s, as shown above. At the south side of the kitchen (bottom), joists were attached without cripples or blocking.

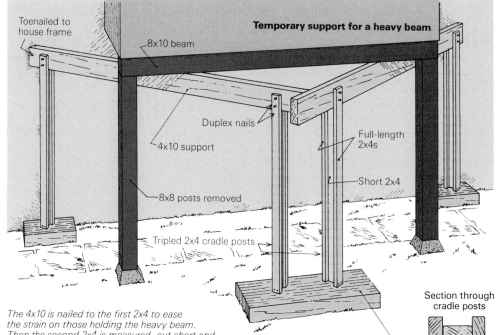

Toenailed to house frame

Temporary support for a heavy beam

8x10 beam

Duplex nails

4x10 support

8x8 posts removed

Tripled 2x4 cradle posts

Full-length 2x4s

Short 2x4

Section through cradle posts

Scrap as base for posts

The 4x10 is nailed to the first 2x4 to ease the strain on those holding the heavy beam. Then the second 2x4 is measured, cut short and nailed in place. The final 2x4 completes the cradle.

sawn 3x10s. This way we could use the old framing as bracing while using the same sandwich approach to beef up the posts at the beam ends. After the 3x10s were bolted in place, we removed the stud frame. To complete the beam we bolted a 4x4 between the 3x10s, flush with their bottom edges (drawing, above left).

The upstairs bedroom floor joists extended 4½ ft. beyond the laundry wall to rest on an 8x10 beam (A in the drawing on the previous page), supported by 8x8 posts just beyond a concrete path. Extending the exterior wall to include these posts and beams would gain about 50 sq. ft. of kitchen space without affecting the house's original roofline or proportions—an opportunity we couldn't resist. But we would need to remove the 8x8s temporarily so we could pour a stem-wall foundation and a slab floor.

To support the 8x10, we used two 4x10s extending from the side of the house and meeting at a point beyond the beam (drawing, above right). We supported the 4x10s on four posts, each built up out of three 2x4s. We first nailed one 2x4 to the side of a 4x10. This took most of the weight off whoever was holding the heavy beam, so measuring and cutting the second 2x4, which would sit at right angles to the first to form a saddle for the heavy timber, was easy. The third 2x4 was nailed up full length and parallel to the first to cradle the 4x10.

Once the foundation work was done and the slab poured, we replaced the 8x8 posts, removed the temporary supports, and fitted custom metal window frames in the new wall.

Central wall—Once we finished the north wall of the laundry, we moved on to the area's central bearing wall (C), just north of the small original kitchen wall (E). Removing the plaster ceiling, we were astonished to find cantilevered 2x6 joists only 10 in. long carrying the load of an upstairs bearing wall (photo, center left). Had the 4x6 joists for the bedroom over the laundry been 8 in. longer, they could have carried the

offset upstairs wall without a problem. We could only surmise that some change in plans had produced this structural anomaly. As it was, the 2x6 rim joist was carrying most of the load. Since we were changing the rim joist's end bearing, we needed to extend the 4x6s the extra 8 in. to carry the upstairs wall.

To do this, we bolted half the length of ⅜-in. steel plates, 5½ in. wide by 15 in. long, to each face of the 4x6s. We then bolted 8-in. 4x6s between each set of plates, and nailed a 1x6 rim joist to the ends of these extended beams (drawing, above left). The floor joists over the kitchen had been face-nailed to the studs of the upstairs wall without blocking or cripples beneath them, which we added before nailing up a skin of ⅜-in. plywood to tie everything together.

At the south wall of the kitchen, the same floor joists had been face-nailed to the roof rafters with no bracing (photo, bottom left). Where the joists didn't line up with the rafters, cripples had been inserted at the angle of the roof. I think it was just the lath and plaster that held them in place. We added blocking under each joist to form a new soffit, and nailed a ⅜-in. plywood gusset to the blocking, cripple and joist for rigidity. Then we could get back to the storeroom/kitchen wall (C in the drawing).

The wall's load had been evenly distributed, requiring only modest footings. Our plan to replace the framing with an 8x10 beam spanning 12 ft. meant larger footings to take the two concentrated loads.

A 4x6 carried the 2x8 floor joists under the wall. It was supported in turn by 4x4 posts on isolated piers about 4 ft. on center. The crawl space was barely a foot high at its east end, and the whole thing was clogged with heating ducts, so the easiest approach was to take up the flooring and excavate from above. We undermined about half the bearing of the pier closest to each point of concentration, poured concrete under both, and incorporated them into new footings about 2½ ft. wide by 4½ ft. long and 10 in. deep

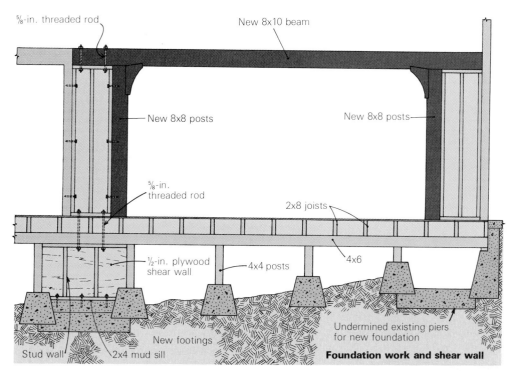

Foundation work and shear wall

Labels: ⅝-in. threaded rod · New 8x10 beam · New 8x8 posts · New 8x8 posts · ⅝-in. threaded rod · 2x8 joists · ½-in. plywood shear wall · 4x4 posts · 4x6 · Undermined existing piers for new foundation · New footings · Stud wall · 2x4 mud sill

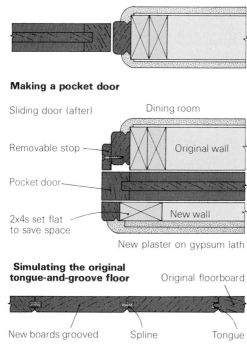

Swinging door (before)

Making a pocket door

Sliding door (after) · Dining room · Removable stop · Original wall · Pocket door · 2x4s set flat to save space · New wall · New plaster on gypsum lath

Simulating the original tongue-and-groove floor

Original floorboard · New boards grooved · Spline · Tongue

(drawing, above). We realized we now had an opportunity to add a shear wall tied directly to the ground to keep the house from racking, so we formed a stem wall on the new west footing directly below the 4x6 beam with anchor bolts and a 2x4 mud sill. We then incorporated adjacent 4x4 posts in a short 2x4 stud wall 12 in. o.c. under the 4x6. Before sheathing it with ½-in. plywood, we ran two ⅝-in. threaded steel rods to the bottom plate of the new west shear wall on the kitchen floor level, binding the new 8x8 post and the 8x10 beam together into a racking panel that carried right down to the new footing.

Pocket door—Fixing our last nagging problem brought our structural work full circle. The house had settled so much that the swinging door between the pantry and the dining room wouldn't pivot more than 90° before it hit the floor and jammed. When it opened into the pantry it was in the way of the stuff stored there. We decided that the best solution was to build a pocket sliding door. So we framed up a new wall in the former pantry out of 2x4s, face side out, covered with gypsum lath and new plaster (drawing, top right). This left us plenty of room to install the original door on its new sliding track, and enough space in the corner to tie up another loose end, the waste line from upstairs.

Re-routing the drain produced three new problems. First, because the upstairs flooring and 4x6 floor joists were to be the finished downstairs ceiling, we had to run the drain line above the upstairs floor. Thus the use of a back-flush toilet, which flushes back rather than down. Its 3-in. drain is about 2½ in. above the floor, and allowed us a 10-ft. horizontal run (at a fall of ¼ in. per ft.) before we would have to penetrate the floor. Our pocket-door corner was 7 ft. away from the toilet, well within range.

Second, some of the flooring under the old toilet needed to be replaced, and numerous calls to lumberyards revealed that 1x6 roughsawn V-joint, tongue-and-groove fir was not a stock

item. We decided to simulate the original material as best we could by using 1x6 rough fir. We would chamfer the edges on a table saw and groove them for splines with a router (drawing, above right). It turned out that 1x6 rough fir wasn't stock either. So I found myself standing at the lumberyard in front of a bandsaw where they were resawing 8x16 fir beams. All I wanted was two 1x6s, 12 ft. long. The operator sent one of his helpers to locate a 2x6, which he brought back on a forklift, and within minutes I drove away with my custom-milled, roughsawn fir planks.

Third, we had to patch the 4x6 beam that had been hacked away by the plumber installing the original drain. This beam would be visible in the new ceiling, so we carefully chiseled and planed a square recess around the damage, then let in a

patch of rough 2x6 with similar grain. This we secured with glue and finish nails.

Our simple-sounding assignment to open up the room for more space led us inexorably to everything from foundation work under the house to installing plumbing on the next floor. We found serious structural flaws that had to be remedied, and had ourselves created conditions that would have been unsafe if we hadn't followed through properly. We'd worked around the unavailability of materials, and had taken advantage of opportunities to improve the structure of the house as we went along. Most renovation work is like that.   □

Eric Rekdahl is a partner in the design/build firm of Rekdahl & Tellefsen in Berkeley, Calif.

In the expanded kitchen, the new carved beams and brackets echo details found throughout the house. Red oak cabinets by Robert Zummwalt harmonize with the oak flooring and trim.

Custom Kitchen Remodel

From the wrap-around buffets to the built-in breakfast nook, an old kitchen gets a new look

by Paul D. Voelker

Deborah Schultz and Penn Fix were planning an extensive kitchen remodel. They wanted something that would blend with their 1926 California-Moorish home and its high-coved ceilings, niches and arches. Architect/builder Gerry Copeland drew the plans; my role was to collaborate with the owners on the layout details, offer ideas for building materials, and then, with a lot of freedom in detailing, create something unusual and artistic (photo facing page).

After seeing quartersawn oak in the front door and in the floors, I suggested quartersawn oak for the cabinets. And once I'd explained to them the difference between quartersawn oak and the more common plain-sawn oak (see sidebar, p. 27), the Fix-Schultzes agreed. We settled up on the other details—the built-in seating, the roll-out shelves and the tambour-door appliance garage—and my brother, Jerry, and I started work.

Taking the bad with the good—The first challenge was to find quartersawn white oak locally—shipping costs from the East coast are horrendous. After calling several suppliers here in Washington, I located one with some in stock. Of the 500 bd. ft. I received, about 100 was totally worthless—firewood to heat the shop. The supplier agreed to ship an additional 100 ft. at no cost, but there were still some major defects to deal with.

Many of the boards showed sticker stains—black stains deep in the wood caused by using stickers of too high a moisture content. To make matters worse, whoever dried the lumber did not place the stickers directly over each other, which resulted in permanent deflection of some boards—more firewood. Furthermore, the lumber was sawn improperly at the mill, resulting in many boards too thin to dress to a full ¾-in. thickness. As a result of all the defects, 500 bd. ft. yielded about 350 bd. ft. of usable stock.

Jerry and I straightened out most of the remaining stock by clamping it to a straight-line ripping jig (see *FHB* #53, pp. 58-61) and running it through the table saw. Then we ripped most of it into 2½-in. to 3½-in. widths (we saved some wider stock for drawer fronts). We ripped it to narrow widths for

three reasons. First, opposing bends could be glued up to straighten each other out. Second, many boards showed quartersawn figure on one side and appeared rift-sawn on the other. We wanted the quartersawn boards for the highly visible areas like door panels, end panels and countertops. And third, the floor in the dining room was also mixed and we wanted to match it.

Cabinet construction—Our first step in building this set of cabinets was to measure the room, including the locations of windows, doors, radiators, light switches and so forth. Back at the shop we cut story sticks to wall or cabinet-run length and transferred all the pertinent measurements—the location and size of windows, doors, chimney, etc.—to them.

We use story sticks because they eliminate mathematical errors in measuring and give us a standard against which to double-check all dimensions. For instance, we cut a story stick the length of the sink wall, located the windows on the stick and centered the future

Shelf-peg holes are drilled in the side of a wall cabinet with the use of a special sliding-table jig, mounted under the drill press. Working the lever with his knee, Voelker advances the table in evenly spaced increments.

sink-base cabinet under its window. Next we marked 24 in. to the right of the sink for the dishwasher. Then we jumped to the end and located the breakfast-nook seat under the second window. The space between the dishwasher and the seat determined the width of the drawer cabinet. The dimensions of the cabinet to the left of the sink were determined the same way.

Standard cabinet elevations have their own sticks, which we keep for repeated use. These sticks are cut to the height of the cabinet side piece and show the location of dadoes for shelves and for cross supports under drawers. We use these cross supports to stiffen the face of the cabinet, take the bow out of the plywood sides (if there is one) and keep drawer stacks a uniform width, top to bottom. They also can be useful for supporting the drawer slide while fastening it to the cabinet side.

Using the measurements taken from the sticks, we wrote up cutting lists for tops, bottoms, sides and partitions. The pieces were cut from ¾-in. birch plywood and marked with a letter to identify the cabinet to which they belonged. We then put the dado blade in the table saw and did all necessary rabbeting and dadoing (drawing, p. 25).

Next we drilled the shelf-peg holes in the sides of the upper cabinets. This is a common operation in our shop, so we have a special jig for it (photo left). On the feed table under the drill press, we installed a jig that rolls on sliding cabinet-door hardware. On the front edge of the jig, we screwed a shelf standard as an index stop. A spring-loaded kneeboard with a bent screwdriver tip in the end engages holes in the shelf standard to ensure a uniform 1-in. spacing of the peg holes.

We assembled the carcases with Franklin Titebond yellow glue and pneumatic fasteners—staples where they wouldn't show and finish nails where they would. After assembling the cabinet sides, bottoms, partitions and cross members, the cabinets were measured for backs, which were then cut from ¼-in. birch plywood and attached with staples and hot-melt glue. We used oak plywood for the backs of the wrap-around buffets; they

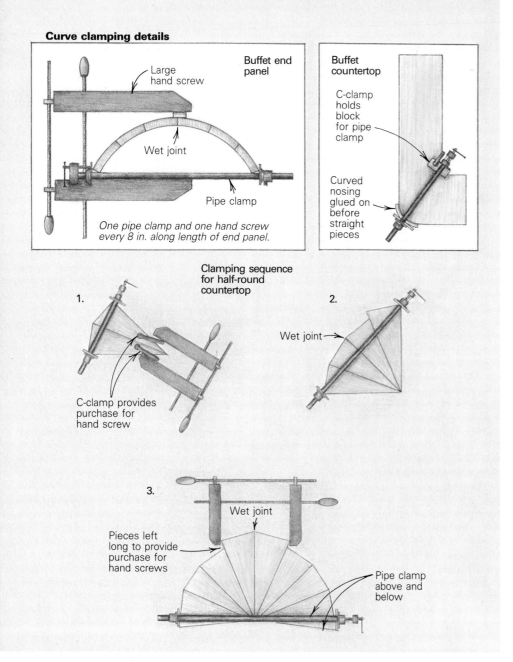

Curve clamping details

Large hand screw

Buffet end panel

Wet joint

Pipe clamp

One pipe clamp and one hand screw every 8 in. along length of end panel.

Buffet countertop

C-clamp holds block for pipe clamp

Curved nosing glued on before straight pieces

Clamping sequence for half-round countertop

1.

C-clamp provides purchase for hand screw

2.

Wet joint

3.

Wet joint

Pieces left long to provide purchase for hand screws

Pipe clamp above and below

The tilt-front bin and the roll-out drawer on full extension slides provide easily accessible storage under the kitchen sink (photo left). Glued up from pie-shaped pieces of quartersawn oak, the round counter beside the stove (photo below) was roughed out on the bandsaw and finished with a router mounted in a circle-cutting jig. The nosing was cut the same way, but the thin walnut inlay was flexible enough to bend around the curve.

have glass doors so the inside of each cabinet would be fully visible.

Next, base supports were attached and strengthened with glue blocks. The base supports are ¾-in. plywood, 4 in. high and were set back 3½ in. from the finished face of the cabinet. This allowed a 2¾-in. deep toe space after the finished kick was installed. The finished kick covers any shimming of the base cabinets made necessary by uneven floors and provides some leeway (¾ in.) for the finished flooring. We ripped the finished kicks from ¾-in. oak plywood and made it ¼ in. less than the height of the toe space so they could be easily slipped into place. These pieces were stained and lacquered in 8-ft. lengths. They were cut to size on the job and installed by Copeland's crew after the floor tile had been laid.

We faced the carcases with strips of oak ripped and planed to ⅜ in. thick. We used ⅜-in. stock because it is strong enough to scribe where a cabinet butts into a wall and thin enough to be trimmed with a router. We let the facings extend 1/32 in. past the outside edge of the cabinet sides. This created a 1/16-in. gap between adjoining cabinets and permitted a tight face joint when attaching carcases together.

Cabinet doors—Our first step in making the raised-panel doors was to glue up ⅝-in. thick panels, oversize 1 inch in width and 2 inches in length, and set them aside for a week or so to give them a chance to shrink or swell before being cut to finished size. Panels were of randomly selected quartersawn stock to correspond to the oak floor; the owners liked it that way.

In the meantime, we ripped rail and stile stock (once again, slightly oversize) and cut it to length. We cut the rails in each line of cabinets from a single board for continuity of grain and color. Wherever we could, we did the same with adjoining stiles.

Stiles were cut to door height plus ⅛ in., and rails were cut to exact length, plus 1/16 in. The rails were coped (the ends were cut on a shaper to be a negative image of the pattern later shaped on the inside edge of the frame) with a cope and pattern set (#MC-50-030) from the Freeborn Tool Co. (E. 3355 Trent Ave., Spokane, Wash. 99202-4459). That removed 1/32 in. from each end, shortening them by 1/16 in. overall.

Next we cut an ogee pattern on the inside edges of the stiles and rails using the shaper. This molding process also cut the panel groove in the edge of the stock. Then we moved the stock to the table saw and ripped it to 2 9/16 in. wide. This extra width, along with the ⅛ in. added to the stile length, allowed for trimming 1/16 in. off the door on all four sides to clean and square it up, resulting in 2½-in. wide rails and stiles. We take these extra steps because on most jobs we use matched rails and stiles, and one ruined piece may mean a lot of extra work.

The pieces were moved to our horizontal-boring machine and drilled for dowels at the

Drawings: Michael Mandarano

joints. We once used two dowels per joint, but have found that one is plenty if done right. We use ⅜-in. dowels, fluted spirally and longitudinally. As with shaping and coping, we keep the stock face down so that any variation in wood thickness will not misalign the cope with the pattern.

Next we returned to the panels, which we cut ⅛ in. undersize to allow a 1⁄16-in. gap between the edges of the panel and the bottom of the groove in the door frame. This gap allows the panel to shrink and swell during seasonal humidity changes.

We sanded the panels flat and shaped the edges with a panel-raising cutter on the shaper. Then we sanded the edge profile with a finish sander and eased the edges for easier installation. Because the panel fits snugly into the grooves, the easiest sequence for assembly seems to be stile, rail, panel, second rail, second stile. We centered the panel in the frame by wedging a short piece of ⅛-in. thick balsa wood into the bottom of each groove before the panel was installed. After they had been glued up, the doors were cut to final size, and the edges and corners were routed with a 3⁄16-in. radius quarter-round bit and finish sanded.

Drawers and tambours—We made the sides, front and back of the drawer carcase of ½-in. ApplePly (States Industries, Inc., P. O. Box 7037, Eugene, Ore. 97401)—an excellent product. It's extremely dense nine-ply alder-core plywood, with no voids. It comes in a variety of face veneers; I use maple. We used ¼-in. birch plywood for the bottoms. The sides were rabbeted to accept the front and back, with the bottom held in a dado set up ¼ in. from the bottom. We glued and stapled the drawer carcases together. The bottoms were fixed in place with ⅝-in. brads. Rather than install adjustable shelves behind the double-door base cabinets, I built roll-out drawers for them (left photo, facing page).

The drawer faces are simply solid oak boards with the corners and edges radiused to match the doors. Whenever possible, adjoining or stacked drawer faces were cut from a single board. We attached the faces to the drawer carcase with Mepla drawer-face adjusters (Mepla, Inc., P. O. Box 1469, High Point, N. C. 27261). These are 25mm dia. by ½-in. thick ribbed plastic inserts that house a steel nut (detail drawing, this page). They are installed in a 25-mm dia. hole drilled ½-in. deep in the backside of the drawer faces. After the adjusters are tapped into place (friction fit), a machine screw is run through the drawer carcase into the nuts in the adjusters. They allow about 3⁄16-in. movement of the face until the screws are tightened, which allows enough play to adjust the faces precisely.

For this set of cabinets we used KV 8505 side-mount drawer slides, full extension plus 1-in. overtravel (Knape & Vogt Manufacturing Co., 2700 Oak Industrial Dr. N. E., Grand Rapids, Mich. 49505). Admittedly, these are overkill for cabinet drawers because the slides

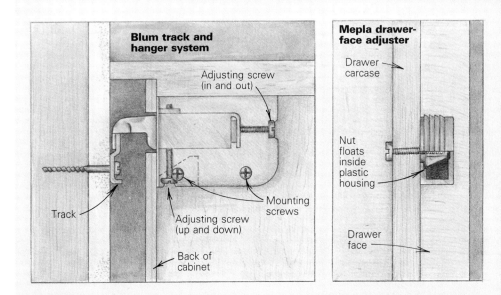

Blum track and hanger system

Adjusting screw (in and out)

Track

Adjusting screw (up and down)

Mounting screws

Back of cabinet

Mepla drawer-face adjuster

Drawer carcase

Nut floats inside plastic housing

Drawer face

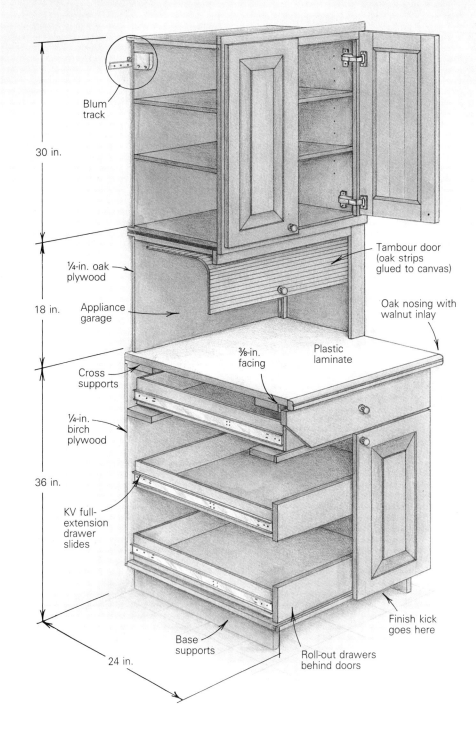

Cabinet construction

Blum track

30 in.

¼-in. oak plywood

Appliance garage

18 in.

Cross supports

¼-in. birch plywood

36 in.

KV full-extension drawer slides

Base supports

24 in.

Tambour door (oak strips glued to canvas)

Oak nosing with walnut inlay

⅜-in. facing

Plastic laminate

Finish kick goes here

Roll-out drawers behind doors

Built-in window seats and a freestanding trestle table create the breakfast nook at the back end of the kitchen (photo above). The walnut grilles behind the righthand seat back and in the toe space allow heat from a hidden radiator to circulate. Although the wrap-around buffets and the round counter beside the stove have oak tops, the main work areas, such as around the sink (photo below), have plastic-laminate countertops, which are more serviceable.

have a load rating of 150 lb., but they are excellent, heavy-duty, smooth-acting slides, allowing easy access to the back of drawers. They are simply screwed to the sides of the drawers and to the insides of the cabinets.

Most people store their blenders, toasters and other appliances on top of the counter, so we built an additional cabinet between the upper and base cabinets, just to the right of the stove, expressly for this purpose (left photo, p. 24). It's called an appliance garage, and like a garage, it has an overhead door. I made the tambour door, using ¼-in. thick by ¾-in. wide strips of oak glued to a piece of canvas. Rather than routing a track in the cabinet sides, I used plastic track from Outwater Plastic Industries (4 Passaic St., Woodridge, N. J. 07075). The track is dark brown, comes in straight and curved sections, and is simply nailed in place.

Wrap-around buffets—Where the dining-room buffets wrap around the sides of the arched opening into the kitchen, we had to make curved end panels for the two cabinets. Oak veneer glued to curved plywood backing would have been the easiest construction method, but would not have matched the door panels. Instead, we glued up the curved panels from 3-in. rippings of solid stock, clamping them in pairs (with a combination of pipe clamps and large hand screws) until the full curve was completed (drawing, p. 24).

The outsides were sanded to a smooth curve with a belt sander run diagonally—an effective method if done carefully. We then cut the pieces to length on the table saw and routed a rabbet on the inside of the ends to accept a ¾-in. plywood top and bottom. Then we attached the unit to the buffet. The process was fairly time-consuming, but well worth it.

Countertops—Although the main work areas have plastic-laminate countertops (bottom photo) with ¾-in. medium-density particleboard substrate and oak nosing, there were four tops made from 4/4 oak: the breakfast-nook table, a half-round top for the cabinet to the left of the range, and one each for the two wrap-around buffets. The basic construction was pretty straightforward. First, we edge-glued the boards (Titebond, again) into rough size, sanded the glued-up panels flat and trimmed the edges on the table saw. The curves were then roughed out on the bandsaw and trimmed to final size with a 3-hp plunge router attached to a circle-cutting jig with an adjustable pivoting arm.

Next we ripped the 8/4 nosing, glued and splined it to the tops. The curved nosings were roughed out on the bandsaw in quarter-arc segments, then they were clamped to the workbench and the inside edges were routed with the same jig. We carefully shortened the cutting arc by exactly ½ in. to compensate for the width of the ½-in. dia. router bit. We mitered the ends of the curves, adjusting the angle slightly as needed for a tight fit, then glued and pipe-clamped the pieces in place.

We attached the straight edging pieces in the same way. The outside edges of the curved nosings were cut with the router and jig after the tops were assembled.

After sanding the nosings flat we routed the groove for the walnut inlay using a face inlay bit (Norfield Tools and Supplies, P. O. Box 459, Chico, Calif. 95927), which cuts a channel ½ in. wide by ³⁄₁₆ in. deep. We then cut and planed walnut strips ⁷⁄₃₂ in. thick by a hair over ½ in. wide. We sanded the inside edges slightly, cut them to length, put glue in the channel and carefully pounded in the strips, using a block of wood and a hammer. With the snug fit, no clamps were needed. The thin walnut would bend around the larger radiuses, but we had to bandsaw curved pieces for the smaller ones. We sanded the inlay flush, routed a ½-in. radius on the top and bottom of the nosings and finish-sanded all the tops.

The half-round top to the left of the stove differed from the others in that the front was made of wedge-shaped pieces of solid oak (right photo, p. 24). The wedges were glued together in pairs, then the pairs were glued together (drawing, p. 24), as with the curved end panels. The piece was then sanded smooth, the curve roughed out on the bandsaw and finished with the router and circle-cutting jig.

As a general rule, when working with solid wood it is not advisable to band end grain as we did by running solid nosing on the ends of the countertops. Wood movement is greater across the grain than it is along it, so banded end grain will often crack, split, or swell and cause the edging joint to fail. We got away with it because the oak was quartersawn, dried to 6.5% moisture content, and the length of the banded end grain was, for the most part, relatively short.

The breakfast nook—Dimensions for the window seats in the breakfast nook were adapted from guidelines in *Architectural Graphic Standards* (John Wiley & Sons, Inc., 605 3rd Ave, New York, N. Y. 10158, 1988; 8th edition). The guidelines call for a seat height of 18 in., so we built the seats 16 in. high, allowing for 1 in. of compression when sitting on a firm 3-in. thick cushion. The top of the back is 36 in. high to correspond to the height of the kitchen countertop. The front facing was extended ½ in. above the seat to prevent the seat cushion from sliding forward. We built the seat as a single unit, but made the back in two pieces and screwed them to the seat on the job site.

Because there was an existing radiator behind one of the seats, we made walnut grilles and installed one in the kick space under the seat and one in the top behind the seat to allow for air circulation.

Instead of using hinged tops to gain access to the storage space under the seats, we opted for drawers, which were constructed in the same fashion as the other drawers. The only differences were that the window-seat drawers had angled front faces, and the oak faces were extended about ½ in. below the bottom of the seat to be used as handles,

since we didn't want any protruding hardware for people to bump with their legs (top photo, facing page).

Finishing and installation—To finish the cabinets, we first wiped on Watco natural oil and let it stand for a few minutes before wiping the surface dry. It's important that the oiled wood be allowed to dry for at least three days before lacquering, otherwise the oil interferes

Quartersawn oak

A cross section of a tree will show the obvious annual rings and the less visible medullary rays, which are groups of cells that conduct moisture to and from the sapwood. For economic reasons, most lumber is plain-sawn—cut from a tree by squaring a log and cutting several boards from one side, then rotating the log 90° and repeating the process. An end section of a plain-sawn board will show the annual rings roughly parallel to the face and the medullary rays perpendicular to the face.

Quartersawn lumber can be sawn from a log in several ways. One way is to quarter the log, then saw the quarters into boards with the face of each board being at right angles (or nearly so) to the annual rings. The medullary rays are then nearly parallel to the face. These rays are well pronounced in oak so that when they appear on the face of the board at a slight angle they produce the beautiful figure for which quartersawn oak is so well known.

In addition to being beautiful, quartersawn lumber is also very stable. When wood dries, the greatest shrinkage occurs in the direction of the annual rings. A plain-sawn board will experience the most shrinkage in width, with very little in thickness and a negligible amount in length. A quartersawn board, on the other hand, will shrink mostly in thickness and very little in width. As a result, tops and panels laid up of quartersawn boards will be very stable. Also, a plain-sawn board upon drying and shrinking may cup, whereas a quartersawn board will not. —*P. D. V.*

Annual rings

Medullary rays

Plain-sawn log and board

Quartersawn log and board

with the lacquer and results in a blemished surface. Next we applied three coats of precatalyzed semi-gloss clear lacquer—a durable finish—lightly sanding between coats.

We installed the wall cabinets first, using the Blum track and hanger system (Julius Blum, Inc., Blum Industrial Park, Highway 16—Lowesville, Stanley, N. C. 28164). The hangers are fastened inside the cabinets in the upper corners, and a metal arm protrudes through a rectangular hole cut in the back (left detail drawing, p. 25). The track is screwed to the wall, and the cabinets are simply hung on the track. The hangers, which slide along the track, have adjustment screws to move them up and down, in and out. With adjoining cabinets, we hung them loosely on the track and screwed them together with 1¼-in. drywall screws run through the sides, just behind the facings. Then we snugged them to the wall as a unit. The hanger system simplifies installation considerably, saving more than enough time to pay for itself (hangers cost me $1.70 each and rail runs $5 for 6 ft.).

The base cabinets were installed after the uppers. We removed the doors and drawers, set the carcases in place, shimmed them up as necessary to keep everything level and screwed adjoining units together. These assemblies were then screwed to the wall. We checked the faces with a framing square to make sure that the cabinets hadn't been twisted when fastened to the wall. Where they had, we shimmed between the back of the cabinet and the wall or between the floor and the base of the cabinet. If the cabinet faces are out of square it is difficult to adjust the doors and drawers for equal spacing between them.

We then set the countertops in place, scribing them to the wall with 36-grit paper in a belt sander. Since the backsplash covered any small gaps, a tight fit was needed only where the front edge of the top touched the wall. We fastened the tops to the cabinets from underneath, screwing through the cross members.

After the tops were set we replaced the drawers and doors, adjusting for even spacing between them. We used Blum concealed hinges with opening angles of 125° or 170°, depending on the application. Their use requires boring a 35mm dia. hole in the back of the door, and they are considerably more expensive than conventional cabinet hinges. But the advantages are several. The door can be removed simply by pulling up a little tab, and reinstalled by snapping the hinge back onto the hinge plate, which makes for easier moving and installation. And the hinges are adjustable in six directions—an important feature when you consider that there is a ⅛ in. or so gap between all doors and drawer faces.

Next we installed the door and drawer pulls (through both the drawer face and carcase), put plastic caps (also from Outwater Plastic Industries) over the heads of the visible screws, then cleaned and polished everything. □

Paul D. Voelker is a cabinetmaker in Chewelah, Washington.

Kitchen Overhaul

Easy maintenance, abundant storage and plenty of workspace in 100 sq. ft.

by Gillian Servais

Shortly before Christmas a few years ago, I received a frantic call from a couple in Berkeley. They had just bought a lovely old house that had been built in the 1920s. Other than a few minor repairs and the usual repainting, it was ready to occupy—except, that is, for the kitchen. It needed a total transformation, and they were expecting their first child in two months.

The existing kitchen was cramped and inefficient. In addition to lacking adequate storage space, light and charm of any sort, its counter peninsula projected awkwardly into the center of the room (drawing, p. 30). The stove was at the other end of the counter, crammed into a corner that left no work room to the left of the burners (photo right). As a gesture to ventilation, a small fan had been stuck in the wall behind the stove. Unfortunately, there was no hood to collect the cooking vapors. A 2-ft. dia. table and two chairs took up the remaining space. They were in a small bay with three windows overlooking the backyard garden to the south. The view from the east-side window was into the neighbors' kitchen, just beyond a nearby fence.

Priorities—Before I meet with my clients to begin design work, I ask them to prepare a wish list that includes the most important features in the new room. The list gives us a starting point, and once we get into discussing the project a hierarchy of priorities usually emerges.

In this case, speed was on my clients' minds. They didn't want a construction project and a new baby, so the kitchen had to be completed in two months. Next, the kitchen had to be an efficient workspace for people who enjoy preparing meals, with durable, easy-to-clean surfaces and high-quality cooking equipment. They wanted the new kitchen to have a modern appearance, but without clashing with the 1920s decor in the rest of the house. Also, it had to have plenty of light and storage space. The clients had a lot of

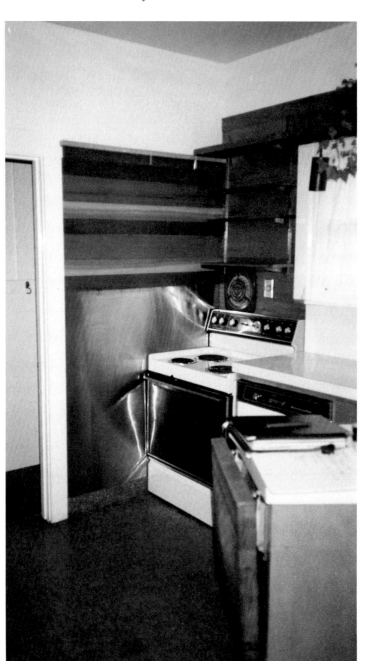

Inadequate storage and a cramped workspace made the original kitchen (above) unsuitable for people who like to cook a lot. A view in the same direction of the remodeled kitchen (facing page) shows the extent of the changes made in this room. White painted surfaces and cabinets get the most from the available light, while track lighting illuminates the work areas. The floor is covered with 12-in. square tiles of heavy-duty vinyl flooring. Drawer pulls of brushed stainless steel complement the stainless hood and sink. To the left of the oven, a marble countertop serves as a pastry surface.

small appliances and specialized gadgets for exotic cooking. While they don't use them very often, they needed places to keep them out of sight. Finally, the kitchen needed a corner to do pastry work.

A tight budget wasn't an issue in this project, so we could have added onto the house to expand the size of the kitchen. But that would have taken the completion date well beyond our deadline. Consequently, our first decision was to avoid any structural changes by staying within the existing space. To gain a little more room, we decided to annex the bay window area occupied by the round table. This still left us with only about 100 sq. ft.—not a very large kitchen for people who cook a lot. Clearly, we had to exploit all the available space.

Because light was a precious commodity in this room, white walls and cabinets were a must. To make it easy to clean the tiny handprints to come, we all agreed that plastic laminate cabinets were the right choice. Their stark simplicity would also lend a feeling of open space. The adjacent dining room has wood trim painted pale grey, so we repeated the grey trim in the kitchen to relate the two rooms. This palette, while durable and bright, borders on the antiseptic. For some highlights and warmth we added stainless steel and natural wood (photo facing page).

A deep wood counter—First we took out all the existing cabinets and the appliances that we wouldn't be reusing in the new kitchen. Then we removed the angled counter and put the sink under the windows that overlook the garden (drawing, p. 31). Because the other window provided some light but no aesthetic value, we made it fade away by covering it with a grey Levelor blind.

The new cooktop and oven are below this window, installed in a 30-in. deep, butcherblock counter. Some of my clients who request butcher-block counters want them only for their

Photo this page: Gillian Servais

The cleanup center now occupies the bay window, giving the person at the sink a view of the backyard garden. A hinged shelf below the sink hides pot scrubbers and sponges, and the drawer below provides easy access to kitchen cleanup items and the trash bin.

A 30-in. deep counter allows enough room for extra-long drawers. This one was sized to hold pot lids, and divided to make them easy to find. Cookie sheets and pizza pans are stored under the oven.

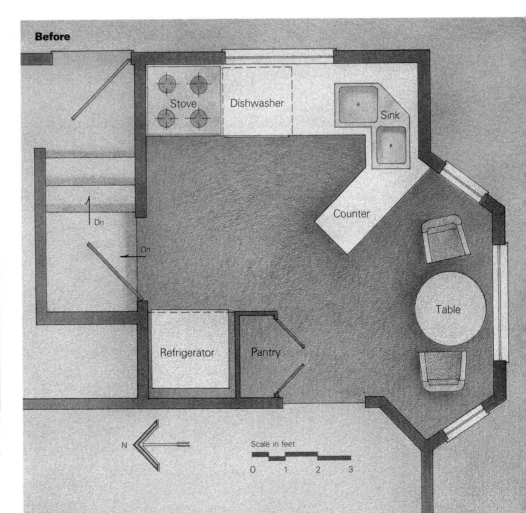

Before

Stove

Dishwasher

Sink

Dn

Dn

Counter

Table

Refrigerator

Pantry

N

Scale in feet

0   1   2   3

looks, rather than their intended use—a chopping surface. Sometimes a client will want to put a sink in a butcher-block counter, which is inviting trouble because the wood will inevitably rot and delaminate around the sink rim. I think this installation strikes the right note between utility and style when it comes to wood counters. This one is separate from the the sink counter, so moisture isn't an issue. It is also used as a chopping surface, taking on the textures and colors that come with using a work surface that is built to be used for a long time.

Evidently some of the companies that make wood counters assume that their products will never feel the sharp edge of a knife, because countertops are often finished with polyurethane varnish or lacquer. In this situation, I have the finish removed with a thickness planer or a belt sander. Then I have the counter refinished with a few coats of mineral oil. I've got a wood counter in my own kitchen, and I touch up the spots that get chopped on about once a week. I just soak a paper towel with some mineral oil, and mush it around on the areas that need it.

Wood counters can get stained. Sometimes a cast-iron pot will leave an ugly black ring on the wood. When this happens, I cut open a lemon and squeeze its juice on the stain. The juice will remove the mark, leaving the wood a little lighter than the surrounding surface and ready for a mineral-oil touchup.

Although a 30-in. deep counter doesn't sound like a big improvement over the traditional 24-in. counter, it is. For one thing, the extra depth provides enough space at the back of the counter to keep appliances and foodstuffs that are in constant use, while still allowing workspace

along the front of the counter. The extra 6 in. also allows added drawer space. For this kitchen, we asked cabinetmaker John Banks to make the drawers the full depth of the counter. Mounted on full-extension drawer glides, the drawers are divided in halves. Frequently used items are in the front sections—seldom needed utensils are stored in the back.

To supply power to the appliances along the back of the counter, we installed a strip of Plugmold (Wiremold Co., 60 Woodlawn St., West Hartford, Conn. 06110). Plugmold is a linear housing that has electric outlets every 6 in. or 12 in. The strips come in 5-ft. lengths, and they are designed to carry 20 amps for every six outlets. I like to use these strips for groups of plug-in appliances because they cut down on power cords draped across the counters.

A stove and a hood—Both the cooktop and the oven were made by Gaggenau, a West German company that makes high-quality appliances (Gaggenau USA, 5 Commonwealth Ave., Woburn, Mass. O1801). While the two are separate pieces, they are made to be used in tandem as built-ins. These are expensive appliances. The cooktop lists for about $550, and the oven costs a bit over $1,200. But for people who love to cook, the capabilities of these appliances may outweigh their expense.

The cooktop burners are sized according to the tasks they most often perform. The front right burner is rated at 12,700 Btus—hot enough to do a real stir fry or sauté. The back left burner performs at 9,520 Btus for boiling water in a hurry. The other two burners are rated at 6,350 Btus, which is the size of the typical burner on a

residential stove. To turn them on one must push in the knob and turn it at the same time to engage the electronic ignition and open the gas valve. This makes it virtually childproof.

The oven is the convection type, which uses a fan to circulate the heat. This kind of oven is especially good for cooking breads and pastries, and it makes for crispy skins on chickens and roasts. The oven door swings to the side instead of down so that you can really see into the oven without hitting your knees on the door. On the other hand, the feature called "continuous cleaning" doesn't really clean very well. Fortunately, the interior walls are easily disassembled, and they will fit into a dishwasher for cleaning.

The stainless-steel hood was custom built to overlap part of the window without overwhelming the space. It houses a Trade-Wind 1501 Ventilator by Thermador, which is rated at 290 cfm.

A good vent is important in a kitchen for two reasons: not only will it cut down on grease and odors, but it will also carry away potentially dangerous combustion by-products from gas cooktops. As a rule of thumb, the vent should move 100 cubic feet of air per minute, per square foot of cooktop. The hood is most often installed 30 in. above the cooktop. Tall people need hoods a bit higher to keep from banging their foreheads when they peek in the soup pot. Thermador (5119 District Blvd., Los Angeles, Calif. 90040) publishes a useful brochure for people who are interested in kitchen ventilation. It's called "Basic Concepts of Residential Kitchen Ventilation," and it's free for the asking.

A place for everything—Before I drew up cabinet details, we took an inventory of everything the clients planned to keep in the kitchen. We measured oversize pans, decided what could be stored vertically and measured lineal feet of cookbooks. Big cookie sheets and pizza pans fit in a short but wide space under the oven (bottom photo, facing page). To its right, a tall drawer with dividers contains pot lids.

The upper cabinets run all the way to the ceiling, where they house infrequently needed pots and pans. At the intersection between the cabinets on the north and east walls, two-piece doors joined with piano hinges allow full access to this otherwise awkward hollow.

The cleanup center now occupies the bay window (top photo, facing page). Banks built this complicated cabinet knowing that he would have to fit it into a three-sided space that was neither plumb nor square, and it was still an installation nightmare for him. To make the necessary scribe cuts in the laminate edges, he first made plywood templates of the wall contours, then used his router along with the templates.

A big drawer fits into the space under the sink, making it easier for grownups to get at the trash bag but harder for toddlers. To its left, an angled drawer ekes out a bit more storage room. Since there was still a little room remaining to the right of the dishwasher, Banks built a special cabinet to house a stepstool for reaching the things in the upper cabinets. □

Gillian Servais is a custom kitchen designer based in Berkeley, Calif.

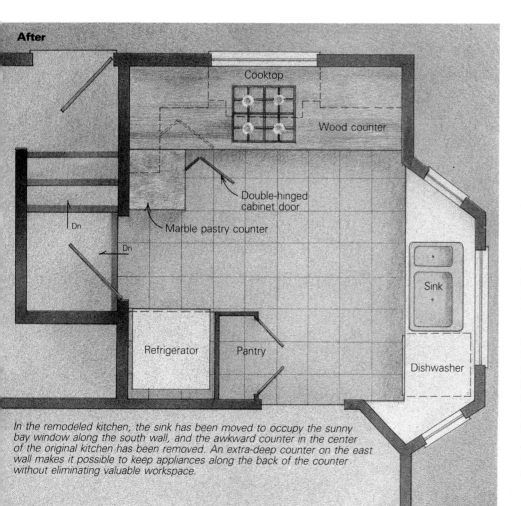

After

In the remodeled kitchen, the sink has been moved to occupy the sunny bay window along the south wall, and the awkward counter in the center of the original kitchen has been removed. An extra-deep counter on the east wall makes it possible to keep appliances along the back of the counter without eliminating valuable workspace.

Recipe for a Kitchen Remodel

Natural materials, top-shelf hardware and tasteful leftovers accent an Arts and Crafts motif

by William E. Roesner

In 1979, my wife and I were the lucky winners of a Scottish-Baronial/American Arts and Crafts-style house in Newton Centre, Massachusetts. At least, it seemed that way when our sealed bid on the house beat out the competition. The robust three-story house, designed in 1912 by prominent Boston architect James H. Ritchie for himself, was replete with dark-stained beamed ceilings, Tiffany windows, quartersawn white oak floors, a Grueby tiled fireplace, an oak-paneled den and other details that placed it stylistically in that period.

Strongly emphasizing class distinction, the Scottish-born Ritchie divided the house into two distinct domains: a simple, functional kitchen and pantry with a bedroom and bathroom above it for the servant (who did all the cooking), and the rest of the house for himself and his family. The two domains were clearly distinguished by their level of detailing. For in-

stance, all the doorknobs in the main part of the house are made of crystal. In the servant's section, they're plain white porcelain. Also, a separate stair, spare in detail, links the kitchen with the servant's quarters. The owner's staircase, on the other hand, is embellished with an artful balustrade, complete with a hand-carved newel post.

For our purposes, however, we thought the servant's bedroom would make a perfect guest room. But for the kitchen to assume a prominent and complementary position in our house, a major remodel was in order.

Once the domain of servants, the kitchen was refurbished to meet contemporary demands and to reflect the Arts and Crafts detailing found in the rest of the house.

Cooking up the plan—Having practiced architecture for more than 25 years, I had always worked to fulfill the wish lists of others. Now I had the chance to design something for myself. The only "client" I had to satisfy was my wife, Elizabeth, who generously volunteered to stay clear of most aesthetic decision making. As a gourmet cook, though, she had plenty to say about how the kitchen would be organized, including how and where food would be prepared, where the dishes would be washed and where storage would be provided.

With Elizabeth's stamp of approval, I organized the kitchen into a food-preparation area and a dishwashing and storage area, with an island counter in between (photo above). The food-prep area has a double sink set in a 6½-ft. long counter, with a refrigerator on one side and a microwave and cookstove on the other. Opposite this sink, the island stores common foodstuffs and portable appliances.

As food is prepared, it's placed on the island counter and then moved to either the small dining table for two located at the end of the island or to the formal dining room. Dirty dishes are returned to the single sink on the opposite side of the kitchen and loaded into an adjacent dishwasher. Dishes and silverware are stored on this side of the kitchen as well as in the pantry (bottom photo, p. 35), which also provides storage for table linens, liquor and wine.

My design brief called for the extension of the Scottish Arts and Crafts tradition into the kitchen through the use of details influenced by Charles Rennie Mackintosh, Scotland's premiere turn-of-the-century Arts and Crafts designer (see *FHB* #54 pp. 36-41). This meant fitting the cabinets with white-colored door and drawer fronts, cross-shaped door pulls and leaded-glass panels, as well as introducing to the kitchen dark wood doors, casings, trim and other finish details. The cabinets would be European-style; they're more accessible than standard cabinets.

The new kitchen appliances would be supplemented with several of the old ones from the original kitchen, including a six-burner, two-oven Magic Chef gas stove dating from about 1930, a kitchen-window exhaust fan dated 1912, a 6-volt intercom system and an old hot-water radiator.

Lighting would be provided primarily by rheostat-controlled, low-voltage incandescent fixtures and by fluorescent fixtures mounted beneath the upper cabinets. Other amenities would include display niches (top photo, p. 35), granite countertops, stainless-steel sinks and chrome-plated faucets.

Of course, my detailed plans would be futile without the handiwork of top-flight craftspersons. I chose Nathan Rome, a member of the Emily Street Woodworkers Cooperative in Cambridge, Massachusetts, to build the cabinets. On Rome's recommendation, I hired William Iacono of Thorpe Construction (also a member of the cooperative) as general contractor. Iacono's team included foreman John Patriquin, a master furniture builder and finish carpenter, and cabinetmaker Jonathan Wright, who would be responsible for most of the shop-built millwork such as doors, jambs and baseboards.

Roughing it out—Iacono's first step was to gut the existing kitchen and pantry down to bare studs and joists. Even the subfloor was removed. It was replaced with ¾-in. exterior-grade plywood panels installed between the joists; the panels were glued and screwed to 2x ledgers fastened to the sides of the joists, positioned so that the tops of the panels are flush with the tops of the joists (drawing at right). This effectively dropped the subfloor about 1 in., allowing the new terra-cotta tile floor to finish out coplanar with the adjacent hardwood floors.

The 8-ft., 1-in. high kitchen ceiling was too high to butt the upper cabinets against, so an 11-in. high soffit was framed around the perimeter of the kitchen. The soffit not only drops the upper cabinets to a convenient height (18 in. above the countertops) but also serves as a plumbing chase for the rooms above and is a means for introducing mahogany trim at the ceiling, thus generating a visual relationship with the beamed ceilings in the living room.

With the soffit completed, the exterior walls were insulated with 3½-in. fiberglass batts, then covered with a 4-mil polyethylene vapor barrier. The ceiling and most of the walls were finished with ⅝-in. gypsum blueboard and skim-coat plaster.

Originally, the cookstove's two ovens were vented into a small duct inside the wall that ran up through the house and out the roof. During demolition it was discovered that sometime in the past, the wall framing had charred slightly from overheating, though somehow it had never caught fire. The building inspector insisted on fire-resistant construction behind the stove and directed us not to hook up the old exhaust duct. The plastered wall behind the cookstove received a double layer of ⅝-in. fire-rated drywall affixed to ⅞-in. metal furring channels nailed to the existing studs. Then we installed an exhaust hood over the stove to absorb heat from the open stove duct.

After the plastering was finished, the existing windows were refurbished. This included straightening the existing zinc weather stripping, installing new wooden guides and replacing the old counterweight ropes with copper-dipped, 75-lb. steel "bag chain." The bag chain (available from Turner & Seymour Manufacturing Co., P. O. Box 358, Torrington, Conn. 06790; 203-489-9214) cost $26.20 for a 100-ft. length, the minimum amount available. Also, a few cracked window lights were replaced with antique glass, saved during demolition, to preserve the wavy view through the windows.

Coved baseboards and fumed oak—While the rest of the work was in progress, Rome and Wright were busy with the millwork. Doors, casings, baseboards and soffit trim were made out of African mahogany to match existing details in the house.

The coved baseboards (photo below) were milled from 1¾-in. by 4⅜-in. stock. The cove was produced by plowing a 1½-in. dia. flute down the length of the stock using a shaper, and then running the stock top-edge-down through a table saw to rip the baseboard to finished thickness. The roundover at the top was produced by routing a 45° bevel along the top edge and then easing it with rasps and sandpaper. Almost all the millwork and cabinetry were prefinished in the shop with three

The coved mahogany baseboards were produced by using a shaper to plow a 1½-in. dia. flute down the length of solid mahogany stock, then ripping off the excess with a table saw. The roundover at the top was shaped by hand using rasps and sandpaper. All the millwork was prefinished with three coats of urethane lacquer.

Dropping the subfloor

The existing subfloor was replaced with a new one, installed flush with the tops of the joists. This allowed the new tile floor to be installed coplanar with the adjacent hardwood floors.

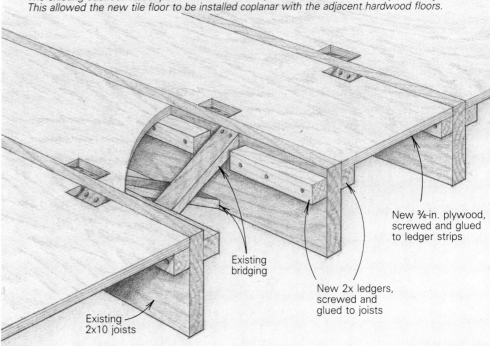

New ¾-in. plywood, screwed and glued to ledger strips

Existing bridging

New 2x ledgers, screwed and glued to joists

Existing 2x10 joists

coats of Lacthane quick-drying, water-resistant urethane lacquer (Eastern Chem-Lac Corp., 1100 Eastern Ave., P. O. Box 266, Malden, Mass. 02148; 617-322-8000) prior to installation.

Wright also milled a supply of unfinished quartersawn white oak door thresholds as well as floor boards for the maid's-stair landing, where the oak would alternate with African mahogany (left photo, next page). To replicate the dark coloration of the existing oak floor, I placed the oak flooring inside a large plastic-bag tent out in the yard overnight and slipped in a small pan of powerful ammonia (ammonium hydroxide) from my blueprinting machine. The tannin in the white oak reacted with the ammonia fumes to produce a rich brown color that, when finished with polyurethane varnish, turned a beautiful golden brown. This is by and large the same principle used by Arts and Crafts artisans at the turn of the century. Please be forewarned, though, that this ammonia is extremely powerful stuff and should not be used indoors or without protective respirators, goggles and gloves.

Composing the cabinets—The cabinets in the kitchen and pantry are built out of a combination of solid African mahogany and mahogany plywood. Complete with sturdy dovetailed drawers and bridle-jointed doors, ball-bearing, full-extension drawer slides and concealed hinges, they're furniture-quality inside and out. Special features include a spice drawer, a bread drawer, an under-the-counter wine rack, a tray-storage cabinet with vertical dividers and two appliance garages tucked into the end of the island (top right photo, next page). Each garage contains a MEPLA mechanical swing-up shelf supplied by Frederick Shohet, Inc. (51 Concord St., N. Reading, Mass. 01864; 508-664-5775): one supporting a food processor and the other a mixer, plugged in and ready for use. Roll-out drawers below hold the accessories.

I originally wanted the Mackintosh-inspired, cross-shaped door and drawer pulls to consist simply of four square holes, each big enough for a finger to slip through. My wife objected, though, so I decided instead to notch 1x crosses into single square openings and to cover the backs of the openings with ¼-in. mahogany plates screwed to the door and drawers (top right photo, next page). The solid-mahogany

A pair of display niches, formed out of mahogany and granite, are illuminated with low-voltage incandescent fixtures. A continuous stainless-steel plugmold, concealed beneath the upper cabinets, gives maximum flexibility in the placement of countertop appliances.

Adjacent to the kitchen, the pantry (photo above) echoes its detailing except that its countertop is of African mahogany instead of granite. The original 6-volt intercom seen in the foreground still works. In the kitchen (photo facing page), the dining table consists of a 2¼-in. thick slab of African mahogany supported by a carved mahogany column. The existing gas cookstove was protected for years by a layer of grease. Scrubbed clean, it's as good as new.

doors and drawer fronts were painted by Johnson Brothers, a furniture-restoration shop located here in Newton, with multiple coats of white lacquer to maintain the wood-grain texture and the bridle-joint "read through."

The leaded-glass inserts for the upper cabinet doors were fabricated and installed by Lyn Hovey Studio in Cambridge, Massachusetts. The glass is imported, hand-blown restoration glass. This "antique" glass has the character-

istic distortion of old handmade glass, but it's actually new. It's made by hand-blowing molten glass into cylindrical shapes and then cutting the cylinders to length while they're still hot. After cooling, each cylinder is cut lengthwise, reheated in a furnace and flattened into rectangular sheets that measure approximately 24 in. by 36 in. The glass, typically used for colonial restoration, averages ⅛ in. thick. Apparently, the glass is hard to find. Ours was made in Germany and imported by S. A. Bendheim Co., Inc. (61 Willett St., Passaic, N. J. 07055; 800-221-7379). The restoration glass was set in 5/16-in. lead came, matching in profile that found in the den, but the new came was also given a copper-colored decorative foil face.

Base cabinets were fitted with continuous plywood tops to support granite countertops (African mahogany countertops in the pantry) and to allow the sinks to be mounted under the granite in routed openings. There's a dining table for two at the end of the island opposite the appliance garages (see photo facing page). It's simply three 2¼-in. thick African mahogany boards edge-glued to form a 28-in. by 33-in. slab. The slab is supported on one end by a cleat screwed to the face of the island and on the other by a single column of white-painted mahogany, carved to match in abstracted form the existing newel post at the foot of the main stair.

Both table and column are notched to slip together, and the base of the column is secured by a ⅛-in. steel pin set into the tile floor.

Topping with granite—With the cabinets in place, the most expensive phase of the remodel—fabrication and installation of the countertops—could begin. After weighing the virtues of both granite and marble, I picked granite because it's four to six times harder than marble, and hence is less likely to chip or stain. The granite would also be used for backsplashes, sidesplashes and window stools.

It was important that the countertops complement the African mahogany, the white-colored walls and cabinets, and the tile floor. After a trip to the stoneyard, I settled on a ¾-in. thick, $18 per sq. ft. stone called "Turquoise," which was quarried in Saudi Arabia, cut and polished in Italy and fabricated in Charlestown, Massachusetts, by Louis Mian

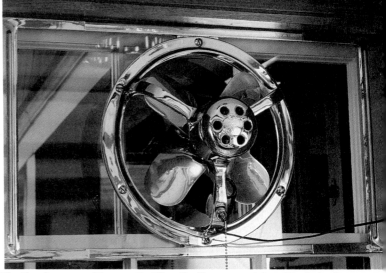

The solid-mahogany door in the kitchen corner conceals a stairway that leads to the old servant's quarters upstairs. Above the door a radiused recess in the soffit, trimmed with mahogany, accommodates the swing of the door. The landing consists of African mahogany alternating with ammonia-fumed white oak.

Floating in a sea of terra-cotta tiles, the European-style cabinets harbor a number of amenities, including the spice drawer, appliance garage and full-extension storage trays shown in the top photo. The original kitchen fan (photo above), dating from 1912, was restored and chrome-plated by a local shop. The job cost $200.

Inc. (547 Rutherford Ave., Boston, Mass. 02129; 617-241-7900).

Because of the complexity of the granite work, I had Thorpe Construction produce in place full-size, ¾-in. plywood templates complete with sink cutouts, sills for the display niches, window stools and splashes. The templates consumed five sheets of ¾-in. CDX plywood and took 149½ hours to make. Mian was called in to review and approve the completed mock-up. I also photographed it and produced a mounted photo montage that was used with the templates for reference back at Mian's shop.

Mian was responsible for shipping, handling and installing the granite. Each of the 29 pieces was fabricated slightly oversize so that it could be ground to an exact fit on the job site. Finish grinding was accomplished outside the house with the use of portable angle grinders fitted with #60 industrial-grade diamond-grit wheels, which cut the granite like it was wood. Once Mian's stoneworkers achieved a perfect fit, the pieces were bedded in epoxy. Installation took two stoneworkers two days to complete.

Oiled terra-cotta—The final phase of construction was the installation of the terra-cotta tile floor. I ordered French-made, unsealed Coverland tiles, called CMPR—French Terra Kotta, from Tile Creations (400 Arsenal St., Watertown, Mass. 02172; 617-926-0559). The rich golden hue of the tiles was achieved by heating them in an oven to about 350° F, removing them with the aid of a pair of insulated ski gloves, and then immediately applying boiled linseed oil to the tops of the tiles with paper towels. The paper towels allowed me to apply the oil in controlled doses, preventing the oil from dripping over the edges, which would have inhibited the grout bond. The oil was absorbed by the tiles to a depth of about ⅛ in., effectively sealing the tiles and preventing them from staining.

The tile was set on a 1½-in. thick mortar bed reinforced with expanded metal lath set perpendicular to the floor joists. The only special concerns during installation were to create a pleasing color pattern and to maintain directionality (the tile has a distinct grain pattern created by machine extrusion and wire cutting). Unlike most terra-cotta tile, French Terra Kotta has a smooth surface, which we maintain by applying an occasional coat of Butcher's Wax Bowling Alley Paste (The Butcher Co., 120 Bartlett Street, Marlborough, Mass. 01752-3013; 508-481-5700). It's a turpentine-

based carnauba wax that's wiped on, allowed to dry and then buffed to a shine.

Saving the best for last—For the most part, all that remained was to restore the original stove, fan, intercom and radiator. We were delighted to discover that the Magic Chef cookstove had been thoroughly preserved by a thick layer of cooking grease. Once we dismantled, cleaned and reassembled it, it looked almost like new.

The kitchen fan (photo above right) was restored by William Sweeney of The Yankee Craftsman in Wayland, Mass. Sweeney scrubbed it clean, polished it, installed a new cord, replaced its cracked glass and, finally, sent the fan to a local shop for chrome-plating. The total cost of the job was $200.

The 6-volt house intercom (bottom photo, previous page) simply needed polishing and it was ready to use for calling the basement, guest room or upstairs hall. The hot-water radiator was delivered to Tim Harney at T. O. C. Finishing Co. For $100, he sandblasted and refinished it. The radiator (photo, p. 32) was relocated in the kitchen next to the back door.□

William E. Roesner is an architect in Newton Centre, Mass. Photos by Bruce Greenlaw.

The Kitchen Cabinet

How to design and build one with basic tools

by Will Hasson

The fundamental building block in every successful kitchen is the below-the-counter cabinet. It supports the work surface above and makes for organized storage beneath. Though this essential built-in can take on a multitude of styles and refinements, at heart the construction requirements are all the same. A sturdy case and framework, easily operable drawers, doors that fit and proper scale are common to good cabinets, whether made of painted plywood or expensive hardwood. In this article, I will describe the basic steps involved in building an uncomplicated, yet handsome, kitchen cabinet unit for about $140 in materials.

The cabinet shown above is the standard 24-in. depth, and is designed for the typical ¾-in. thick by 25½-in. plastic-laminate countertop. Its 35¼-in. height, also standard, accommodates appliances such as dishwashers and trash compactors, and presents the countertop at a level on which most people can work comfortably. These dimensions are used widely in the trade, but you can change the height to suit yourself just by adding or subtracting an inch or so. The 54-in. length here is arbitrary, but it makes good use of a single sheet of plywood and has room enough for a small sink to be let into the countertop. Also, a cabinet of this general size is small enough to move easily from shop to site—an important consideration.

Starting out—Constructing cabinets should always begin with a drawing of exactly what you have in mind. The drawing is indispensable for working out proportions, making cutting lists and for seeing the relationships between the different parts. You can use the drawings and cutting lists on the facing page as models for preparing your own design and material requirements. If you do as much as you can on paper before you cut any wood, you'll save yourself a lot of time and frustration.

Almost all cabinets have the same parts: a case (or carcase), a face frame, doors and drawers. The cabinet shown here is designed to feature wood, and therefore has a carefully joined face frame and panel doors. The face-frame members are doweled together, and the whole frame is then applied to the front of the case. It provides jambs for the cabinet doors, defines the openings for the drawers and generally stiffens the carcase and helps it resist lateral racking. The doors and drawers have ⅜-in. rabbeted inner edges so they overlap the face frame ⅜ in. to form a lip on all sides, and so the drawer fronts and door frames project ⅜ in. beyond the plane of the face frame. This arrange-

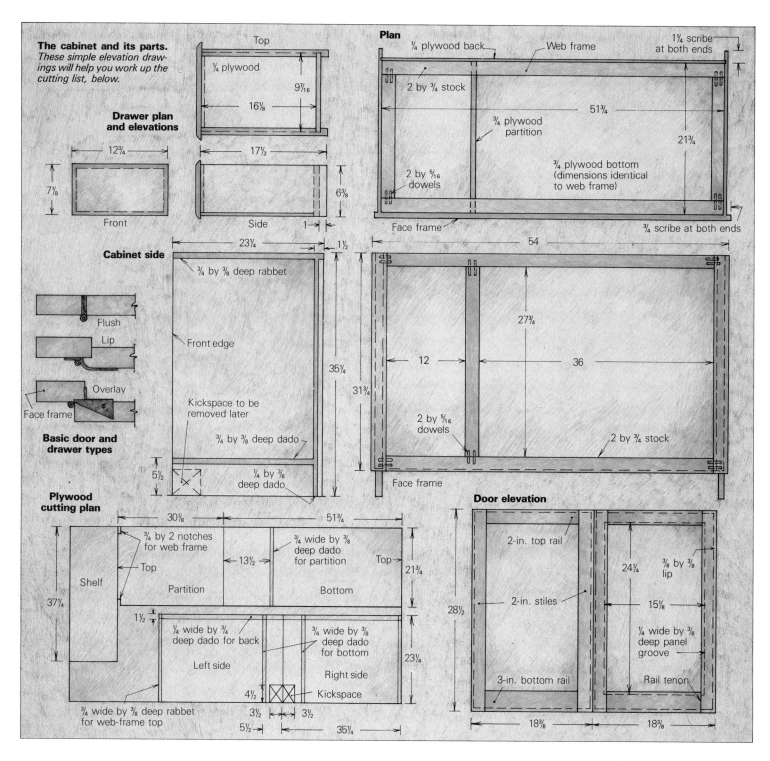

The cabinet and its parts. *These simple elevation drawings will help you work up the cutting list, below.*

ment looks good, and the rabbets allow considerable latitude in fitting doors and drawers into the cabinet. Once the face frame is made and attached, however, you can choose between either overlay or flush detailing, as shown in the drawing above.

In our shop, we make the face frame extend ¾ in. beyond the sides of the case so the cabinet can be scribed to fit snugly against interior walls and against other adjacent cabinet units.

You can build the entire cabinet unit with just a few tools. A table saw or radial arm saw is useful for ripping frame members and drawer sides to width and for crosscutting them accurately to length. The case sides and back, however, are best cut with a skill saw, since in many cases it's almost impossible to wrestle a full sheet of ¾-in. plywood onto a saw table. You will also need an electric drill with a sharp

⁵⁄₁₆-in. bit (preferably a brad-point bit) and a doweling jig for joining frame members.

It's possible, but not advisable, to get the job done without a table saw or radial saw. Without standing power tools, you would have to use a circular saw for all the ripping and crosscutting and a router for cutting the grooves, rabbets and dadoes. By hand-planing the frame members and drawer sides to finished width, you could certainly get accurate results, though it would take you considerably longer this way than if you were to use a standing power saw.

Making the face frame—Construction begins with the face frame. Rip ¾-in. solid stock into 2-in. wide strips and cut them to length. A crosscut jig for your table saw can be a great help in cutting accurate 90° angles. One way you can build a jig like this is described in the

Cutting list

Part	How many?	Size (in.)
Case		
Partition	1	30⅛ × 21¾ × ¾-in. ply
Bottom	1	51¾ × 21¾ × ¾-in. ply
Sides	2	35¼ × 23¼ × ¾-in. ply
Shelf	1	37¼ × 14 × ¾-in. ply
Back panel	1	51¾ × 30½ × ¼-in. ply
Web frame	2	51¾ × 2 × ¾
	2	17¾ × 2 × ¾
Face frame	2	50 × 2 × ¾
	2	31¾ × 2 × ¾
	1	27¾ × 2 × ¾
Doors		
Stiles	4	28½ × 2 × ¾
Rails	2	15⅛ × 2 × ¾
Rails	2	15⅛ × 3 × ¾
Panels	2	15⅛ × 24¼ × ¼-in. ply
Drawers		
Fronts	4	7⅛ × 12¾ × ¾
Sides	8	6⅜ × 17½ × ¾
Backs	4	6⅜ × 9⁷⁄₁₆ × ¾
Bottoms	4	16⅛ × 9⁷⁄₁₆ × ¼-in. ply
Kickplate	1	54 × 3½ × ¾
Hanger bar	1	37¼ × 3½ × ¾

The frame. With the doweling jig indexed on the pencil mark (1) Hasson bores out the end grain in a frame member. The hole is bored to the proper depth when the electrical tape on the drill bit is flush with the top of the jig, which is a self-centering dowel-guide made by Dowl-It (Box 147, Hastings, Mich. 49058).

For joining face-frame members, a single pencil line (2) marks the intersection of an upright. Lines to mark bore centers have been extended with a combination square down the edges to ensure accuracy in locating holes.

Crosscut jig

A simple table-saw attachment is especially useful for cutting frame members to length. We have four different versions for cutting various angles and sizes of work. The one drawn below is for making precisely square cuts in stock up to 2 ft. wide.

The guide rails on the bottom of the jig fit into the two miter grooves milled into the saw table on either side of the blade. We use oak or maple for the rails because these woods are hard and slippery. The runners should slide easily without any side-to-side movement.

The rails must be exactly perpendicular to fence A, which is rabbeted on its underside. In our latest version, I placed the rails in the table grooves and put a dab of glue atop their ends. Then I positioned fence A on the glue points and adjusted it perpendicular to the rails with a combination square. When the glue had set up, I applied glue to the edge of a ½-in. plywood panel and carefully slid the edges into the rabbet at the bottom of fence A, clamped it in place, and screwed the plywood to the runners, without moving the assembly from the table saw. Later I glued fence B to the top of the plywood. It keeps the ends of the plywood from flopping around and gives ballast to the front of the jig.

Passing the jig over the sawblade a few times will cut a workable slot in the plywood table. If you use the jig with a dado blade, make several shallow cuts to form the blade slot.

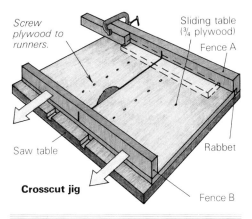

Screw plywood to runners.

Sliding table (¾ plywood)

Fence A

Saw table

Rabbet

Crosscut jig

Fence B

sidebar at left. Lay the frame members on a flat surface in the positions they belong in and label both sides of each joint. Holding one piece tightly in position with your fingers or a clamp, draw two lines across the joint. These lines mark the centers of the $5/16$-in. dowel holes, so don't put them too close to the edges of the stock—about ½ in. in is good. Next, carry the marks over the edges and ends of the strips with a combination square. A doweling jig is crucial to this operation because it ensures that the dowel hole is square to the surface and in just the right spot. Center the indexing mark of the doweling jig (mine is self-centering) on the lines and bore $5/16$-in. dia. holes slightly more than 1 in. deep for 2-in. dowels (photo 1, above). Drill a test hole to the right depth, and mark the drill shank with a piece of electrical tape where it's flush with the top of the jig. The tape will mark the depth for all the holes.

Before you join the frame members, think which parts should go together first. Generally, the rule is to work from the inside out. With large, complicated frames it is sometimes useful to glue up the frame in sections, letting the glue in each section dry before assembling it into a complicated whole. After drilling all the holes, baste the dowels on one end with a thin coat of yellow (aliphatic-resin) glue, and drive them home (2). To assemble each section, apply glue first to the end-grain edges, letting it soak in and reapplying as necessary. Then coat the dowels and close the joint.

Clamp the frame together with bar clamps, and use wooden pads between the clamp jaws and the face frame to avoid crushing the edges and to direct the clamping force to the joint area (3). Small pieces of paper between the clamp and the frame will prevent the glue from reacting with the metal and staining the wood black. Don't rush. Work steadily and carefully, making certain that everything is flat and square. After the glue dries, tool off the squeeze-out with a sharp chisel or paint scraper. Plane or sand the face frame with a belt sander to even out the joints; then set it aside.

3

4

When gluing up the face frame (3), check for square, and position clamp blocks to direct clamping pressure across joint lines.

The basic case (4): ¾-in. plywood sides, bottom and partition are glued and nailed in place with 6d cement-coated nails. Notches in the top of the partition will receive the web-frame top.

Apply the face frame (5) with the cabinet laid on its back. Before gluing face frame to carcase, check the scribe depth (the amount by which the frame overlaps the sides). Re-check periodically while tightening the clamps. The web-frame top has already been glued and nailed into notches in the partition and into rabbets in the case sides.

5

The case—The case or carcase determines the interior space of the cabinet. The sides, bottom and interior partition and shelf in this cabinet are all ¾-in. plywood, and the back is ¼-in. plywood. We use lauan plywood for these parts because it's easy to work, and has an unobtrusive color and grain pattern that doesn't clash with the solid woods on the face of the cabinet. A web frame, similar to the face frame, is fitted into rabbets and holds the carcase together at the top. The bottom of the case is housed in dadoes in the sides.

Now lay out the cabinet sections on the plywood in the most economical fashion (drawing, p.38). Cut the plywood for the sides, bottom and partition, and mark the positions of the dadoes and rabbets. Remember there are two opposing sides, one the mirror image of the other. Avoid making a pair of identical sides by accident, and having to scrap one.

Set your table saw or router to cut a groove ¾ in. wide by ⅜ in. deep. Now rabbet the tops (inside) of the case sides and dado the bottoms

as shown in the drawing on p.38. Then cut ¼-in. wide by ⅜-in. deep grooves for the plywood back.

Next, dowel-join and glue up the web-frame top just as you did the face frame. It has the same outside dimensions as the plywood bottom panel, and is held in the rabbets cut into the top of the case sides and in two notches cut into the partition top. The web frame holds the top of the case together, and serves as a cleat for attaching the countertop.

When the carcase components are cut to size, nail and glue them together from the bottom up (4). Use 6d cement-coated nails, and draw a centerline opposite the dadoes to aid in locating the nails. Lay the partially assembled case on its back and align the side and partition while nailing the web frame in place. Make sure the distance between the partition and the sides is equal at the top and bottom.

After assembling the case, attach the face frame (5). If the cabinet is to be painted or if nail holes are not objectionable, the face frame

can be glued and face-nailed to the body with 6d finishing nails. A neater way is to glue and clamp the face frame to the case, though this requires a good supply of bar clamps and C-clamps. Whichever method you use, leave an equal overlap at each side for scribing. When the frame is glued in place, saw out the kickspace notches.

Drawers—Doors and drawers fall into one of three categories, depending on how they relate to the face frame. Lip doors and drawers are the traditional choice. Overlay doors and drawers are used almost exclusively in mass-produced kitchen cabinets, mainly because they are so quick and easy to install. But they also give a kitchen a clean, solid look. Flush doors and drawers (they fit flush with the face frame) make the cabinets look like furniture, and are by far the most difficult to install, as each one must be hand-fitted.

The details for drawer construction depend upon the type of drawer (lip, overlay or flush)

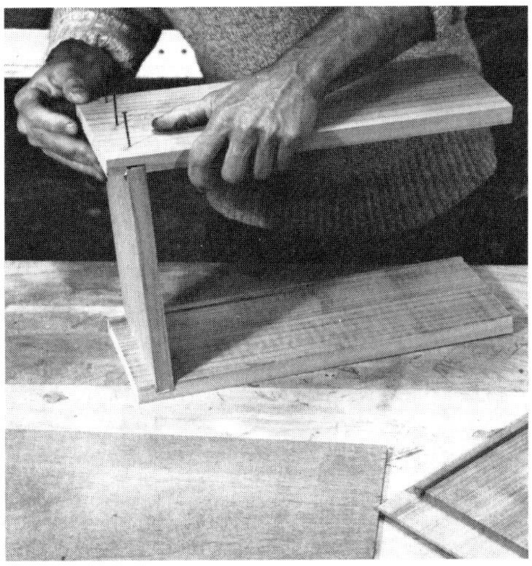

6

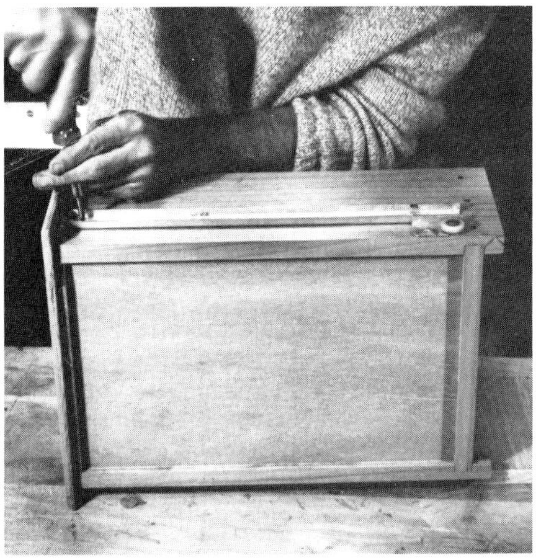

7

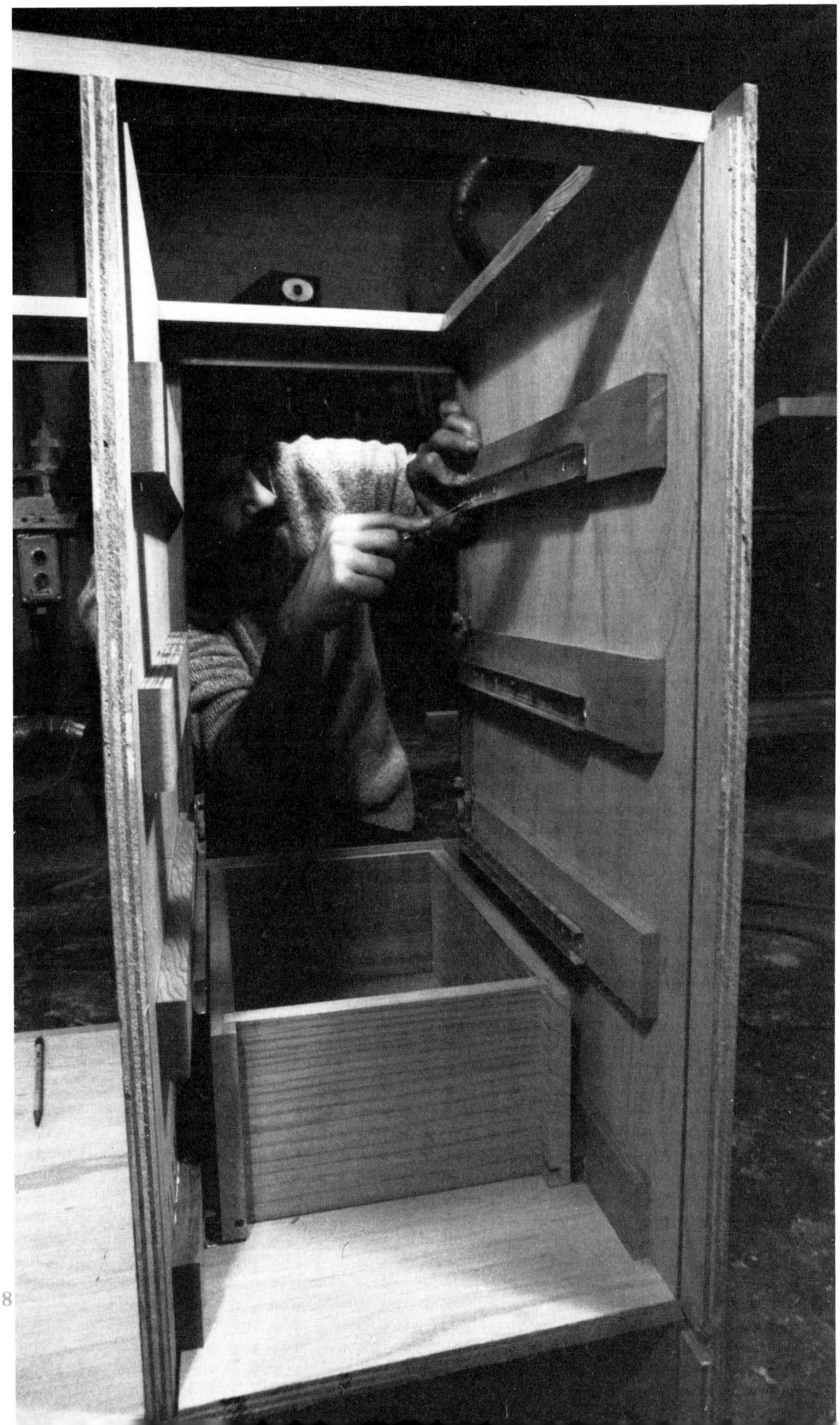

8

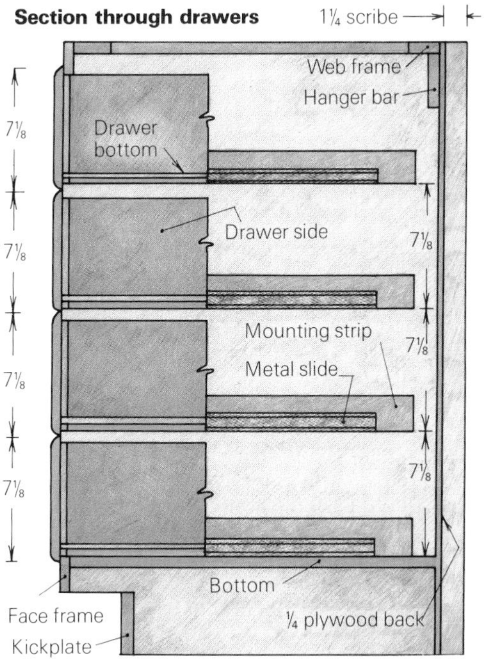

Section through drawers
1¼ scribe
Web frame
Hanger bar
Drawer bottom
Drawer side
Mounting strip
Metal slide
Bottom
Face frame
Kickplate
¼ plywood back
7⅛
7⅛
7⅛
7⅛
7⅛
7⅛
7⅛

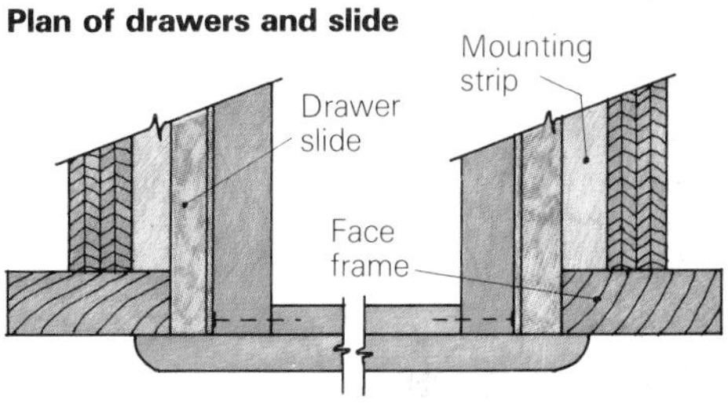

Plan of drawers and slide
Drawer slide
Mounting strip
Face frame

Drawers. **After cutting the components (drawing, above), assemble the drawer by gluing and nailing the dadoed sides to the back (6). Slide the drawer bottom into its groove, and cap the box with the drawer front. Bore pilot holes for nailing the sides into the rabbeted front to avoid splitting the wood. The front edges of the drawer front have been shaped with a router and a ⅜-in. rounding-over bit.**

Screw the slides to the drawer sides (7). The wheel flange should be flush with the side's bottom edge, and the track parallel to the edge.

Inside the cabinet (8) drawer slides are fixed to a mounting strip that holds them flush with the face frame. The mounting strips are glued and screwed to the case sides.

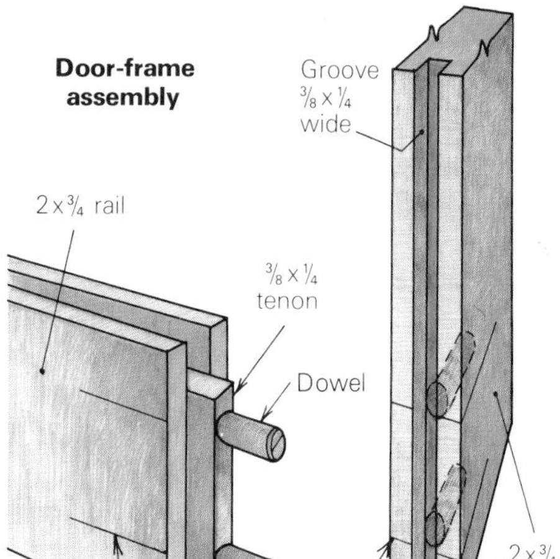

Door-frame assembly
Groove ⅜ x ¼ wide
2 x ¾ rail
⅜ x ¼ tenon
Dowel
2 x ¾ stile
Witness-mark face side and edge.

A bottom rail, with doweled tenon and panel groove. The stubby tenon adds strength and lets you plow unstopped grooves in the stiles.

and the kind of drawer-slide mechanism you use. We use metal slides with nylon rollers for mounting the drawers because they are easy to install and because drawers glide smoothly and quietly on them. The slides come in a number of sizes, based on the dimensions of the drawer and the expected weight of its contents. Each drawer requires a pair of slides, which fit into a corresponding pair of tracks mounted on the inside of the cabinet. The slides in this cabinet are Grant #336 (Grant Hardware Co., High St., West Nyack, N.Y.; and 16651 Johnson Dr., City of Industry, Calif. 91745).

Begin laying out the drawers by considering the inside dimension of the opening in the face frame into which they will fit. In this cabinet, the drawer opening is 12 in. wide and 27¾ in. high. To keep things simple, we'll construct four identical drawers (drawing, previous page, top). Add the opening height plus the width of two lips (27¾ in. + ⅜ in. + ⅜ in. = 28½ in.) and divide the total by four to determine the height of each drawer front (7⅛ in.). The length of the drawer front is the width of the opening plus the width of two lips (12¾ in.).

Cut out the drawer fronts and calculate the width of the rabbet on the inside of each drawer front required to overlap the drawer sides, the metal slide and the face frame. The side thickness is ¾ in.; almost all metal slides require 17/32 in. between the drawer side and the face frame; and the lip width is ⅜ in. This adds up to 1 21/32 in.

Cut the rabbets in the drawer fronts, and set them aside while you make the other drawer parts. The width of the sides will be the drawers' front height less the width of the two ⅜-in. lips (in our case, 7⅛ in. – ¾ in. = 6⅜ in.). The drawer length of 17½ in. in this cabinet is arbitrary. Drawers can be as long as the depth of the cabinet will allow.

The drawer sides, back and front are grooved along their bottom inner edges to receive the ¼-in. plywood bottom. Plow the groove ¼ in. deep and ⅜ in. from the bottom edge. The sides have a ¾-in. wide dado cut 1 in. from the rear edge to house the drawer back. Nail and glue

the drawers together, making sure they are square (6). Apply glue to the joints but not to the bottom panel, which should float freely in the groove. This is especially important if the drawer bottom is made of solid wood rather than plywood, because gluing it will cause it to crack eventually.

Half of the drawer slide is screwed to the drawer sides (7); the other half is attached to the sides of the cabinet on a spacer strip that brings it flush with the face frame. Locate the bottom edges of the spacers the same distance apart as the height of the drawer fronts. This will give you a guide for attaching the slides (8). All metal slides come with slotted holes to allow up-and-down and in-and-out adjustments. Use the slotted holes until the drawers run properly, and then drive the rest of the screws to lock the slide in place. You'll probably have to shave the top and bottom edges of the drawer fronts with a plane to regularize the spaces between them.

Panel doors—Frame-and-panel construction is common to most cabinet doors because it can be varied in so many ways. The inner edges of the frame may be molded with a router or shaper, be treated with applied molding or just be left square. The panel may be flat or raised, or glass may be used instead of wood.

Construction is basically the same regardless of the details. The first step, again, is to make a cutting list. Door stiles should be equal to the height of the door opening plus ¾ in. for the lips top and bottom. Calculate the width the same way. For a pair of doors, the opening plus ¾ in. is divided by two to get the width of each individual door. The length of the rails equals the width of the door less twice the width of the stile plus twice the depth of the panel groove for cutting a short tenon on the rail ends. In this cabinet, rail length is 15⅛ in. (18⅜ – 4 + ¾). Typically stiles and top rails are 2 in. wide. Bottom rails are 1½ times as wide to add visual weight and to increase the amount of wood involved in the joint.

After ripping the stiles and rails to width and

cutting them to length, arrange the pieces on a flat surface and mark the joints for dowels. Keep the holes far enough from the edges to prevent cutting into the dowels when rabbeting the outer edge for the lip and grooving the inner edge for the panel (drawing previous page, bottom). Mark the inner edge of each piece so rabbeting, grooving and drilling get done in the right spots. Then bore for dowels.

Make a ¼-in. wide groove in a scrap piece of wood for testing the thickness of the rail tenons. Now cut the tenons ¼ in. thick by ⅜ in. wide on both ends of the rails. Do this on a table saw or with a router, or clamp the rail in a vise and cut the tenon with a good backsaw. Make sure the tenons fit snugly, but not too tightly in the test groove.

The next step is to groove the inner edges of the frame members to receive the panels and tenons. Be certain to mark the outside face of each member and hold that face against the saw fence when plowing the grooves for the panels. Cut the ¼-in. plywood panel to fit, and then assemble the frame around it. Again, don't glue the panel into the groove. Be sure the doors are square and flat; otherwise they won't lie flat against the cabinet when closed.

Once the glue has dried, cut the ⅜-in. by ⅜-in. rabbet all around the door's inner edges (9), and you're ready to put on the hinges. Hinges are made for all three kinds of doors, and each style requires a specific type of hinge. It is best to install the hinges for lip doors on the doors first, spacing them one hinge length down from the top and the same up from the bottom. Next, set the cabinet on its back, put the doors in place and mark the position of the hinges (10). Drive one screw into each hinge and see if the door swings freely and lies flat. If it does, drive in the rest of the screws. If the fit is skewed, remove the screws, readjust the hinges as necessary, and try again. Now install catches to keep the doors flat against the face frame. Mount the catches opposite the door pulls. We use the common roller variety. Screw the male half to the top of the door stile, engage the two halves and screw the catch plate to the mount-

Lipping. A ⅜-in. lip is cut around the inner edges of the door (9) after the outer edges are rounded over. A wooden auxiliary fence makes it easy to expose the right amount of the dado head to get the ⅜-in. rabbet.

Hinges are first mounted on the doors, and then the doors are held in place against the face frame while screw centers are marked (10).

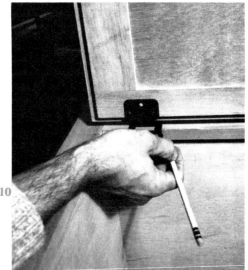

9

10

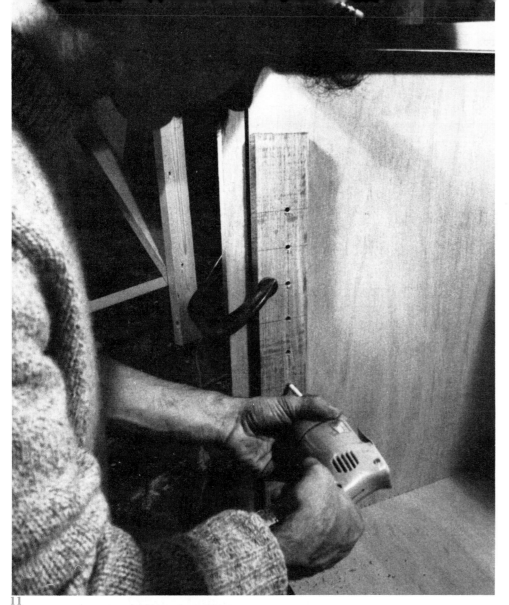

ing block with the door closed. Magnetic catches are also good, but best of all are self-closing hinges, which let you do away with catches all together.

While the back is still off, bore holes for the shelf rests. Make a drilling jig like the one shown in photo 11 with ¼-in. dia. holes, 2 in. on center, for press-in shelf rests. Use a piece of tape on the drill bit to regulate the depth of the hole. I drill the vertical rows of holes about a foot apart toward the back of the cabinet. The shelf should be about 14 in. wide, rather than span to the front of the cabinet. This narrower shelf lets you get at pots and other stuff stored in the rear of the cabinet.

A 1x4 hanger bar for installing the cabinet should now be nailed and glued to the bottom of the web frame and to the sides of the cabinet (12). Finally, slide the ¼-in. plywood back into its groove and nail it in place. Give everything a good sanding, and protect the wood with the finish of your choice. For wood finishes, we prefer Watco Danish Oil or lacquer, but for cabinets that are used frequently, polyurethane is the best choice.

Installation—Chances are good that the space your cabinet will occupy is neither level, square nor bordered by perfectly flat walls. These imperfections are usually slight and of no structural consequence, but they can drive the meticulous installer crazy. A few tips:

First, measure the highest and lowest points in the room and determine the differential. If the difference is an inch or less, I shim up the bottom of the cabinets, starting at the lowest point in the room. If the difference is more than 1 in., I split it by adding shims at one end and cutting the bottoms off the cabinets at the other. When the cabinets are level, pull them away from the wall and attach 1x4 ledger strips to the wall opposite the hanger bars.

Return the cabinets to their intended positions and check any counter-to-wall intersections for fit. If the wall is irregular, plane the scribing strip to match the wall contour (for more on scribes, see *FHB* #9, pp. 39-41).

When the cabinets are scribed and level, clamp the neighboring face frames together (if you've got more than one cabinet) and attach them with three counterbored drywall screws. Don't worry about plugging the counterbores—they won't show, and you can easily remove the cabinets if you decide to take them with you. Once the face frames are joined, screw the hanger bars to the wall ledgers, filling any gaps between the two with shims. It doesn't take a lot of screws for a solid connection; two per cabinet should do it.

Cut the kickplate to fill the gap at the back of the toe-space, and attach it in place with 6d finishing nails. We recommend finishing the juncture between the flooring and the kickplate with dark-colored vinyl coving. The coving makes this busy but hard-to-reach kitchen cranny easier to clean, and protects the kickplate from scuff marks.   □

Will Hasson is a partner in Fourth St. Woodworking, Berkeley, Calif.

A template (11) makes drilling holes for shelf rests quick and accurate.

The hanger bar for attaching the cabinet to the wall is glued and nailed to the bottom of the web frame (12). The kickplate overlaps the side by the same amount that the face frame does.

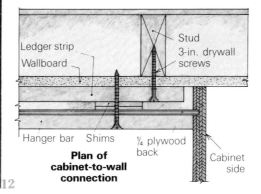

Ledger strip
Wallboard
Stud
3-in. drywall screws
Hanger bar   Shims
¼ plywood back
Cabinet side
Plan of cabinet-to-wall connection

Attaching adjacent cabinets

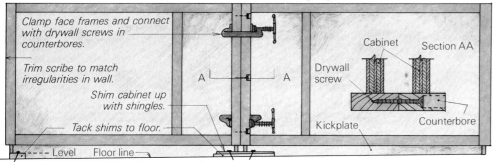

Clamp face frames and connect with drywall screws in counterbores.

Trim scribe to match irregularities in wall.

Shim cabinet up with shingles.

Tack shims to floor.

Level   Floor line

A   A

Drywall screw

Cabinet   Section AA

Kickplate   Counterbore

Kitchen Cabinets from Components

With careful layout and efficient assembly, you can piece together affordable cabinets from mix-and-match doors, drawers and boxes

by Sven Hanson and Joel Wheeler

Wood adds the custom touch. This bright, Santa Fe-style kitchen is dressed up with cabinet doors and drawer fronts made of pickled maple. The cabinets behind them are affordable modular boxes made of laminated particleboard.

For more than 13 years we've been building premium furniture and custom cabinets in Albuquerque, N.M. In that time, costs have risen, but competition has kept our prices low. About five years ago, we began looking for a partner who could help us stay competitive. That partner turned out to be not just one but a group of companies that make cabinet components.

Component manufacturers make everything from a single, simple square box to elaborate assemblies that will cover the wall. The cabinets arrive in tightly packaged bundles of flat panels (called knocked down, or KD). Large retailers such as IKEA sell KD cabinets to brave and thrifty do-it-yourselfers. The retailers include extensive instructions with the components, and market them under the category RTA, which means ready-to-assemble. We often get calls from do-it-yourselfers to help them to complete their jobs, so we don't mind the competition.

Some fabricators deal in machined components made of particleboard veneered with vinyl, polyester or wood. Others carry solid-wood components such as face frames, boxes, doors, drawer fronts, shelves, and drawer sides and bottoms.

Manufacturers show their wares in well-organized catalogs. For some (Components Plus), you specify what you want, and they tell you what you need and give you the prices. Others (Cab-Parts) let you pick from a huge assortment

Photo this page: Robert Reck

of shapes and sizes. Then, you add up the costs based on the price list and order the parts by catalog designation.

Typically, we buy KD cabinets and drawers from one manufacturer, doors from another and hardware from our local mail-order distributor (TJ Hardware Inc., P.O. Box 30308, Albuquerque, N.M. 87190; 800-462-4266). If we need a hardwood drawer, we go to another fabricator. The result is a set of cabinets that combine the look of custom woodwork with the efficiency of modular construction (photo facing page). As a ballpark price, you can figure the base cabinets will cost about $70 per running ft. and the upper cabinets $60 per ft. This price includes the carcases, drawers, raised-panel doors and necessary hardware. All these parts fit together because the dimensions are standardized and we are meticulous in our specifications.

They call it Eurostyle—Component makers offer the greatest cost savings when supplying frameless cabinets predrilled with two vertical rows of holes spaced on 32-mm centers (photo right). These holes, about 1¼-in. apart, accept shelf pins and hardware-mounting screws.

This style of cabinet construction is called Eurostyle because it was developed in Europe as a response to the devastation of World War II. Europeans needed to get back into the 20th century quickly, and they had to do the job with limited resources. Fractured forests yielded more particleboard than solid lumber, and a decimated work force didn't have time to rebuild an entire continent using their traditional hand craftsmanship. So cabinetmakers and manufacturers of machinery and hardware worked to standardize all aspects of cabinet dimension and construction. That standardization included ditching traditional face-frame cabinets in favor of slab construction.

The hinge hides on the backside of the door, and the flanges that secure the hinge to the cabinet have screw holes on 32-mm centers. The doors hide all but about ⅛ in. of the edge of the carcase. The universal nature of the door-to-hinge-to-cabinet relationship permits a complete remodel of the cabinets for the cost of a new set of doors and the time it takes to install them. For cabinetmakers, that's a good way to sell around the "I'm not sure I'll like it forever" objection.

By ordering premachined parts, we run a safer, cleaner, quieter shop. Each job ties up the shop floor for less than half the time that it takes to build cabinets from scratch. But you've got to knock them together fast. Even more importantly, you must take the basics of a floor plan, turn it into a functioning design and, from it, order the correct parts.

Ordering the cabinets—We begin the cabinet layout with a plan of the room and place center lines on counter-mounted fixtures such as sinks and range tops. Then, we draw in boundaries for areas reserved for stove, refrigerator, compactor, dishwasher and microwave (consult the appliance manuals for clearance requirements). We're also careful to note the positions of walls, doorways and windows on the plan.

Hardware first. Before assembling the boxes, Michael Fratrick screws the hinges and the drawer tracks to the sides of the cabinet. The holes to the left of the slide receive the doweled drawer divider.

From these fixed positions, we determine the unbroken runs of cabinets and figure out how many it will take to fill out the run. Cabinets are sized in 1½-in. or 3-in. increments, depending on which company we're ordering from. Any gaps left over are finished with filler strips.

We prefer to keep cabinet doors in the range of 20-in. wide. Doors that are wider than 22 in. to 24 in. have a tendency to warp, and their manufacturers won't guarantee them for flatness. For a

kitchen to look right, the majority of the doors need to be taller than they are wide.

We can order cabinets that have nonstock dimensions, but there's a hefty penalty to pay. A typical premium is $5 to $10 for a change in width or depth, and $15 for a change in height. And if you've got a base cabinet with nonstandard drawers, you can figure an additional charge of about $3 per drawer. So when the dimensions get odd, the costs mount quickly.

Glue secures the back panel. Karen Umland runs a bead of hot glue around the back panel to affix it to the cabinet's sides, back and bottom. The plywood strip on the right is a hanger bar for the cabinet.

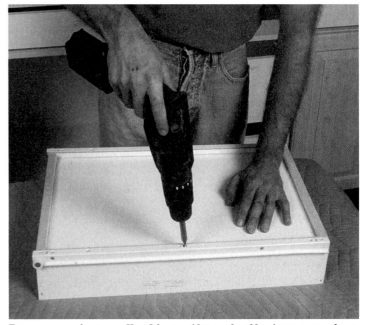

Building a box. Hardware installed, the box is ready to assemble. Here, the last side is aligned with dowels in the top, the bottom and the drawer divider. The back panel will tuck into the dado in the cabinet side.

Drawers are just small cabinets. Also made of laminate-covered particleboard, the drawer boxes have the same construction details as their cabinets. Here, a drawer slide is being affixed to the bottom of the drawer.

Ideally, the doors of the upper cabinets should line up with doors and drawers of the lower cabinets. In practice, however, this is tough to accomplish. Windows, sinks and other obstacles often derail the strictly aligned approach.

At inside corners it's important to use adequate filler strips (at least 2-in. wide) to allow drawers and doors on both sides of the corner to pass each other. Clients can more easily forgive oversize fillers than cabinet doors that can't be opened. We also want fillers at wall intersections to allow us to scribe to the curvy walls typical of New Mexico's residential architecture. In Euro-style, we don't have an overhanging face frame to provide scribing room.

Basic dimensions figured, we go to the appropriate catalog—or, in the case of Components Plus, we just fax them our list of sizes, and they fax us back our list and the prices. One way or the other, the business of estimating a cabinet installation is greatly simplified by having the first half or our cost computed exactly. The Compo-

nents Plus order can even include the hardware, and that might sway a first-timer or a builder working in a remote location. But you'll save more money by buying in bulk (25 slides or 50 hinges) from a hardware supplier.

Quick assembly is the key—We win or lose the time/money part of this deal at the assembly stage, so we set up the shop to allow our best mechanics to work at full speed. When the parts arrive, we put them into groups: drawer sides; individual cabinet sides and tops; backs; and miscellaneous parts. After this step, we drive the dowels into the horizontal members—cabinet bottoms and drawer dividers. The dowels are held fast by a glue supplied by the manufacturer.

Our cabinet assemblers work on a smooth, 18-in. high bench, assembling the boxes according to a set of instructions provided by the manufacturer. With two cabinet sides laid flat and placed top to top, mechanic Michael Fratrick lightly pencils in positions for hardware. Fratrick uses the

Magic Wand, a layout tool made by Blum. If you don't have one of these tools, you can use a good ruler with enhanced markings to show the 32-mm centers and the positions of the hinges and drawer slides.

On a base cabinet, Michael positions the drawer slides and hinge mounting-plates (photo p. 45). He fastens them into the holes with 5 mm stud screws. He then squirts a bit of glue into each of the dowel holes on one cabinet side and wrestles the horizontal parts into proper position. He drives them down by striking the dowels on the other end with a rubber hammer.

The back goes in next, then the other side goes on (left photo, above) and the rubber hammer slams it home. Instead of clamping, we staple the joint, which provides additional reinforcement.

Michael places the cabinet face down and squares it up by comparing diagonal measurements. Meanwhile, our other mechanic, Karen Umland, glues the hanger bar (a strip of plywood that reinforces the cabinet back where the mounting screws will attach it to the wall) along the top edge by pressing it into a wavy bead of hot glue. With the same hot glue, she puts a bead, or fillet, around the back-panel perimeter (top right photo, facing page). The result: a square, sturdy cabinet. We have never gotten a customer complaint on carcase quality.

Next, the drawers—The drawers go together in the same manner as the cabinet carcases. It may seem like a small thing, but the repetitive process means we don't have to change tools or mental gears. No doubt the similarity of material and structure saves time at the factory, too.

After sliding the bottom into place, Michael hammers on the other side. Then, he checks the drawer for square and runs a bead of hot glue around the bottom-to-side connection. He next installs the tracks with ⅝-in. #6 nickel-plate deepthread screws (bottom right photo, facing page).

Ordering and drilling the doors—The doors make up the vast majority of visible surface on a true Eurostyle-cabinet job, so we put a lot of energy into helping the client choose the doors. Ordering doors is simplest when done through your carcase suppliers. They'll automatically make the doors to fit, but you're usually limited to particleboard and laminated work, albeit some fancy styling including rolled edges and running edge pulls. For a more traditional look, we order raised-panel doors from another source.

Various manufacturers offer a wide selection of wooden doors. Most species are familiar North American hardwoods, but some you may never have heard of. Door manufacturers also offer scores of panel profiles, edge profiles and inside edge-bead profiles. Some suppliers will finish doors for you, and they also will drill for hinges and pulls.

The usual dimensions are the same height as the case, but ⅛ in. (3 mm) shorter and narrower. That leaves an ⅛-in. reveal between doors in a run of cabinets. We leave a minimum ³⁄₁₆-in. gap at a wall to ensure room for the door to open.

Our doors arrive without the holes drilled for mounting the hinges. That way, the door suppliers haven't had to concern themselves with which way the doors open, which cuts down on costly mistakes. Now comes the part where the assembler displays some true craftsmanship, or at least a talent for accurate measurement.

The European-style hinge needs three holes to attach to the door (middle photo, right). In the center is a 35-mm (1⅜-in.) by 13-mm deep hole that receives the hinge cup. The edge of this hole is 2 mm to 3 mm from the edge of the door. In addition to the 35-mm hole, the hinge needs two ⁷⁄₆₄-in. dia. holes for the #6 mounting screws.

We do our drilling with a three-spindle machine costing roughly $2,600 and made by Blum (top photo, right). Other hinge suppliers offer a similar device.

To mount hinges using an ordinary drill press, you first install the 35-mm bit, rotate one cutter next to the fence and move the fence ⅛ in. away from the bit (check the specs for your hinge). Clamp the fence in place. We adjust the table to

This machine drills three holes at once. When it's done boring the holes for the hinge, this specialized drill press inserts the hinge into the circular mortise.

Hinges are adjustable. Slots in the hinge-mounting plates allow the hinge to be moved in and out, and up and down, which makes it easy to get the door to lay flat, square and centered on the cabinet.

Installing the doors. Once the boxes are assembled, Fratrick snaps the doors onto their hinges and tinkers with their final positioning with a screwdriver. Sink bases make up the top tier of cabinets. They sit atop a row of base cabinets.

Fitting a drawer front. Drawer fronts in a European-style kitchen must be installed accurately. Two threaded, adjustable inserts are let into 20-mm holes in the back of a drawer front (above), which is then attached to the box with machine screws run into the inserts (below).

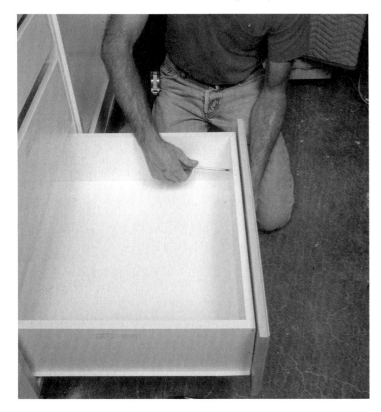

Affixing the drawer front. The adjustable inserts allow the drawer front to be moved ⅛ in. in each direction. When alignment is right, drywall screws make the positioning permanent.

hold the work 1 in. below the bit and set the depth stop to drill to a depth of ½ in. + ¹⁄₃₂ in. That give us a little allowance if we have thin stock or dust in the hole.

For the majority of the doors, the center of the 35-mm hole is 3³⁄₁₆ in. to 3¾ in. from the top and bottom of the door. So we set the appropriate stops on the drill-press table to let us quickly register the hinge positions. Special-purpose cabinets sometimes need different hinge positions, and tall doors will need additional hinges. A glance at the positions of the hinge-mounting plates on the cabinets tells us whether we are using the correct set of stops on our hinge machine.

To test the accuracy of our stops, we drill hinge-mounting holes in a 2-in. wide scrap cut to the length of the door. Then, we screw the hinges on the test stick and install the stick on the cabinet. If it sits right and opens cleanly, not hitting cabinet edge or adjacent door, we know the setup is ac-

curate, and we go ahead and drill and attach the doors (bottom photo, p. 47).

Cabinet ends and drawer fronts—Picture the classic window over the sink. Now, glance to the side at the upper cabinets, and you'll likely see a surface that the neophyte designer forgets about. Without some additional treatment, the cabinet sides are probably gleaming white or champagne polyester.

An attractive alternative includes peel-and-stick veneer, prefinished to match the doors and applied to a clean, flat end panel. For a slight additional cost, we apply a raised panel to those ends. To make this look right you've got to make sure the visible edge of the panel is finished, and the door has to be wider by the thickness of the panel's frame. The hinge position has to be adjusted accordingly by using a different base plate.

Drawer fronts are the same widths as the doors. Two typical heights for drawer fronts are 5 in.

and 6 in. Aligning drawer fronts so that the gaps between adjacent drawers are equal is a finicky business. Back in the old days, we used to rely on tricks such as putting small tabs of double-sided mirror tape on the drawer box. Then, we'd slide the drawer into its box, position the drawer front so that it looked right and press the drawer front to the box, hoping it would stick long enough to anchor it with a couple of screws driven from inside the drawer. Now, we use "drawer-front adjusters" to attach fronts to boxes. The adjuster has a threaded-steel insert floating inside a slot in a 20-mm barbed-plastic dowel (top left photo above).

We put one of the adjusters at each end of the drawer front—about 3 in. from the end and roughly centered. The adjusters nest in 20-mm holes that are 10.5-mm deep. We drop 20-mm dowel centers into the holes, press the drawer front to the drawer box and slam it with a fist to mark the drawer box. Through these marks, we drill 5-mm holes using a brad-point bit and a backer block to reduce tearout in the drawer.

Then, we press the adjusters into the holes in the drawer front and attach it to the drawer box with a couple of machine screws (bottom left photo, facing page). The inserts in the adjusters allow the drawer front to be moved up and down, and side to side about ⅛ in. in all directions. Once we complete final on-site adjustments, we affix the drawer fronts with a couple of 1¼-in. drywall screws (right photo, facing page).

Installation notes—In a true Eurostyle job, the upper cabinets hang from a metal Z-bar attached to the wall. Installers hang and adjust the cabinets using special cam-action hangers inside the boxes. The hanger-bar system lets a single worker hang cabinets. I suppose these are clever devices, but we don't mess with them. The hardware costs extra, and the cabinets inevitably have to be notched in places to fit over the bars.

Instead, we install the upper cabinets by screwing through the hanger bars that we've glued to the backs of the cabinets. One installer holds the bottom aligned with a line drawn level from a point 54 in. above the floor, while the other shoots in the screws. That's American style.

Most of the manufacturers sell a combination leg and leveler for their base cabinets. You adjust the levelers with a screwdriver passed through a small access hole inside the cabinet. A press-on cover then hides the hole. After leveling cabinets, you snap the toe kick onto the front leg levelers.

For a couple of reasons, leg levelers have not received wide acceptance in the United States. In Europe, cabinets typically belong to the household, not to the house. Far fewer Europeans own their own homes than Americans, and when Europeans move, they take their cabinets.

The levelers cost only about $8 per set, but with labor added, that's too much for single use. We construct 4-in. tall bases of ¾-in. CDX plywood. To level the bases, we crawl the floor with a 4-ft. level until we've determined the highest point in the runs. We start there and level all the bases to that point using shims, construction adhesive and 2x4 blocks glued and nailed to the floor and screwed to the bases. This makes our foundation strong (to learn more about installing cabinets, see pp. 80-85).

We still build cabinets from scratch when they have to be customized to fit a particular installation. But for the straightforward jobs, using components effectively doubles the size of our shop and lets our skilled cabinetmakers concentrate on the one-of-a-kind projects that they relish.

We can't claim that cabinets from components will turn you into a master cabinetmaker. And we can assure you that making cabinets from components won't work if you like to fake it as you do a job. But if you understand basics of cabinet design and if you can measure accurately and assemble in an orderly fashion, making cabinets from components can really work. □

Joel Wheeler and Sven Hanson are friendly competitors in New Mexico's furniture and cabinet market. Photos by Sven Hanson except where noted.

Cabinet-component suppliers

The manufacturers listed below offer a range of cabinet components, from KD (knocked down) cabinet carcases to hardwood frame-and-panel doors. In addition to these suppliers, which all ship nationwide, there are countless other regional or local shops too small or too busy to advertise nationally.

Accent Manufacturing
1585 Mabury Road, Unit B, San Jose, Calif. 95133; (408) 926-3667, Fax 408-926-0890. Cabinet-box components, shelves, drawers, hardware, drilled doors in laminates with custom radii, wood-slab and veneer doors. Sell to cabinet shops, builders and related trades.

Cab Parts
716 Arrowest Road, Grand Junction, Colo. 81505; (303) 241-7682, Fax (303) 241-7689. Component cabinets including drawers, adjustable shelves, roll-out drawer boxes. Simple line of cabinets with comprehensive catalog of sizes and styles. Sell to cabinetmakers and contractors who make their own cabinets only.

Components Plus-Vass Inc.
3405 Walnut St., Denver, Colo. 80205; (303) 292-1040, Fax (303) 292-1041. Line of melamine cabinet components featuring 1½-in. width increments. Dowels are preinstalled in horizontal pieces. Doors and drawers are predrilled for European hardware. Edge

banding available in pvc, laminate, wood tape or solid wood up to 12 mm thick. Sell to cabinetmakers and contractors who make their own cabinets.

Conestoga Wood Specialties Inc.
245 Reading Road, P.O. Box 158, East Earl, Pa. 17519-0158; (215) 445-6702, Fax (800) 722-0427. Comprehensive line of frameless and face-frame cabinets, doors, drawers including dovetailed wood. Mind-boggling list of merchandise. Sell to cabinetmakers and manufacturers only.

Hutchinson Products Co.
P.O. Box 12066, Oklahoma City, Okla. 73157; (800) 847-0091, Fax (405) 946-4446. Wood or MDF door and drawer fronts in slab or frame-and-panel. No finishing, drilling or hardware.

Mar-Flo Inc.
8 Fox Court, Dumont, N.J. 07628; (201) 742-4765, Fax (201) 742-9471. Solid wood doors in more than 100 styles, finished or unfinished. Sell to

cabinetmakers, contractors and savvy owner-builders.

Porta Door
65 Cogwheel Lane, Seymour, Conn. 06483; (203) 888-6191, Fax (203) 888-5803. Doors, drawer fronts and drawer boxes. Finishing available. Sell to cabinetmakers and contractors.

Scherr's Cabinets
5315 Burdick Expressway East, Rt. 5, Box #12, Minot, N.D. 58701; (701) 839-3384, Fax, (701) 852-6090. Box components, drawers (including dovetailed solid wood) hardwood doors, raw or stained and finished. Drilling and hardware optional. Sell to cabinet makers, contractors and savvy owner builders.

Top Drawer Components Inc.
700 N. Neely St., Suite 4, Gilbert, Ariz. 85233; (800) 745-9540, Fax (602) 926-9601. Dovetailed drawers of wood and melamine in sizes from 2-in. to 14-in. high. Assembled or RTA, the wood is finished with two coats of vinyl sealer and one coat of precatalyzed lacquer. Sell to anyone.

Cabinet-hardware suppliers

European-style cabinets require hinges, drawer slides, fasteners and assorted jigs and tools that aren't always readily available. Here's a list of manufacturers who can steer you to a local supplier, or to mail-order houses that can fill your order.

Alfit America Inc.
7801 Redpine Road, Suite J, Richmond, Va. 23237; (800) 451-0444. Drawer slides, assembly fittings and adjustable attachment blocks.

Amerock Corp.
4000 Auburn St., P. O. Box 7018, Rockford, Ill. 61125-7018; (815) 963-9631. USA-made European and traditional hardware.

Julius Blum Inc.
Highway 16, Lowesville, Stanley, N.C. 28164; (704) 827-1345. European hardware, jigs and tools.

Grass
1202 Highway 66 South, Kernersville, N.C. 27284; (910) 996-4041. Full range of hinges and hardware.

Mepla Inc.
909 W. Market Center Drive, High Point, N.C. 27260; (910) 883-7121. Full range of European hardware, tools and jigs.

Salice America Inc.
3301 Woodpark Blvd., Suite P, Charlotte, N.C. 28206; (704) 598-7258. Full range of European hinges.

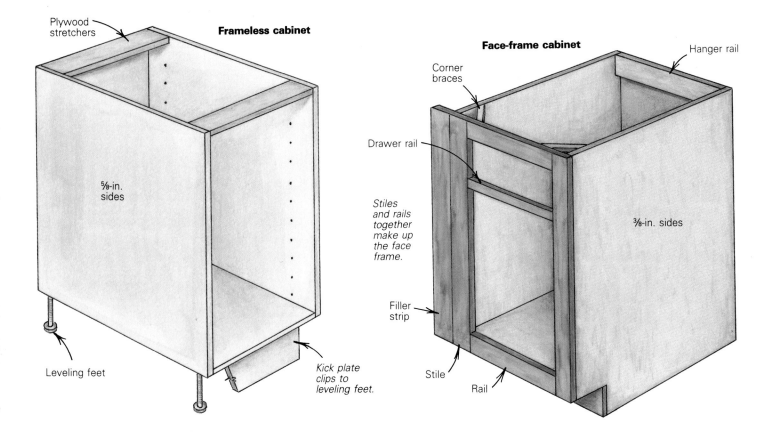

Plywood stretchers

Frameless cabinet

⅝-in. sides

Leveling feet

Kick plate clips to leveling feet.

Face-frame cabinet

Corner braces

Drawer rail

Stiles and rails together make up the face frame.

Filler strip

Stile

Rail

Hanger rail

⅜-in. sides

Manufactured Kitchen Cabinets
Given all the choices, separating function from fashion can be tough

by Kevin Ireton

"When you open the lower cupboard door, our patented Base Shelf Extender automatically brings the shelf out with it." No, this isn't the latest cabinet innovation from some high-tech European manufacturer. It's a standard feature advertised by a cabinet manufacturer in a 1917 issue of *The Saturday Evening Post*. Given the number of companies manufacturing cabinets today and the enthusiasm with which they promote their products, I must admit to getting some perverse satisfaction from learning that roll-out trays in base cabinets are nothing new, and what's more, that 70 years ago they came out automatically when you opened the doors.

Last year more than 200 cabinet manufacturers each sold over $1 million-worth of cabinets, with the top six companies each selling over $100 million. Most of these companies have two or three lines, in a dozen or more styles. And prices are even more diverse. You can spend $50 for a stock 24-in. one-drawer base cabinet bought from a home center, or

you can go to a kitchen dealer and spend $400 for the same size cabinet in a custom line from a European manufacturer. In this article I'll take a close look at cabinet materials and construction in an effort to explain what accounts for such diversity and how to select cabinets in the face of it.

Hoosier cabinets—The kitchen cabinet industry was born at the turn of the century and founded on the manufacture of "hoosier cabinets." A relative of the baker's tables used in the late 1800s, the typical hoosier cabinet was about 40 in. wide and 5 or 6 ft. tall. It consisted of a deep base cabinet, usually with a door on one side and a column of drawers on the other, a wood or porcelain countertop and a shallower upper cabinet outfitted with flour sifters, spice racks and sugar containers. As often happens, the generic name "hoosier cabinet" derived from the company who made more of these cabinets than anyone else, the Hoosier Manufacturing Company, which by

1920 had built over two-million cabinets.

Hoosier cabinets dominated American kitchens until the 1930s when built-in cabinets began to compete for space, beginning a movement toward streamlined kitchens with continuous working surfaces. By the late 1930s most manufacturers of hoosier cabinets were out of buiness. Modular factory-made cabinets as we know them have been the dominant kitchen storage system ever since.

Face-frame versus frameless—In the U. S., face-frame cabinets are the standard (top photo, facing page). They typically employ ½-in. or ⅜-in. plywood or particleboard for the carcase and have a ¾-in. hardwood face frame that frames the door and drawer openings (drawing above). This face frame hides the exposed edges of the carcase, stiffens the cabinet and provides a place to attach hinges. Often the back of a face-frame cabinet is a non-structural ¼-in. plywood or hardboard panel. A wood hanger rail runs across the top of the back,

Drawings: Michael Mandarano

Face-frame cabinets with raised-panel doors and drawers are the bread and butter of the cabinet industry. And even stock, such as those pictured above, employ solid hardwood for their face frames, doors and drawer fronts. *Photo courtesy of Aristokraft, Inc.*

Some proponents of European-style cabinets argue that the lack of face frames makes these cabinets more accessible and easier to clean. *Photo courtesy of Läger Kitchens.*

providing some substance through which to screw the cabinet to the wall.

Frameless cabinets (bottom photo), also called 32mm cabinets or European-style cabinets, use thicker material for the entire carcase, usually ⅝-in. or ¾-in. particleboard. The back provides the ridgidity and racking resistance that other cabinets get from their face frames.

Developed in Germany during the 1950s, the 32mm system reduced cabinet manufacturing down to the processing of flat panels and introduced standardized measurements based on increments of 32mm. For instance, holes for shelf pegs are 32mm apart. The efficiency of the system stemmed in part from drilling these holes simultaneously, and the 32mm dimension came about simply because that was as close together as the spindles on a multiple-spindle boring machine could be.

Europeans have a history of taking their cabinets with them when they move, so the 32mm cabinets, in Europe at least, are seldom attached to the walls. Base cabinets stand on adjustable leveling legs, which are hidden by a kick plate that clips over them (drawing facing page). Upper, or *wall*, cabinets are hung from a steel rail screwed to the wall.

It used to be that face-frame and frameless cabinets differed stylistically as well—face-frame cabinets had wood doors and drawer

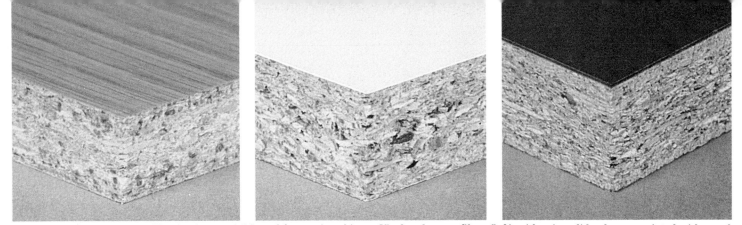

There are three basic ways of laminating particleboard for use in cabinets. Vinyl and paper films (left), either in solid colors or printed with wood grain, are the least durable and are common on stock cabinets. Melamine (center) is particleboard covered with a layer of paper saturated in melamine resin. High-pressure laminates (right), like those used on countertops, are the most durable. *Photos by Kevin Ireton.*

fronts, and frameless cabinets had laminate doors and drawer fronts. But that's no longer true. You can now get face-frame cabinets with laminate doors and frameless cabinets with wood raised-panel doors.

As for which type of cabinets is better—face-frame or frameless—I'm inclined to think it's a Ford-or-Chevy kind of issue. Keep in mind, though, that frameless cabinets weren't designed to work *better* in your home than face-frame cabinets; they were designed to streamline the manufacturing process.

Stock versus custom—Within the realm of manufactured cabinets, there are three categories of cabinet lines: stock, semi-custom and custom. If the distinction between them was ever clear, it no longer is.

Stock cabinets are mass-produced and are stockpiled by distributors, who sell them to lumberyards and home centers. Most are made of particleboard, with hardwood face frames, doors and drawer fronts. They come in standard heights and depths, and are available in 3-in. increments of width. Stock cabinets usually require fillers to fit a specific space. If your stock cabinets happen to end 2 in. shy of the wall, for instance, a filler strip, finished to match your cabinets, would be cut down and screwed to the face frame of the last cabinet in order to cover that 2-in. gap.

The first thing to understand about the other two categories is that when people in the kitchen business say "custom" cabinets, they don't mean one-of-a-kind cabinets made by a small, local, woodworking shop. Custom and semi-custom cabinets are produced in large quantities on assembly lines. What distinguishes them from stock cabinets is, first of all, that they're made to order.

Semi-custom and custom cabinets are usually sold through kitchen dealers who order the cabinets you need directly from the manufacturer. The manufacturer then makes them specifically to fill your order. Among other things, this means a longer lead time—how long depends on the manufacturer (I've heard everything from three weeks to 12 weeks).

Although semi-custom and custom cabinets offer a larger selection of styles, finishes, woods and accessories than stock cabinets, you're still selecting from choices presented by the manufacturers. You can have the cabinets made in whatever size or shape you want, but

you can't go to these companies with your own design for the doors and drawer fronts.

In general, semi-custom and custom cabinets are more expensive than stock cabinets, they're made of higher-grade materials, employ sturdier construction techniques and sport better drawer slides and hinges. The distinction between semi-custom and custom themselves is less clear, in part because each company seems to define the terms differently. But a few examples will give you some idea.

Wood-Hu Kitchens, Inc. (343 Manley St., W. Bridgewater, Mass. 02379; 508-586-8050) makes a line of semi-custom cabinets, called Woodbridge, and a line of custom cabinets, called Wood-Hu. When I asked Ralph Grillone, the company's vice president, about the difference between them, he pointed out three things. First, the interior of the semi-custom cabinets is an Asian mahogany; the custom cabinets have maple-veneer interiors. Second, drawers in the semi-custom line are ½-in. thick Asian mahogany with dovetailed corners. The custom drawers are dovetailed out of ⅝-in. maple. And third, at the front corner of the cabinets, the face-frame stile on their semi-custom cabinet overhangs the side of the carcase by ³⁄₁₆ in.—a common detail. On their custom cabinets, the corner is flush. Given that both lines have the same hardwood face frames, doors and drawer fronts, the differences struck me as pretty minor, and I came away wondering why anyone would pay 25% more for the company's custom cabinets.

Here's another example. If you order the Decora line of semi-custom cabinets from Aristokraft, Inc. (P. O. Box 420, Jasper, Ind. 47547-0420; 812-482-2527), you're still limited to standard sizes in 3-in. increments, but rather than have to use a filler strip, a particular cabinet would be made up with an extended stile—a wider-than-normal stile on the face frame. This means one less seam in the face frame. If you order Aristokraft's custom cabinets, which they call ACTUA, you can have the cabinet made slightly bigger and eliminate the need for a filler or extended stile altogether.

Cabinet carcases—Even stock cabinets typically have hardwood face frames, doors and drawer fronts. Where cabinets differ most is in the carcases and drawers. That's where stock manufacturers cut costs to keep their prices down, and that's where semi-custom and cus-

tom manufacturers beef up the quality to woo customers and justify their prices.

Carcases of stock cabinets, both face-frame and frameless, are usually made of particleboard because it's less expensive than plywood. Face-frame cabinets in semi-custom and custom lines usually have plywood carcases—not necessarily because it's a better material from which to make cabinets, but because the general public perceives it as better. In the jargon of cabinet marketing, a carcase made of plywood qualifies as "all wood" (not "solid wood") whereas one made of particleboard does not, despite the fact that both are man-made products composed of wood and glue and that particleboard itself is 90% wood.

Curiously, the common perception of particleboard as an inferior material in a face-frame cabinet doesn't extend to its use in frameless cabinets. Nearly all frameless cabinets—stock, semi-custom and custom—use particleboard for the carcase because it provides a smooth substrate for laminate.

There are three basic ways of laminating material to particleboard used in cabinets (photos above). The least durable treatment is to cover it with a vinyl or paper film, not unlike the contact paper used to line shelves. These films can either be printed with wood grain for use on face-frame cabinets or they can be solid colors for use on frameless cabinets.

A better method, used chiefly for semi-custom and custom frameless cabinets, is to cover the particleboard with a single layer of paper saturated in melamine resin (called a low-pressure laminate). Although the resulting lamination is no thicker than a vinyl or paper film, the melamine resin creates a tougher, more durable coating.

Still, the very thinness of the lamination makes melamine somewhat prone to chipping. The best frameless cabinets will have high-pressure plastic laminate on their exposed parts, such as doors and end panels, and melamine on the interiors. High-pressure laminates (such as those made by Formica or Wilsonart) are the ones used for countertops. Melamine involves one layer of paper, but high-pressure laminates have 20 or more layers, forming a stiff plastic sheet.

Shelf material varies from ⅜-in. particleboard to ¾-in. plywood. In general, the thicker the shelf, the less likely it is to sag. In their certification tests, the Kitchen Cabinet Manufactur-

Inset cabinet doors, like those in the kitchen pictured above, sit inside the cabinet face frame and are flush with it. They are rarely done these days because they leave little room for error, but they do have an old-fashioned look. Photo courtesy of *Plain 'n Fancy Kitchens, Inc.*

ers Association loads shelves at 15 lb. per sq. ft. for seven days and rejects any that sag more than 1/16 in. per ft. (1/4 in. total regardless of length). For more about the KCMA's certification program, see the sidebar on p. 56.

In most wall cabinets, the shelves are adjustable, supported by pegs or clips that fit into holes drilled in the side of the cabinet—a detail adopted from frameless cabinetry. Metal shelf standards are an option with some custom and semi-custom cabinets, but holes in the cabinet work fine.

A bad reputation—Two issues are chiefly responsible for particleboard's public-relations problems. The first is offgasing from the urea-formaldehyde glue used to bind the wood particles. This isn't the appropriate article in which to explore that issue, but I can say that formaldehyde emissions from particleboard have been greatly reduced over the past 10 years. And according to the National Particleboard Association (18928 Premiere Ct., Gaithersburg, Md. 20879; 301-670-0604), even the vinyl and paper films laminated to particleboard are something like 90% effective in containing the offgassing. Low- and high-pressure laminates are even better.

Still, the EPA does classify urea-formaldehyde as a "probable human carcinogen." Therefore, the less exposure the better. The hardwood plywood used for cabinets is also manufactured with urea-formaldehyde glue, but contains much less of it than does particleboard. Also, the outer plies effectively limit offgasing to the edges of the plywood.

The other common complaint about particleboard is that it doesn't hold up well when exposed to moisture—the "grain" raises and the particles eventually delaminate if exposed to water for too long. But it's worth noting that there are 10 grades of particleboard, and the

industrial grade used for cabinets is more moisture-resistant and holds fasteners better than the particleboard builders see at the lumberyard. Also, plywood and solid wood have their own problems if exposed to water for too long. Regardless of what your cabinets are made of, it's a good idea to run a bead of silicone caulk inside your sink base, around the bottom. If the plumbing ever leaks, this will help keep water out of the joint.

Face frames—The structural integrity and the beauty of face-frame cabinets depends in large part on the face frame. From stock to custom, nearly all the manufacturers that I know of use solid hardwood for their face frames—no plywood or particleboard here. How the frames are joined, however, varies a good bit.

During a visit to Aristokraft's manufacturing facilities, I learned that the face frames on their stock cabinets are joined with mortises and tenons, while those on their semi-custom and custom cabinets are butted, glued and screwed. (The screws are pocket screws inserted from the back of the face frame.)

When I expressed surprise at this seeming heresy, I was told that Aristokraft's testing had shown the screw joint to be as strong as the mortise and tenon under most circumstances, and strong enough for a face frame under all circumstances. But the reason they use it for semi-custom and custom cabinets is that it lends itself more readily to the frequent set-up changes necessary in made-to-order cabinets.

When assessing the quality of a face-frame cabinet, look for cross-grain scratches on either the stiles or the rails of the face frames. Assembled face frames are usally fed into a giant belt sander. Because the stiles and rails are at right angles, one or the other gets sanded perpendicular to the grain. Better cabinets will have the cross-grain scratches sanded out.

Drawers will tell—If I had to judge a cabinet based on a single detail, I'd open a drawer. At Aristokraft I saw two drawers that struck me as defining the extremes of the subject. Their best drawer (bottom photo, next page), the one on their ACTUA line, is dovetailed together from 9/16-in. maple, with a 1/4-in. plywood bottom let into a dado on all four sides and a separate drawer front screwed in place. The top inside edge of the drawer is radiused all the way around.

At the other end of the spectrum (but still meeting KCMA standards) is the paper-laminated particleboard drawer on their stock cabinet (top photo, next page). It's a three-piece drawer with the sides attached directly to the hardwood drawer front. The sides engage dados in the drawer front and are held in place by 3/4-in. staples. In fact the whole drawer is held together with staples and a bead of hot-melt glue, applied like caulking around the underside of the drawer bottom.

During my plant tour, I stood in front of a pneumatic clamping/stapling machine and watched a woman assemble one of these drawers about every 10 seconds. When I questioned their strength, Bob Wright, Aristokraft's quality-control manager, told me, "You could jack up a car and set it on one of those drawers." Later, when I recounted Wright's quote for the guys from research and development, they fidgeted a bit and finally said it depends on what kind of car you're talking about.

Between these extremes of drawer construction exist myriad combinations—particleboard drawers doweled and glued together; hardwood drawers rabbeted and stapled together. But manufacturing costs and marketability have as much to do with their construction as does strength. Wood-Hu once used a sliding dovetail joint to join their drawers. It was plenty strong, but customers couldn't see it so it couldn't be used as a selling point. Wood-Hu switched to standard dovetails.

To keep up with foreign competitors and with each other, most American cabinet manufacturers provide epoxy-coated steel slides with nylon rollers, even on stock cabinets (I'd be wary of any drawer that's still riding on a single slide centered under the bottom). The epoxy coating looks better than unfinished steel, is easier to clean, quieter and makes a smoother operating drawer. As you go up in price, you find slides made of better steel that will carry more weight, are full-extension (as opposed to 3/4 extension) and even self-closing (though you do have to nudge them).

Ball-bearing slides are available on some custom cabinets—often for an "up charge" (i. e., more money). These are arguably the strongest and most durable type of slide, but may be overkill in a kitchen drawer. When examining drawers, look for slides that are quiet and that don't have much play side to side with the drawer fully extended.

Why doors look alike—Cabinet manufacturers often buy doors, and to a lesser extent drawers and other components, from outside

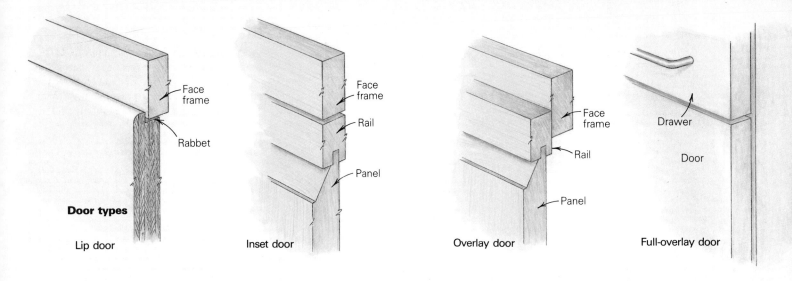

Door types

Lip door — Face frame, Rabbet

Inset door — Face frame, Rail, Panel

Overlay door — Face frame, Rail, Panel

Full-overlay door — Drawer, Door

vendors. Conestoga Wood Specialties is probably the largest door manufacturer in the country. They make doors in 102 different styles and in 20 different woods, which they sell only to cabinet manufacturers.

I called Conestoga and asked if they made doors in a range of quality levels for use on different lines or makes of cabinets; they don't. One door might cost more than another because of the wood it's made from (cherry versus oak, for instance) or because of the design (raised-panel versus flat) but all the doors are equally well made. So a stock cabinet might very well have the exact same door on it that a custom cabinet has (which explains why many stock, semi-custom and custom cabinets look alike). The doors are sold unfinished, however, and a custom manufacturer may take greater pains with the sanding and finishing. Door backs are another place to look for cross-grain scratches, by the way.

Basically, there are four types of doors (and drawers), which are shown in the drawing above. Inset doors, like the front door to your house, fit inside the face frame and are flush with it. This is the hardest type of door to execute because it demands very close tolerances. If the door is too small for the opening, it looks bad; if too big, it will stick. Only a few custom manufacturers, like Rutt (1564 Main St., P. O. Box 129, Goodville, Pa. 17528; 215-445-6751) Plain 'n Fancy Kitchens (P. O. Box 519, Schaeferstown, Pa. 17088; 717-949-6571) and Heritage Custom Kitchens (215 Diller Ave., New Holland, Pa. 17557; 717-354-4011) offer cabinets with inset doors (photo previous page).

Lip doors are pretty rare these days, too. The flat plywood doors common in the 1950s and 60s were lip doors. They have a rabbeted edge all the way around and sit half inside the face frame and half over it.

Most cabinets today have overlay or full-overlay doors on them—the entire door hangs in front of the cabinet. On a face-frame cabinet, an overlay door allows the face frame to show all the way around. Because they have no face frame, frameless cabinets must have a full-overlay door—the doors and drawer faces are nearly as wide as the cabinet. Although this look has become popular with the influx

of frameless cabinets from Europe, it's nothing new. The steel cabinets of the 1940s and 1950s all had full-overlay doors.

The raised panels in manufactured doors are glued up from narrow strips whose color and grain may differ radically. And while you'd expect a custom woodworking shop to take great pains to arrange the pieces in the most sympathetic order, you'd be lucky to find a custom manufacturer that did so. Still, some manufacturers definitely do a better job than others of unifying the color of the wood, either with their selection of the pieces or with their finishing process.

Aristokraft makes nearly all of their own doors, so I got a glimpse of door manufacturing when I visited. I was surprised to learn that they are sensitive to the differences between adjoining pieces in a glued-up panel.

The drawers on Aristokraft's top-of-the-line ACTUA cabinets (bottom photo) have dovetailed maple sides. Aristokraft's stock cabinets, on the other hand, have drawers made of paper- laminated particleboard (top photo). *Photos courtesy of Aristokraft, Inc.*

tween adjoining pieces in a glued-up panel. Not only do they reject panels that don't meet their standards, they also have people on assembly lines inspecting doors under the raking light from a bank of four car headlights. Besides looking for defects, they judge which panels are sufficiently uniform for medium and dark stains. Others are marked for finishes that will mask the variations, like white stains.

Some companies use raised-panel doors with hardwood frames and an embossed MDF (medium density fiberboard) panel with a hardwood veneer over it. This originally struck me as a good idea; MDF is more stable than solid wood and a veneer will provide a uniform grain and color in the panel. But all whom I asked about this disagreed, saying it was done to cut costs. They told me that such a door is heavier than one with a solid raised panel; the lines of the molded panel are not as crisp; and there's a possibility of stress cracks developing in the veneer where it folds over the edges of the raised panel. And everyone speculated that the veneer might delaminate.

A new type of raised-panel door, made entirely of MDF, is starting to show up on some semi-custom and custom cabinets. The raised panel design is molded into the door during the manufacturing process, then the door is finished with a PVC coating. These doors are used only on painted cabinets, and their advantage is that they won't crack from the shrinking and swelling of the panel like a painted door of solid wood is likely to do.

Mitered doors have become popular recently. These doors feature a molded edge around the inside of the stiles and rails so they have to be mitered at the corners rather than butted like traditional frames. The miters are usually held together with dowels or splines. Several manufacturers told me of occasional problems with the miters opening up over time, especially in humid climates.

Hinges are another area where European competition has forced American manufacturers to raise their standards. The best hinges are the concealed cup hinges developed for frameless cabinets, which have since been adapted for use with face-frame cabinets. These hinges are completely hidden when the door is closed and allow doors to be easily adjusted. Also, because the cup nestles into a recess drilled in the door (top photo), the weight of the door is carried more securely than if the hinge were simply surface mounted with two or three screws (this is especially important with particleboard doors).

Knife hinges (middle photo) are used on some custom and semi-custom cabinets. Although not fully concealed, only the small pivot point of these hinges shows when a cabinet door is closed. But the pivot protrudes through a notch cut in the edge of the cabinet door, which some people don't find very attractive.

Most stock cabinets have barrel hinges, with a stack of meshing cylinders like those found on a leaf hinge. Some are surface-mounted, screwed to the front of the face frame. The better ones wrap around the edge of the face frame (bottom photo), hiding the mounting screws and usually offering at least some means of vertical adjustment.

Accessories—There are a lot of different accessories available for kitchen cabinets, and I haven't the space here to discuss them all, but I will offer a few comments based on a conversation with kitchen dealer Tom Santarsiero (Kitchen Design Center, 46 Fairfield St., Montclair, N. J. 07042; 201-744-0088).

Like everyone else, I've always been intrigued by those pantry or utility cabinets with layers of swing-out shelf units. I asked Santarsiero to comment on these, and he rolled his eyes. He told me there's a tremendous amount of wasted space in them because of the clearances needed to engineer the cabinet. They're tough to operate, and it's hard to see the back shelves. According to Santarsiero, a much more efficient storage solution is to have a pantry with roll-out shelves top to bottom.

I also asked about roll-outs in base cabinets. He said they're more convenient than fixed shelves, especially if they're mounted on

Hinges. **Concealed cup hinges (top photo) offer the advantages of being hidden and are easily adjusted in three directions. Knife hinges (middle photo) require that a slot be cut into the cabinet door. The pivot point protrudes through the slot and is visible with the door closed. Barrel hinges (bottom photo) are most common on stock cabinets. The better ones have a flange that wraps around the face frame.** *Photos by Kevin Ireton.*

adjustable shelf standards, but that the European approach is better yet. He showed me some base cabinets that simply had wide, deep drawers for holding pots and pans. Why should you have to open doors and then pull out the drawers, he asked me.

If you're on a tight budget, but have a taste for accessories, you might consider buying them from someone other than the manufacturer and installing them yourself. The Woodworkers' Store (21801 Industrial Blvd., Rogers, Minn. 55374; 612-428-4101), for instance, sells roll-out units for trash cans, sink-front tray sets, wire spice racks, swing-up mechanisms for kitchen appliances and even those ironing boards that fold up into a drawer.

How good is good enough?—As I pointed out earlier, you can spend $50 on a one-drawer base cabinet or $400. Both will hold your silverware and skillets. Clearly a dovetailed maple drawer is stronger than a stapled particleboard box, but how strong does a drawer, or an entire cabinet, need to be?

Under normal circumstances over the typical lifespan of a kitchen, will custom cabinets really prove more durable than stock cabinets? Or will they just look better? Aristokraft makes stock, semi-custom and custom cabinets, so I asked several of their employees if they thought Aristokraft's stock cabinets would hold up as well as the company's custom cabinets. They all said yes.

Beyond a certain minimum standard, you're paying for form, not function. You're buying the bragging rights to a dovetailed drawer. And besides, I suspect that most kitchens are remodeled not because the cabinet drawers have fallen apart or ceased rolling on their slides, but because someone wants a new look or a more efficient layout. □

Kevin Ireton is the editor of Fine Homebuilding.

Certified cabinets

The Kitchen Cabinet Manufacturers Association (KCMA, P. O. Box 6830, Falls Church, Va. 22040; 703-237-7580) has a certification program that provides minimum standards for kitchen cabinets. It's a voluntary program in which manufacturers submit their cabinets for testing in accordance with standards developed by the KCMA and the American National Standards Institute (ANSI).

Certified cabinets must first meet 14 general construction requirements. For example, corner or lineal bracing must be provided where needed to ensure rigidity. All exterior exposed construction joints must be fitted in a workmanlike manner. Exposed edges of plywood and composition-board edges must be filled and sanded, edge-banded or otherwise finished.

Then the cabinets are tested in various ways for strength and durability. Shelves are loaded at 15 lb. per sq. ft. for seven days and must deflect no more than $\frac{1}{16}$ in. per ft. (or $\frac{1}{4}$-in. total, regardless of length). Wall cabinets are loaded to 500 lb. and checked for signs of failure. Face frames on base cabinets are loaded to 250 lb. (200 lb. if there's no drawer rail) to ensure that the joints won't open. A 3-lb. steel ball is dropped from 4 in. onto shelves, cabinet bottoms and drawer bottoms. Doors are operated with a 65-lb. weight attached to test door construction and hinges. Drawers are opened and closed 25,000 times while carrying 10 lb. per sq. ft.

Cabinet finishes are tested as well. Doors are placed in a hotbox at 120° F, 70% relative humidity for 24 hours and must show no deterioration afterwards. In another test, doors spend an hour in the hotbox, come out for 30 minutes, then go into a coldbox (-5° F) for an hour. This cycle is repeated five times. Stain resistance is tested by subjecting doors, drawers and face frames to dollops of vinegar, grape juice, coffee, alcohol and the like for 24 hours. In one of the toughest tests, especially for the particleboard doors on frameless cabinets, doors are stood in a basin of detergent formula for 24 hours and must show no sign of swelling, delaminating or discoloring afterwards.

There's a complete description of the certification requirements in the KCMA's Directory of Certified Cabinet Manufacturers, which is free. The directory lists 139 companies along with the particular lines that are certified. But you don't need the directory to identify certified cabinets. They all bear a blue and white seal on the inside of their doors. Most of the lines certified are stock cabinets. By their very nature semi-custom and custom cabinets are more likely to exceed the standards for certification. —K. I.

Building a Butternut Kitchen

Hand-planed hardwoods and high-grade plywood coupled with dowels and dovetails

by Rex Alexander

"Wood is vulnerable; it can be spoiled by a single wrong movement of the tool. It has its textures, luster, rhythms—but only the patient hand and seeing eye can coax these forth. Never inert, wood has a will of its own, the seasonal breathing of which can split rock and burst walls." —James Krenov, in *A Cabinetmaker's Notebook*.

When I first read *A Cabinetmaker's Notebook*, I was deeply inspired by James Krenov's words of wisdom, not to mention his refined woodworking techniques. Since then, I've studied all of Krenov's books (he's written four that I know of), tried out his methods and gone about my work with an enhanced regard for wood.

The turning point in my career as a cabinetmaker came when Glen and Dottie Williams asked me to design and build kitchen cabinets for their new house. The house, designed by Texas architect Kenneth Loose, sits atop a bluff near Traverse City, Michigan, overlooking East Bay. The kitchen occupies the west side of the main floor, two steps above a living room that offers dramatic views of the bay.

I knew immediately that the upper cabinets between the kitchen and living room would need glass-panel doors on both sides to link the kitchen visually to the living room. I also thought the cabinets should be simply styled so as to not detract from the open plan and spectacular views, yet at the same time should quietly display wood and craftsmanship.

In short, here was my chance to apply a dose of Krenovian perspective (at least as I interpret it) to a kitchen-cabinet job. That meant carefully selecting wood for color and figure, doweling carcases, dovetailing drawers and doing plenty of hand-planing (one of my favorite pastimes).

The basic plan—The Williams wanted their cabinets to be made of butternut (sometimes called "white walnut"). Once revered by cabinetmakers, it's a lightweight and moderately soft native North American hardwood (you can dent it easily with a fingernail) that's en-

dowed with rich, chestnut or ginger-brown coloration and delicate figure.

I decided to fuse the subtle beauty of butternut on the outside of the cabinets with the structural integrity of plywood on the inside (photo below). The base carcases (drawing facing page) would consist of ¾-in., A-2 ("A" grade on both sides) birch plywood tops, bottoms and sides tongue-and-grooved together, backed with ¼-in. birch plywood and fitted with butternut-edged, plastic-laminate coun-

tertops. Visible ends of the cabinets would be fitted with solid quartersawn butternut panels instead of plywood, and the bottoms of the cases would be embellished with beveled butternut molding and butternut toe kicks.

The design of the upper cabinets was inspired by a delicate pearwood cabinet featured in one of Krenov's books. Typical of his work, that cabinet has solid-wood tops and bottoms doweled to solid-wood sides. Because butternut is so soft, I decided to dowel solid

Inspired by the work of furnituremaker James Krenov, the kitchen cabinets combine the subtle beauty of hand-planed butternut with the structural integrity of plywood.

butternut sides to birch plywood tops and bottoms. That way, the plywood, and not the soft butternut, would absorb any wear caused by the daily jostling of cookware and dishes.

In theory, doweling solid wood to plywood in this way can cause problems because solid wood tends to shrink and swell across the grain in response to humidity changes, while plywood is relatively stable. But because butternut is one of the most dimensionally stable domestic hardwoods and these cabinets would be finished inside and out for moisture resistance, I figured there would be no risk in joining the two materials (for more on wood movement, see the sidebar on p. 60).

Where visible, the bottoms of the upper cabinets would be masked by solid butternut panels screwed to the plywood. Otherwise, bottom and top edges would be finished with the same beveled trim as that used for the base cabinets. Drawer fronts, door frames, upper-cabinet backs that would be visible through glass-panel doors, and the door panels in the base cabinets would also be butternut.

Of course, kitchen cabinets should be functional as well as attractive. These cabinets would be fitted with such amenities as roll-out

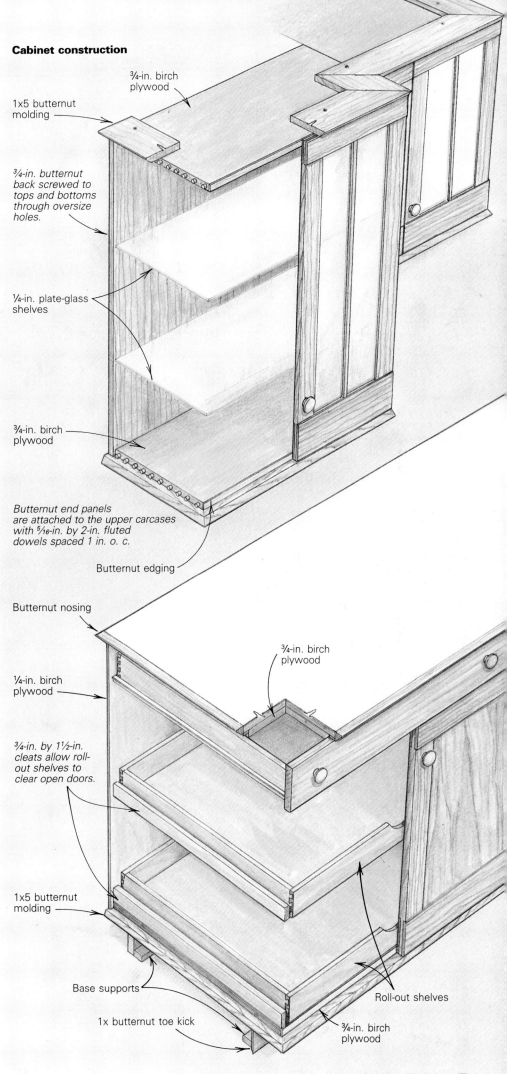

Cabinet construction

¾-in. birch plywood

1x5 butternut molding

¾-in. butternut back screwed to tops and bottoms through oversize holes.

¼-in. plate-glass shelves

¾-in. birch plywood

Butternut end panels are attached to the upper carcases with ⁵⁄₁₆-in. by 2-in. fluted dowels spaced 1 in. o. c.

Butternut edging

Butternut nosing

¾-in. birch plywood

¼-in. birch plywood

¾-in. by 1½-in. cleats allow roll-out shelves to clear open doors.

1x5 butternut molding

Base supports

1x butternut toe kick

Roll-out shelves

¾-in. birch plywood

Drawing: Bob Goodfellow

shelves, a shop-built lazy Susan, display shelves (complete with four hand-dovetailed drawers attached to the underside of one of the shelves), and homemade ceramic knobs and tiles made by Dottie and Glen in their basement shop.

Layout—My first step in building the cabinets was to mark all the pertinent features of the kitchen (including the locations of windows, wall openings and electrical outlets) on story poles (wood sticks cut to the length of each run of cabinets). The Williams' house is a 1½-hour drive from my shop, and the story poles guaranteed accurate measurements. That done, I returned to my shop and made construction drawings for each cabinet. I also mapped out on paper the best way to cut each 4x8 sheet of plywood to minimize waste. Then I produced a cutting list of all the cabinet parts.

With the cutting list completed, I ordered the butternut from L. L. Johnson Lumber Manufacturing Co. in Charlotte, Michigan. The butternut—kiln-dried, surfaced to a thickness of ¾ in. and delivered—cost just 98¢/bd. ft.

Solid-wood end panels—Construction began Krenovian style: slowly. I started by rummaging through 1,000 bd. ft. of random-width

butternut in my shop to select the best stock for the end panels. Then I squared the edges of the panel stock on my 6-in. jointer-planer and removed the knife marks using a 22-in. long homemade jointer plane. This took just one swipe with the plane and produced the optimal surface for gluing. I glued up the panels with yellow glue and scraped off the excess before it hardened.

With the glueup completed, I flattened both sides of the panels by planing them *across* the grain using a #4 Stanley smoothing plane, then *with* the grain using a #3 Stanley smoothing plane. I could have flattened the panels using a belt sander, but I prefer the satisfying sensation of hand-planing to lunching on sawdust. Besides, it takes about the same amount of time either way. Both planes worked best with their irons ground to a 22½° angle.

I finished the job using a Japanese smoothing plane and a Stanley #80 cabinet scraper that had a slightly burred edge. I like Japanese planes because their exceptionally hard cutting edges produce a glasslike sheen. The cabinet scraper was handy for smoothing knots and unruly grain, and with no tearout.

After a final polishing with 600-grit sandpaper, I cut the panels to size and grooved the

base-cabinet panels to accept the tongues on the plywood tops and bottoms.

Lower carcase construction—The plywood parts for the base carcases were assembled with yellow glue and 1-in. pneumatic staples. The T&G joints holding the butternut end panels to the tops and bottoms of the carcases were glued only along a 1-in. long section at the fronts of the cabinets, helping to hold the panels to the carcases while allowing the butternut to expand and contract. After the glue cured, I glued and stapled ¼-in. birch plywood to the backs of the carcases, fitting it into rabbets cut into the butternut end panels.

In retrospect, I'm not convinced that a 1-in. glue line in the front and a glued and stapled back is the best way to secure a solid-wood end panel to a plywood carcase. Seasonal movement of the panel *could* eventually break the glue lines and loosen the staples, especially if the panel is made of wood that's less stable than butternut (after a year in service, there is no sign of problems with these cabinets). That's why I now build most of my base carcases completely out of plywood, then screw solid-wood panels to the visible plywood ends. Installed from inside the cabinets, the screws

---

A simple tenoning jig

The stiles and rails on the cabinet doors are coupled with bridle joints. Cutting these joints was easy, using a table saw and a tenoning jig. A woodworking friend and I built a simple jig for this job over a weekend, using wood scraps and simple hardware. Like commercial jigs, this one is guided by the miter-gauge slot in a table saw. I positioned the saw's standard rip fence to shield my right hand from the sawblade, but that isn't required. The only hitch I encountered was in cutting the 4-in. long bottom tenons on the stiles. My table saw will cut a maximum 3 in. deep, so I cut the top 1 in. of the tenons by lowering the sawblade, laying the stiles flat on the saw table and using the saw's miter gauge to guide repetitive cuts in the stiles up to the shoulders of the tenons. —R. A.

The author's shop-made tenoning jig.

Cutting a tenon.

A completed bridle joint.

pass through oversize holes in the plywood to allow the panels to expand and contract.

The exposed plywood edges of each carcase were trimmed with iron-on white birch veneer. A variety of these easy-to-apply veneers is available from most cabinet- and furniture-shop suppliers. I buy mine, plus all my cabinet hardware, from two reliable distributors; Superior Distributing Co., Inc. (918 Ft. Wayne Ave., Indianapolis, Ind. 46202; 800-622-4462); and Courterco (8098 Woodland Dr., Indianapolis, Ind. 46278; 800-626-2373).

Doweling the uppers—The interiors of the upper cabinets adjacent to the living room would be clearly visible through their glass doors, so I selected A-2 birch plywood for the tops and bottoms with a heartwood face veneer that closely matches the color of butternut. I used a homemade doweling jig to align the dowel holes in the tops and bottoms with those in the sides. This simple jig (as described in Krenov's *The Fine Art of Cabinetmaking*) is simply a length of 1x1 hard maple with a heel on one end and 5⁄16-in. holes drilled through it, spaced 1 in. o. c. The heel allowed the jig to be hooked to the front edge of each board, and a pair of drywall screws held the jig temporarily in place at the ends of the boards during drilling. I drilled the dowel holes using a brad-point drill bit fitted with a wood stop to prevent the bit from running too deep.

Before assembling the upper cabinets, I drilled holes in the cabinet sides to accept brass-plated shelf clips (Knape & Vogt, 2700 Oak Industrial Dr., N. E., Grand Rapids, Mich. 49505; 800-253-1561) and located the holes with the aid of another hole jig. These clips would support ¼-in. thick plate-glass shelves.

When assembling the carcases, I tapped 5⁄16-in. by 2-in. fluted dowels into the holes, allowing each dowel to stick out exactly ½ inch. If you've ever tried to set a bunch of dowels at the same height, you know how exasperating that can be. I did it by drilling a 3⁄8-in. dia. hole clear through a ½-in. thick piece of wood, slipping this jig over each dowel as I drove it home. With glue in the holes of the carcase sides, I pressed the carcases together and pulled the joints tight with pipe clamps.

Finally, I ironed white-birch veneer onto the plywood edges, saw that the veneer's color clashed with the plywood, and ironed it off. I replaced it with a 3⁄16-in. thick strip of solid butternut, adhered with yellow glue and routed flush using a trim bit guided by a ball-bearing.

Stiles into rails—Photographs of Krenov's Swedish ash and solid pearwood cabinets persuaded me to try a sort of reverse door style: that is, stiles butting into rails that are ⅛ in. thicker than the stiles to produce a shadow line (right photo, facing page). For stability, I made the parts from straight-grained, quartersawn wood, cutting the rails for adjacent doors out of a continuous length of butternut so that the grain pattern would flow from one door to the next. The stiles and rails were joined with exposed bridle joints (see sidebar, facing page).

To house the door panels, I cut slots along the inside edges of the stiles and rails, stopping each cut before reaching the ends of the stiles so they wouldn't show. I cut the door panels from flat-sawn stock for maximum figure. At first, I thought ¼-in. thick door panels would do. But I discovered that raising the panels flush with the stiles looked better. Extra-wide panels, as well as panels for double doors, were glued up out of a single piece of butternut for consistent figure. All the panels were sized and raised on the table saw.

The glass-panel doors were built like the others, except they were fitted with a center mullion mortised to the top and bottom rails. The 45° bevels on the front edges of the mullions were cut using the table saw, then smoothed with a 6-in. homemade polishing plane. All the door parts were hand-planed and dry-fitted before the doors were assembled.

The doors were drilled after glue up to receive 125° Grass concealed hinges (Grass America, Inc., P. O. Box 1019, 1202 Highway 66 South, Kernersville, N. C. 27284; 800-334-3512). I wanted to install 176° hinges, which allow doors to swing completely out of the way when opened, but Dottie thought they looked too bulky. When hanging the doors, I hand-planed the edges where necessary to produce a 3⁄32-in. gap between the doors and moldings to allow for expansion.

Dovetailed drawers, roll-out shelves—The base-cabinet drawers are made of hard maple that was hand-planed, scraped and polished with 600-grit sandpaper. I dovetailed the corners using a router and a dovetail bit in combination with a Stanley dovetail jig. Grooves accept ¼-in. birch plywood drawer bottoms, which were secured to the drawer backs with staples. Before assembly, I rounded over the top inside edges of the drawer sides using a ¼-in. roundover cutter on my shaper, adding a nice visual detail while making the drawers more user-friendly. The finished drawer fronts were cut from 5-in. wide by 8-ft. long butternut stock (to produce a continuous grain pattern), temporarily attached to the drawers with double-stick carpet tape and then fastened permanently from inside the drawers with countersunk drywall screws.

The drawers glide on side-mount, Blum 230E self-closing drawer slides (Julius Blum, Inc., Highway 16-Lowesville, Stanley, N. C. 28164; 704-827-1345). I like these slides because they're easy to install, durable and they operate smoothly. They handle up to 88 lb. per drawer. Though full-extension slides would have provided an extra 3 in. to 5 in. of throw, the clients didn't want to spend an extra $15 to $20 per drawer for them.

Roll-out shelves in the base cabinets are basically 3-in. deep drawers located at the bottoms and midpoints of the cases. They're constructed and supported like the rest of the drawers (but without the butternut fronts).

Bending in the shower—There's only one jog in the kitchen cabinets, and that's in the

Craftsmanship on display. Behind the stove (top photo), a solid butternut cabinet displays ornamental ceramics. Its delicate, hand-dovetailed and hand-planed drawers (photo above) hold coffee, teas and dried foods.

Shop-built carousels. The lazy Susan consists of two plywood carousels that rotate independently on 12-in. bearings. The maple edge banding for the carousels was steambent in the author's shower and is reinforced with iron-on oak veneer. Each carousel is held in the closed position by a simple bullet catch (visible on the top shelf, right).

southeast corner of the kitchen. This called for the installation of a lazy Susan to render the corner storage space accessible. Concealed behind a pair of hinged doors, the lazy Susan consists of two 34-in. dia. plywood carousels, each revolving independently on a 12-in. bearing supported by a plywood shelf (bottom photo, previous page). Each bearing supports up to 1,000 lb.; I bought them from Armac Distributing Co. (219 Main St., Garden City, Mo. 64747; 816-862-8600). The carousels and shelves are made of ¾-in. birch plywood, edge-banded with strips of hard maple.

The tight radius of the carousels required that I steam-bend their maple edgings before glue up. I accomplished this by using my shower as a steam box. Twenty minutes of exposure to steam left the edgings pliable enough to bend into a tight circle, and I joined the ends temporarily with spring clamps. When the strips were dry, I unclamped them and attached them to the carousel edges with yellow glue and ½-in. brads. Finally, to reinforce the edgings, I applied iron-on oak veneer over them. This added another grain direction to help prevent splitting.

I also installed a pair of bullet catches (made by Knape & Vogt) to hold the carousels in the closed position. A bullet catch is a small spring-loaded cylinder with a steel ball partially projecting from one end; the ball engages a strike plate. The cylinders are mounted in deep holes in the tops of the plywood shelves, and the strike plates are screwed to the undersides of the carousels.

Dovetails on display—Glen and Dottie wanted a place for displaying pottery, so I built a solid butternut wall-mounted display cabinet (top and center photos, previous page) consisting of a coffee-cup rack and a stack of shelves grooved to hold ornamental dinner plates. Because the stove and microwave would be nearby, I added a series of small, hand-dovetailed drawers for holding coffee, tea and other dried goods.

The cabinet was assembled with dowels, same as the upper cabinets. The dovetailed drawers have ½-in. thick fronts, backs and sides, and ¼-in. thick solid butternut bottoms. Once I glued up the drawers, I hand-planed them for a friction fit, using paraffin and air as the drawer glides.

Trim and tops—The only parts left to make were the plywood bases, the solid butternut toe kicks, the beveled moldings for the tops and bottoms of the cabinets, and the countertops. The molding is made of 1x5 stock with a 30° bevel on the front edge, rounded over using a router and a ⅛-in. roundover bit. The base molding is affixed with drywall screws to the tops of the toe kicks and to the undersides of the base cabinets. The upper moldings are screwed to the plywood tops and bottoms.

The countertops have plastic laminate surfaces and a butternut nosing, which was fastened with 1-in. brads and yellow glue.

My favorite portion of the countertop is next to the stove. That's where I inlaid a square section of Glen and Dottie's homemade tiles

to serve as a built-in hot plate for pots and pans. Made out of a low-fire white clay, the tiles were formed in a wood mold fitted with a CDX-plywood bottom to produce a wood-grain imprint on the tiles. The sandpebble coloring of the tiles was achieved by applying three coats of a commercial glaze before firing.

Finish and installation—Unfinished, lightly oiled or waxed surfaces are Krenov's favorite, but I was hesitant to use any of them in a kitchen. Instead, I applied two thinned coats of Minwax Helmsman Spar Urethane (The Minwax Co. Inc., Montvale, N. J. 07645; 201-391-0253), polishing between coats with 600-grit paper and buffing the final coat with beeswax. This protected the surfaces and produced the satin sheen I was striving for.

The interior surfaces were finished with two coats of Hydrocote sanding sealer and four coats of Hydrocote satin lacquer (The Hydrocote Co., Inc., E. Brunswick, N. J. 08816; 800-229-4937). Hydrocote is a water-base finish that's extremely durable and waterproof. I sanded between coats with 400-grit wet/dry sandpaper. I also sprayed the drawers and roll-out shelves with a six-coat Hydrocote finish, allowing it to cure for 12 hours before polishing it with 4/0 steel wool and Hydrocote rubbing compound. Finally, I installed all the door and drawer knobs, made by Dottie out of the same clay and glazing as that used for the tiles. □

Rex Alexander is a custom woodworker in Brethren, Mich. Photos by Bruce Greenlaw.

Solid wood and humidity

Most kitchen-cabinet carcases are made of plywood or particleboard, both of which are significantly more dimensionally stable than solid wood. In northern Michigan's climate, for instance, an unfinished 12-in. wide Douglas fir plywood panel will typically expand and contract about ¹⁄₁₀₀ in. as it responds to seasonal changes in relative humidity; a solid, unfinished flatsawn Douglas fir panel of the same size will expand and contract about ³⁄₁₆ inch in width. That's why using solid wood for kitchen-cabinet carcases, especially where it will be attached to plywood or particleboard, can be risky. If you plan to use solid wood for carcase construction, here are a few pointers to keep in mind.

Quartersawn wood, which has its annual rings perpendicular to the face, is more stable than plainsawn wood, which is milled with its annual rings roughly parallel to the face (for more on

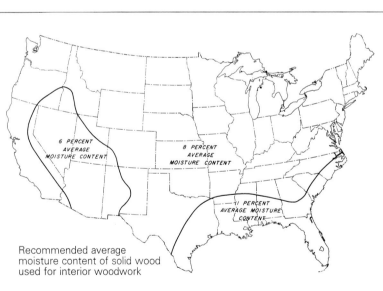

Recommended average moisture content of solid wood used for interior woodwork

quartersawn and plainsawn wood, see *FHB* #58, p. 41).

Before it's converted into cabinet parts, wood should be dried to a moisture content (MC) consistent with the average indoor relative humidity of its final destination (see map above), or about 8% MC in northern Michigan. Relative humidity is the ratio of the amount of water vapor in the air, at a particular temperature, to the maximum amount the air can

hold at that temperature, expressed as a percentage. It determines the moisture content of wood, which in turn determines the final dimensions of the wood (below a moisture content of about 28%, wood shrinks as it dries). Moisture content can be determined by the use of a moisture meter—available from most woodworking-tool suppliers.

Seasonal movement of solid wood can be curbed substantially

by applying multiple coats of a wood finish to all sides. This protects the wood from extremes in humidity, substantially reducing seasonal expansion and contraction. It also prevents the wood from warping, which is caused by uneven moisture absorption.

Different wood species can vary significantly in their response to seasonal changes in relative humidity. For example, a 12-in. wide panel of unfinished quartersawn white oak in northern Michigan will shrink about .13 inch in width from summer to winter, while the same panel made of quartersawn butternut will shrink about .08 inch.

By far, the best book I've read on the characteristics of wood is *Understanding Wood: A craftsman's guide to wood technology*, by R. Bruce Hoadley (The Taunton Press, Inc.). It has all the charts, graphs and formulas you need, and it's written in layman's terms. Also, your local weather bureau can give you statistics on local humidity.
—*Bruce Greenlaw, contributing editor to* Fine Homebuilding

Map courtesy of Forest Products Laboratory

Hybrid Cabinet Construction

This system combines traditional looks with efficient assembly techniques

by Jim Tolpin

By now, most Americans know what a typical European kitchen looks like: unadorned, monochrome surfaces separated by crisp joint lines. Besides the streamlined appearance, European-style cabinets are also noted for their accessibility and ease of cleaning. Nevertheless, the Kitchen Cabinet Manufacturers Association (1899 Preston White Dr., Reston, Va. 22091; 703-264-1690) reports that the market share of plastic-laminate doors, characteristic of European-style cabinets, plummeted from 30% in 1980 to 19% in 1990.

To a woodworker like me who makes his best money building European-style kitchen cabinets, this was troubling news. I've found these cabinets to be incredibly cost effective to build, even in my one-man shop. They have no face frames to make and install; no complex case joints to execute; and no surface-mounted, nonadjustable hinges or sloppy drawer slides to fight with. Instead, modular cases, prefitted with hardware, are assembled quickly and easily using removable fasteners. The hardware, designed specifically for the European 32mm system of cabinetmaking, not only offers ease of installation but also allows the fit of doors and drawers to be fine-tuned without removing and rehanging the components.

When Mark and Martha Ditchfield asked me to build them a "country" kitchen to complete their kitchen remodel, I decided it was time to apply the 32mm system to the creation of traditional, "American-style" cabinets. This would allow me to use all the nifty specialty tools and jigs (not to mention the know-how) that I had acquired over the past few years. The challenge would be to create the look of face-frame cabinets with applied moldings and end panels that would work with the 32mm system.

Design by mail—In preparation for new cabinets, the Ditchfields had gutted their old kitchen and pantry. I drafted two copies of the kitchen's floor plan at a scale of 1 in. to 1 ft., then sketched plan views of the upper cabinets on one copy and the base cabinets on the other. I located the stove, the refrigerator, the dishwasher and the pantry first, then filled in the blanks with cabinets. Not including the pantry unit, lengths of individual carcases would range from 18 in. for a stack of drawers to 43½ in. for the corner units, well within my tolerances (for ease of handling, I never build cabinet sections longer than 60 in.).

Country-style modules—The Ditchfields wanted their cabinets to be built of a light-colored wood with a natural finish, so I chose maple as the primary material. The maple would be lacquered to allow the grain and the color to show through.

Conforming to the 32mm system, the basic carcases would consist of edgebanded, seven-ply, ¾-in. A-3 ("A" grade on the face; "3" grade on the back) maple plywood tops, bottoms and sides (plywood stretchers for the tops of the base units), butt-jointed with knockdown (removable) fasteners and backed with ¼-in. white-vinyl faced fiberboard (drawing next page). I use knock-down fasteners because they're easy to install, strong enough to eliminate the need for rabbets and dadoes and can be quickly removed should the cabinets need to be dismantled and modified on the job site. Instead of displaying the plastic-laminate surfaces usually associated with 32mm cabinets, the visible sides and backs of the base units would be faced with ¼-in. kadama "Beaded Victoria Panels" (States Industries, P. O. Box 7037, Eugene, Ore. 97401; 503-688-7871). Kadama is an Indonesian hardwood that complements maple in grain and color. Also available in red oak, the panels are commonly used for wainscoting. The exposed ends of the upper

Half moons. **The two blind corners in the kitchen are fitted with half-moon slide-out shelves. The shelves swing out of the cabinets, then roll forward for easy access.**

Country metric. Through the adroit use of applied moldings, frame-and-panel doors and applied, beaded-plywood panels, the author created 32mm cabinets with a country-American flavor.

Cabinet construction

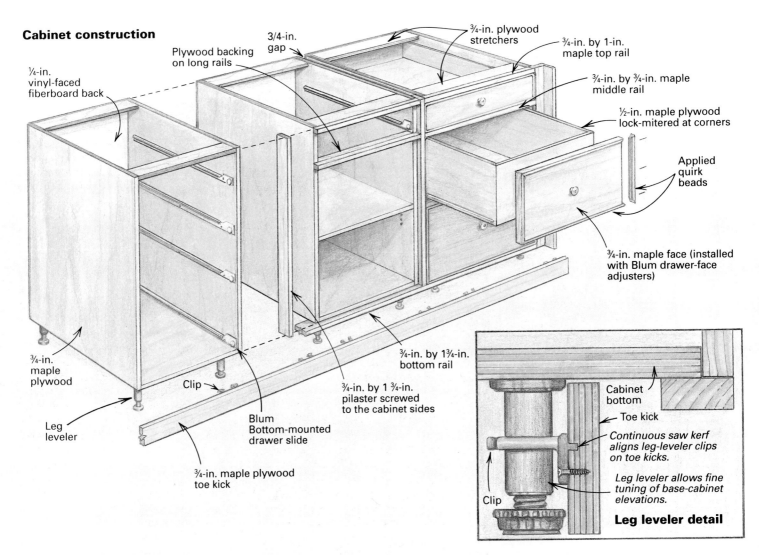

¼-in. vinyl-faced fiberboard back

Plywood backing on long rails

3/4-in. gap

¾-in. plywood stretchers

¾-in. by 1-in. maple top rail

¾-in. by ¾-in. maple middle rail

½-in. maple plywood lock-mitered at corners

Applied quirk beads

¾-in. maple face (installed with Blum drawer-face adjusters)

¾-in. maple plywood

Leg leveler

Clip

Blum Bottom-mounted drawer slide

¾-in. maple plywood toe kick

¾-in. by 1 ¾-in. pilaster screwed to the cabinet sides

¾-in. by 1¾-in. bottom rail

Cabinet bottom

Toe kick

Continuous saw kerf aligns leg-leveler clips on toe kicks.

Clip

Leg leveler allows fine tuning of base-cabinet elevations.

Leg leveler detail

Drawings: Bob Goodfellow

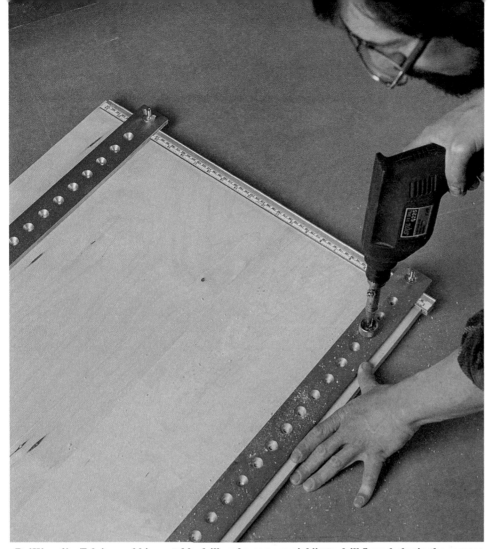

Drilling jig. Tolpin used his portable drill and a commercial jig to drill 5mm holes in the carcase sides for attaching hinge plates, drawer slides and shelf clips. Photo by Patrick Cudahy.

cabinets would be faced with plain ¾-in. A-3 maple plywood panels.

The Ditchfield's cabinets would also feature frame-and-panel doors: solid Eastern hard-maple frames surrounding either ¼-in. beaded kadama panels or double-strength glass panels embellished with applied lead came (see sidebar p. 65). Drawers would have ½-in. maple plywood fronts, backs and sides fitted with ¼-in. maple plywood bottoms and solid-maple faces. All door frames and drawer faces would be outlined by an applied quirk bead. An easy-to-install detail, the applied bead would reinforce the kitchen's country appearance.

Typical of 32mm cabinets, the doors and the drawer faces would overlay the front edges of the carcases, concealing the edges when closed. However, instead of butting end-to-end in the usual manner, the carcases would be spaced ¾ in. apart, with the resulting gaps concealed by solid maple pilasters. Pilasters would also be installed between the three sets of double doors, next to the appliances and at the inside corners of the cabinets. Finally, horizontal top, bottom and middle rails would be nailed to the base cabinets, flush with the pilasters.

The resulting façades would give the appearance of doors and drawer faces flush-mounted in conventional face frames (photo, facing page). Applied cornice and pelmut moldings, a tiled countertop and ceramic pulls would complete the country-American motif.

This hybrid design would allow the use of 32mm-system hardware throughout: concealed adjustable door hinges, bottom-mounted drawer slides, 5mm brass shelf clips and, finally, adjustable legs for the base units covered by removable plywood toe kicks. Amenities would include two space-conserving, half-moon lazy susans and a countertop appliance garage enclosed by a shop-built tambour door.

Carcase cutting—Once the Ditchfields approved my plan, the next step was to develop cut lists for all the cabinet parts. I began by listing on a chart all the components specific to each unit. From this chart, it was easy to develop specific cut lists for the components in each category. Additional charts listed the moldings and the applied panels. I used these charts to develop master cut lists. One list specified the total lineal footage of solid stock that would be required in specific widths. A second list of plywood components was converted to graphic illustrations of 4-ft. by 8-ft. panels layed out for optimal yield.

Armed with this information, I started cutting parts out of a forbiddingly tall stack of plywood. I cut most panels on a table saw fitted with an Excalibur rip fence and extension table (Excalibur Machine and Tool Co., 29 Passmore Ave., Unit 6, Scarborough, Ont. MIV 3H5 Canada; 800-387-9789). Parts that were too narrow to crosscut safely against the fence (anything less than 14 in. wide) were crosscut on a radial-arm

saw equipped with a Biesemeyer sliding stop (Biesemeyer Mfg. Co., 216 South Alma School Road, Suite #3, Mesa, Ariz. 85210; 800-782-1831), carefully indexed to match the indicator on the table-saw fence. Accurate to within ¹⁄₆₄ in., the rip fence and the sliding stop are easy to adjust and eliminate the need for constant checking with a tape measure.

With the panels cut, I hauled all the parts targeted for edgebanding to a production cabinet shop equipped with an expensive, but fast and reliable, edgebanding machine. Edgebanding can be done with a variety of hand-held machines, but I've found them to be excruciatingly slow when working with a large volume of stock. This edgebanding job cost about $100.

Drilling the cases—With the stock edgebanded and back in the shop, I drilled ⅜-in. holes in the bottom panels of the base units to receive standard Blum nylon "leg levelers" (Julius Blum, Inc., Highway 16 Lowesville, Stanley, N. C. 28164; 800-438-6788 or, in North Carolina, 800-222-7551). Next, I drilled a series of 5mm holes in the side panels to provide attachment points for shelf clips, hinge plates and drawer slides. This operation was accomplished easily with the use of a drilling jig designed specifically for 32mm construction (photo left). Made by J and R Enterprises, Inc. (12629 North Tatum Blvd. #431, Phoenix, Ariz. 85032; 602-953-0178), the jig has two graduated steel fences (one that bears against the top edge of the panel and the other against the bottom edge) linked by two brass-colored aluminum drilling templates that rest on the face of the panel. The templates locate the front and rear rows of holes on the 32mm grid, which is essential when drilling for drawer slides and adjustable shelf clips. This jig, which sells for $190, comes with a 5mm brad-point drill bit fitted with an adjustable depth-stop centering collar.

For custom cabinetmakers, there's no need to drill *all* the holes on the 32mm grid. That's why I use a device called "The Magic Wand" with my drilling jig. It's a 1m long, clear plastic scale (marked in inches and millimeters) with 5mm dia. holes on 32mm centers, the same as the drilling jig. A variety of plastic inserts snap into these holes to represent hinge plates, drawer slides, shelf clips and other hardware, which allow me to mock up any hardware configuration. The bad news is that this product (once sold by Blum) is no longer manufactured, although some distributors may still carry it. An alternative is to make pencil marks on the drilling jig itself to indicate locations of the various hardware.

Time to finish—I cut the solid stock for the door frames, the drawer faces and the trim slightly oversized. After jointing the parts to final width, I used a beading bit chucked in a table-mounted router to shape the quirk-bead detail for the doors, the drawer faces and the pelmut moldings, then switched to a chamfering bit to shape the edges of rails, pilasters and other moldings.

After sanding all the cabinet parts with 180-grit sandpaper, I lacquered everything except the drawers and the doors, which would be finished after assembly. Interior surfaces received a coat of sanding sealer followed by two coats of gloss lacquer, while exterior surfaces (and later, the doors and the drawers) received a coat of sealer plus three coats of semigloss lacquer. I used Hydrocote finishing products (The Hydrocote Co., Inc., 77 Milltown Road, E. Brunswick, N. J. 08816; 800-229-4937); they're nontoxic, nonflammable and fast-drying and cure to a clear, durable, water-resistant finish. Each coat was sanded with 220-grit wet/dry sandpaper, and the final coat was buffed with 400-grit wet-dry sandpaper.

Doors and drawers—Before assembling the carcases (which would quickly eat up limited shop space), I tackled the doors and the drawers. Using a ¼-in. slotting cutter and a router table, I cut a groove in the edge of each stile and rail for the kadama panels. The grooves stop short of the stile ends, so they don't show at the tops and the bottoms of the doors. I assembled the door frames using biscuits and yellow glue, cutting the slots for the biscuits on a stationary biscuit joiner (for more on biscuit joinery, see *FHB* #70, pp. 50-53). Because plywood panels are dimensionally stable, I glued the panels into their grooves.

After glue up, I used a router to round over the door frames around the panel perimeters and to rabbet the back sides of the nine glass-door frames so that the glazing would fit flush with the backs of the frames. Small plastic stops (available from the glass supplier) would later be screwed to the frames to hold the panels in place, allowing easy replacement should a panel break. I scraped and sanded all the frames, tacked on the quirk beads and rounded over the inside edges of the frames with a router. I also applied quirk beads around the drawer faces.

Next, I drilled holes in the back of each door for a pair of Blum 125° clip-on cup hinges. A Blum "Juniorpress" drilling fixture attached to my drill press (photo top right) made it easy to drill simultaneously a 35mm cuphole and two 8mm attachment holes for each hinge. An attachment on the device allowed me to install the hinges, too. Though the Juniorpress lists for $600, I've found it to be a worthwhile investment.

Before assembling the drawers, I routed grooves in the plywood sides and fronts to hold the drawer bottoms, then used a Freud lock-miter bit to cut the corner joints. The drawers were assembled with glue and brads, then fitted with Blum 230 bottom-mounted, self-closing drawer slides, which attach to the bottom edges of drawers for rapid installation. Drawer faces were attached with Blum drawer-face adjusters, which are plastic inserts that I install in the backs of the faces to allow adjustment for perfect alignment.

Carcase assembly—Finally, more than 100 hours into the job, it was time to put together some cabinets. I began by fastening the hinge plates, the drawer slides and the leg sockets to the appropriate carcase panels, then tacked the carcases together with finish nails, squared them up and screwed on the fiberboard backs. The side panels were then secured to the tops and the bottoms with "Confirmat" threaded-steel knockdown fasteners (Häfele America Co., 3901 Cheyenne Dr., Archdale, N. C. 27263; 800-334-

Door hinging. A fixture attached to a drill press was used to simultaneously drill a 35mm cup hole and two 8mm attachment holes for each door hinge, as well as to press the hinges into place. Here, the author demonstrates the jig on a sample oak door. Photo by Patrick Cudahy.

Knockdown carcases. Instead of the usual tongue-and-groove assembly, these carcases are butt-joined and held together with knockdown fasteners. Here, the author demonstrates the drilling of pilot holes for the fasteners using a Häfele drilling fixture. Photo by Patrick Cudahy.

Glass and lead

Before installing the glass door panels, I applied a grid of a self-adhering, bronze-colored lead strip (Decra-Led, Ltd., 2601 Portage Road, Portage, Wisc. 53901; 608-742-8386) to the face of each panel to create the illusion of divided lights (photo above). This product, which is available in various colors, was installed by peeling protective paper off the back to expose an adhesive, then pressing the strip in place with a small rubber roller. I drew reference lines on a piece of cardboard and placed it under the glass to help me align the strips before pressing them in place. Where strips overlapped, I used a small plastic tool (supplied with the came) to mash them together to mimic a solder joint. — J. T.

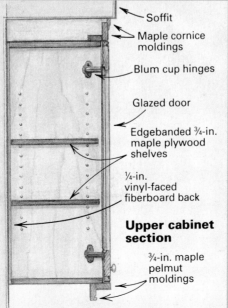

Soffit
Maple cornice moldings
Blum cup hinges
Glazed door
Edgebanded ¾-in. maple plywood shelves
¼-in. vinyl-faced fiberboard back

Upper cabinet section

¾-in. maple pelmut moldings

1873). Pilot holes were drilled using a "Zentrix 40 + 50mm" drilling system (also available from Häfele) attached to my electric drill. This device (bottom photo, facing page) sells for about $285 and made it easy to drill perpendicular holes the proper distance from the panel edges.

Once the carcases were assembled, I flipped them onto their backs and, using a pneumatic finish nailer, installed the pilasters in the double-door openings. Then I installed the middle rails and the plywood backing for the cornice moldings. Next, I installed half-moon slide-out shelves in both corner units and a tilt-out sink tray for more storage. Designed for blind corners (corner spaces that don't turn the corner), the slide-outs (photo p. 61) swing out of the cabinet, then slide forward for easy access (Rev-A-Shelf, Inc., P. O. Box 99585, Jeffersontown, Ky. 40269-0585; 800-626-1126 or, in Kentucky, 502-499-5835). The last step was to install the drawers and the doors.

Installation—To prepare for installation of the cabinets, I snapped level chalklines 34½ in. and 53½ in. up from the high point of the floor around the perimeter of the kitchen to indicate the tops of the base units and the bottoms of the upper units. I established these elevations using a reservoir-type water level (Price Brothers Tool Co., 1064A Machin, Novato, Calif. 94945; 415-897-3153), which can be operated by one person.

I installed a corner base unit first by tapping its four adjustable legs into their sockets, sliding the unit into position and then backing out the legs until the top of the unit was level with the lower chalkline. Next, I fastened a pilaster to either end of the unit with 1¼-in. drywall screws, positioning the pilasters so that their front edges jutted ¾ in. beyond the front edge of the cabinet. For each subsequent unit, it was a simple matter to slide the carcase against the pilasters, level it to the chalklines and screw it to the pilasters with 2-in. drywall screws. I continued around the kitchen until all the base units were in place. I then fastened them all to the wall studs with 2½-in. drywall screws angled through the top frames and into the studs, using shims to fill any gaps.

The upper units were fastened to the walls with 2½-in. long, #10 oval-head wood screws, and to each other (through pilasters) with drywall screws. End and exposed back panels were attached to the cabinets with drywall screws driven from inside the cabinets.

I fastened the various horizontal moldings to the cases with 1¼-in. finish nails. The toe kicks were then cut to length and attached to the leg levelers with plastic clips hammered into saw kerfs along the backs of the kicks. These clips allow the kicks to be removed later to trace plumbing leaks, exterminate pests or lay a new floor.

Once the shelves were installed, the doors and the drawer faces adjusted and the porcelain pulls screwed on, I filled the visible nail holes with putty and snapped almond-colored plastic caps over the visible screw heads. ☐

Jim Tolpin is a cabinetmaker and writer in Arcata, Calif. His book, Working at Woodworking, *is available from the Taunton Press, Inc.; (800) 888-8286. Photos by Bruce Greenlaw except where noted.*

An old material lends a sense of warmth to a new kitchen. The longleaf pine used to make these cabinets, commonly called heart pine, originally was cut from old-growth forests in the South and the Southeast. The wood was salvaged from old buildings and was remilled.

Making Heart-Pine Cabinets

Recycled wood brings a warm glow
to a Virginia kitchen

by Daniel Foster

A fellow I worked with in Vermont some years ago was a third-generation carpenter. "Brad," his grandfather once said to him, "we weren't any better carpenters than you. We just got all the good wood." Almost ten years after Brad told me that story, the words are even more true. Good wood is getting scarce. It was a welcome opportunity, then, when I had my first chance to work with wood of grandfather's day.

My client and I had been discussing the merits of various woods for his kitchen cabinets. He was pushing for pine, which I said was too soft. When I asked what color he wanted, he pointed to a small table and said, "Pumpkin pine." "Oh, that's different," I said. "That's heart pine."

Many salvaged-wood dealers carry heart pine—Longleaf pine, also called heart pine, is one of 11 species of southern yellow pine. The recycled wood available now was harvested from frames and floors of buildings built in the past century. The trees from which this wood came grew slowly, in part because of the competitive nature of virgin forests. Mature trees often were up to 300 years old. In the wood I purchased for this kitchen, it was not hard to find over 30 growth rings to the inch. Longleaf pine still is found in forests in the Southeast, but most old-growth trees were cut in the 1700s and 1800s.

Heart pine is far denser than any other cabinet-grade pine and is available in several grades, from knotty to perfectly clear. Because it's from dense, old-growth stock, the wood used for these cabinets should be more stable and more likely to wear well. Its durability is enhanced by the way it was milled. Most of the recycled timbers were quartersawn, which results in a greater percentage of boards with vertical grain.

Antique heart pine's working characteristics include stability, high density or hardness (for a softwood), high resin content and a tendency for brittleness. It's a great source of splinters.

When I purchase wood for cabinets or for furniture, I usually make it a point to select boards by hand. In this case, I ordered the wood sight unseen from Mountain Lumber (P. O. Box 289, Ruckersville, Va. 22968; 800-445-2671). The supplier had assured me of the wood's quality. At nearly $8 per board foot, I expected the wood to be good, and I wasn't disappointed.

Easy to cut, harder to shape—I had little difficulty cutting or planing heart pine. I received the stock in rough form and ran it through a planer with little tearout. The boards were so straight hardly any truing was required prior to ripping, and I used the joiner hardly at all. I have a high-quality Forrest combination blade (Forrest Manufacturing Co., 461 River Road, Clifton, N. J. 07014; 800-733-7111) on my table saw with a

stabilizer, a flat metal disk installed alongside the blade to reduce vibration. This combination produced cuts ready for glue up.

Routing, though, required more attention. For the raised-panel cabinet doors (photo facing page) I made on a router table, I used matched rail-and-stile cutters and a vertical panel-raising bit. At this point I found that the wood had a strong tendency for tearing out and splintering. This problem was especially bad with smaller-diameter cutters, such as the one I used to make the small astragal molding that covers the joints between cabinet face frames and side panels. Until I made a zero-clearance fence for this profile, I was getting terrible tearout every few feet.

A shop-made fence reduces tearout—The zero-clearance fence is simply a piece of smooth medium-density fiberboard (MDF) attached to the router-table fence and then moved into the rotating cutter until the fence and cutter are positioned for use (photos below). With some router bits, I cut away some of the MDF with a jigsaw first to allow the bearing to clear. This fence eliminated nearly all of the tearout.

I used a similar fence with most of the router bits, including the vertical-panel raiser, the bead-forming bit and the rail-and-stile sticking cutter (the half of the two-piece set that cuts the profile along the long edges of the rails and stiles). Only the rail-and-stile coping cutter didn't need one; it

Keep the router bit from biting off too much material. The author made a zero-clearance fence from MDF for router bits used to fabricate the face frames and raised-panel doors. The MDF fence was carefully swung into the spinning cutter until the fence was in line with the bit's guide bearing. Very little tearout occurred as the workpiece was fed through the router table (above) because there was no gap between the cutting edges of the bit and the fence.

only cuts end grain. A piece of scrap used for backup eliminated tearout in this case.

In making raised panels, it is relatively common practice to remove some of the stock from the shoulder of the panel with a table saw before running the panel through the router table. This technique was particularly useful with heart pine, again reducing tearout (photos below).

High resin content slows sanding—Because of the high resin content of the wood, sandpaper clogged quickly. A belt sander can be cleaned with a crepe-rubber cleaning stick, but orbital sanders are a different story. The only solution there seemed to be to change paper fairly regularly. The use of stearate-coated paper (stearates are anticlogging "lubricants") helped, but not a lot. Some boards contain higher than average resin content. They literally are heavy with clear, hard resin, and they clog paper especially badly. On these boards, I found a scraper to be more effective at removing resin. Although heavy resin makes the wood hard to work with, I find it beautiful. The resin creates a stunning dimension of depth.

I thought the high resin content of the wood might create difficulties in gluing, but it did not. My wood supplier recommended ordinary yellow carpenter's glue, and it worked well.

The relatively brittle nature of heart pine means that nearly invisible cracks parallel to the growth rings can exist in the wood. If the wood isn't carefully examined, cracks can go unnoticed until you're preparing to put on finish.

You can biscuit-join narrow face frames—I am a believer in biscuit joiners. In my opinion, a biscuit joiner is to cabinetmaking what a nail gun is to carpentry. I wouldn't want to do either job without the appropriate tool. Both the birch-plywood carcases and the face frames were joined with biscuits. My assistant and I used three biscuits in each joint of the wall cabinets and six in each joint of the wider base cabinets.

Our techniques for joining the face frames were a little unusual. Although many of these members are only 1½ in. wide, we used #20 biscuits, which are more than 2 in. wide, to join them. I prefer the larger biscuits because they reach deeper into the boards being joined, thus providing considerably more gluing area. I used a bandsaw to cut off as much as ½ in. from each end of the biscuits, reducing them to just less than 1½ in. long. Lamello (Colonial Saw Co., 845 Milliken Ave., Suite F, Ontario, Calif. 91761; 800-252-6355) makes a small, round biscuit that would have worked within these parameters, but these biscuits have to be ordered from a Lamello dealer and require cutting round slots on a router table. In general I prefer to use a standard biscuit joiner.

One result of this approach is that the slots cut into the stiles and rails for the large biscuits are visible at the inside edge of the finished face frame. We covered these slots with narrow beaded trim that wraps around the inside of every opening (top photo, facing page). The visual effect of these face frames with the inner bead is much like that of beaded rails and stiles. I find this technique to be much easier, and the speed and strength of biscuits is a big plus.

When attaching the bead to the face frames, I allowed it to extend slightly beyond the face of the rails and stiles. This approach did two things: It provided a greater level of depth to the cabinet detail, and it broke up the plane that otherwise would have extended uninterrupted across the face frames and inset doors. We also were allowed a margin of error in case a door was not exactly flat or perfectly hung. Inset doors are fussy enough; I like to have this slight assistance.

The face frames were glued, clamped and face-nailed to the carcases. The astragal molding that conceals the joint between cabinets covered most of the nail holes in the face frames. To hide the brads holding the astragal, we used a mixture of shellac and fine heart-pine sawdust as filler. The resulting color closely matched the tone of the finished cabinetry.

A better grain match is possible with custom-made doors—Some people think I'm crazy to make doors and drawer fronts when

First, rough out the raised panels on the table saw. The author fabricated the raised panels in three steps. First, he defined the outline of the raised panel with a table saw by cutting a shallow kerf in the panel's face. Then, still using the table saw, he removed most of the stock from the shoulder of the panel.

Then run the panel by the panel-raising bit. Each panel was milled to its final shape with multiple passes along a router table and vertical panel-raising bit. The tall fence helped the author keep the panel vertical.

they can be purchased inexpensively. That argument is good for paint-grade work. But for me, it's better to have control over how individual boards are used. There should be a good match in the grain on a series of drawer fronts. On a cabinet with two doors, those doors should go well together. Until I learn otherwise, I will continue to believe this situation can be controlled only if I make these components myself.

The drawer boxes, also of heart pine, were assembled with machine-cut, through dovetails (bottom photo). All of the drawers have birch-plywood bottoms and are mounted on full extension slides.

Clear finish brings out the beauty of heart pine—After some experimentation with finishes, I found white, or clear, shellac to be a perfect first coat for heart pine, followed by a nonyellowing, water-based urethane. Despite its name, clear shellac has an amber tone, and it brings out the color in heart pine. Some urethanes contain ultraviolet blockers that keep sunlight from deepening the wood's color. We chose one, Hydrocote Polyurethane (77 Milltown Road, E. Brunswick, N. J. 08816; 800-229-4937), that allows the sun to reach the wood. Heart pine ages gracefully, and I wanted to let it do so.

I experimented with finishes on both the heart pine and the birch cabinet carcases to make sure that the two would go together well. The two woods clearly differed in color, but I thought they looked good together. The use of clear shellac as a sealer on both the pine and the birch helps give a compatibility in tone and results in a good color match where there are dark heartwood areas in the birch.

Flooring and trim to match the cabinets—We also ordered heart-pine flooring, baseboard, casing and crown molding for the kitchen from Mountain Lumber. We ordered the flooring in a lesser grade, select prime, that contained some solid knots and a larger percentage of holes from pulled nails and screws. This lower grade adds character, sometimes too much. We found that the need to make decisions on the acceptability or placement of imperfections increased the time it took to lay the recycled material, as compared with conventional strip flooring.

Both the clients and I are pleased with the kitchen. It is warm and relaxing, but at the same time rich in detail. Although many of the details are derived from the look of contemporary English cabinetry, including the beaded openings, complex drawer fronts and astragal moldings, the heart pine makes the kitchen seem unmistakably American. □

Daniel Foster is a cabinetmaker and contractor in Leesburg, Virginia. Photos by Reese Hamilton.

Bead hides the biscuit slot. The cabinets' face frames appear to have been made of beaded stiles and rails. In fact, the bead was installed after the frames were assembled. The decorative bead covers the exposed biscuits that result when biscuit-joining narrow rails and stiles. Joints between face frames and raised side panels were covered with astragal molding.

Dovetails display vertical grain. Drawer boxes were made of pine boards joined with through dovetails. The bottoms of the drawers are 1/4-in. birch plywood.

Frameless Cabinets With a Traditional Look

A professional cabinetmaker describes his simple methods for making cases and doors

by Paul Levine

Frame-and-panel doors provide a traditional look. These cherry cabinets with a lacquer finish employ cup hinges, so the doors hang on the cases instead of from a separate frame. The moldings that frame the door panels emphasize the traditional appearance.

I had a little memory-jogging experience the other day when I visited a friend who rebuilds car engines. "Pull my finger," he told me, but I knew that old joke. "No, really, take a look at this," and he put his finger on a device he had bought to measure drill-bit diameters. The device has a needle gauge marked in 1,000ths of an inch, and every second or so, the needle jumped. "That's my pulse," he said. Marveling at the sensitivity of the new instrument, I remarked that 20 years ago I thought I needed that kind of precision in my cabinetmaking shop. Ah, the folly of youth.

I no longer rely on precise measurements and setups. Over the years I've developed a cabinet-building system in which, rather than trying to make a cut perfect the first time, I make the piece too big and then pare it down slowly to get the cut just right.

I've also learned to disregard nominal dimensions. For example, when making grooves to house ¾-in. plywood shelving, I take out the ¾-in. dado, right? No. I ignore the nominal dimension and set the dado to ⅝ in. Then I incrementally widen the groove until the plywood just drops in. The setup takes a little longer, but the results are great.

Here I'll describe how I use these methods to build frameless cabinets, also called European cabinets (photo above). Frameless cabinets have no integral face frames and use 32mm cup hinges and drawer slides. This hardware lets doors and drawers be attached directly to the case. It's the style of doors and drawer faces that can give frameless cabinets a traditional look.

The traditional look I'll build here is a full-overlay frame-and-panel door. Full-overlay doors cover the edges of the case, as opposed to half-overlay doors, which leave part of the case's edges exposed. If I were building a traditional cabinet with a face frame, I might leave that frame totally visible by using inset doors, which hang within the face-frame openings. But face-frame cabinets with inset doors and drawers are tougher to build and give you less storage space than the frameless cabinets I'll build in this article.

Loose-tenon joints are quick and strong—In my small shop, I build doors first because they take up less space than cases. If I built the cases first, I'd be wallowing in them as I built the doors.

When I build a frame-and-panel door or drawer face, I join stiles and rails (the vertical and horizontal parts of the frame) with a loose-tenon butt joint (top photo, facing page). This joint is as strong as a conventional mortise and tenon, yet it takes much less time to execute because I don't need any special tools, just a router and a table saw. In this joint the rails butt into the stiles, and both members are mortised so that a separate tenon may be slipped into these mortises like a dowel. After assembling the frames, I rabbet the inside edge, drop in a panel and hold it in place with panel molding.

I use 5/4 stock for frames not just because it looks good but also because the thickness gives more bearing surface for clamping. The thinner the stock, the more likely it is that a clamp may pull a frame out of flat. After jointing and planing the stock, I rip it into 2½-in. widths, then cut it to length on a chopsaw.

There's a ¹⁄₁₆-in. reveal all the way around the door or drawer face, which means its size equals the case dimensions minus ⅛ in. If I'm hanging two doors in a single opening, the doors will be half the case width minus ⅛ in. Because the rails butt into the stiles, the rails are cut 5 in. less than the overall widths just cited. I save a few cutoffs for setting up the mortising fixture.

Mortising fixture locates mortises accurately—With the best faces of the stiles and the rails facing me, I set the frames on a flat surface and mark across the center of each rail onto the stile. These marks indicate where mortises will go. The ends of the rails and the top and the bottom edges of the stiles get mortised.

I do the mortising with a fixture that I designed for use with a plunge router (sidebar p. 73). I clamp a stile or a rail in the fixture and then run the router against the fixture's stop blocks to cut an oblong mortise.

I make all my mortises starting ⅜ in. from the edges of the stock. Any less, and I could open up the mortise when routing the outside edge detail. Typically, mortises are ⅜ in. wide, 1¹⁄₁₆ in. deep and 1¾ in. long.

Pare down tenons until they just slip into mortises—Because the tenons are buried in the frames, they don't have to be pretty. They do, however, have to be strong and stable, so I make tenons from poplar, an inexpensive hardwood. I rip tenons from 4/4 stock on the table saw, deliberately ripping them about ¹⁄₁₆ in. thicker than the mortise.

The strength of a loose-tenon joint comes from a tenon of perfect thickness. I get precisely the right thickness by thinning tenon stock on a table saw or a planer until the tenon just slips into the mortise with light force.

The tenon's length and the width aren't as critical, so these dimensions are undersized to allow for glue runout and to compensate for any imperfections. I round over all edges of the tenon stock with a ³⁄₁₆-in. roundover bit in the router and cut the tenons in 2-in. lengths.

Assembling the frames—Now I put glue in all four stile mortises, swish the glue around with a stick to coat the inside walls of the mortise and drive in four tenons with a mallet (photo center right). I also swab glue into the rail mortises and onto the ends of the rails.

Then I slip the rails onto the tenons and clamp the frame with pipe clamps (photo bottom right). There should be excess glue at every joint; if no glue squeezes out, I didn't use enough glue. The clamps are positioned at the tenons to apply pressure through the center of the frame stock. If the clamps are too high or too low, they'll pull a stile out of flat.

Next, I scrape away excess glue. The joint will set up faster with this extra moisture removed, and it's easier to remove glue now than when it hardens. Then I set the frame aside to dry overnight.

Rabbet the inside edge to hold the panel—To get all the joints flush, I rough sand the frames with 80-grit paper on a random-orbit sander. When the surface is flat, I shape the inside and outside edges of the frame. I use an ogee curve on the outside edge. Although I use a shaper to cut this decorative edge detail, there are router bits that do the same job.

I shape a test piece to see if it will allow space for 32mm cup hinges. If the shaping bit cuts too deeply into the edge of the frame, it may cut into a hinge mortise. After shaping the edge, I move to the drill press and bore the back of the door frames for the 32mm cup hinges (bottom photo, p. 72). Next, I rabbet the inside edge of the frame. The depth of the rabbet depends on the thickness of the panel and the panel molding. I use a ⅜-in. bearing-guided rabbeting bit in the router (top photo, p. 72) and square the radiused corners with a chisel. Then I sand the frame up to 220 grit.

The center section of the door is called the panel; it's seated within the rabbeted door frame. I make solid-wood panels from ½-in. stock, which, unlike thinner stock, has a substantial feeling that enhances the quality of my doors. I cut panels from a single piece of wide stock. Even 36-in. wide cabinets, which are very wide, only require about 12¾-in. wide panels. Stock this wide and wider is readily available from any decent lumber supplier. Door panels are installed with the grain running vertically. I crosscut the panel stock so that it fits precisely in the frame, but I rip panels about ³⁄₁₆ in. narrower than the frame to allow for the panel to expand. Because I use such thick stock for panels, I rabbet the edges of the panel so that I can seat it and

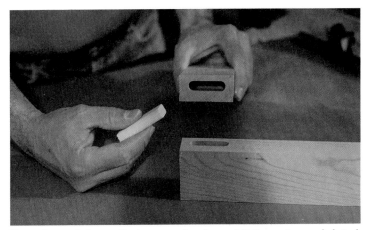

Door-frame joinery features a simple, quick loose-tenon joint. A loose tenon ripped from solid poplar fits into mortises in the stiles and the rails. Mortises are cut with a ⅜-in. straight bit in a plunge router.

Loose tenons are tapped in with a mallet. Loose tenons are pared down on a table saw until they fit snugly in the mortises. Here, the tenons are inserted into the stile mortises, which have been coated with glue. The rails are then slipped onto the tenons.

Assembled frames are clamped with pipe clamps. It takes about a day for the frames to set up. Pressure blocks prevent clamps from damaging the frames. Clamps must be centered through the thickness of the frame, or they may pull the frames out of flat.

A rabbeted edge to hold the panel. Instead of a groove to house the panel, a rabbet creates a ledge against which the panel is seated. Rabbeting is simpler because it allows you to assemble frames first without the panel to complicate assembly. The rounded corners are squared with a chisel.

Panel molding is rabbeted to fit over frame. The depth of the rabbet in the frame depends on the thickness of the panel plus the seated depth of the panel molding. The panel molding holds the panel in place.

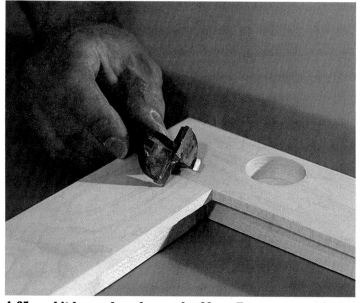

A 35mm bit bores door frames for 32mm European cup hinges. The edge of the bore is 3 in. or less from the end of the door. The back of the door is bored, and the bore does not penetrate the frame.

the panel molding in the frame. The panel's rabbeted edge interlocks with the frame's rabbeted edge like a shiplap joint.

I rabbet panels on a table saw with a dado blade, sending the panel on edge past the blade. I make several passes, deepening the rabbet until it's just deep enough for the panel molding to hold the panel snugly in place.

Shaped to fit over the door frame and the panel, panel molding looks something like cove molding with a rabbet on the back edge (photo center left). I make my own panel molding on a shaper, but you can get panel moldings milled up at a good lumberyard. I cut the panel molding on a chopsaw, mitering the ends, and then sand the molding and the panel by hand. Then I reset the panel and pin the molding in place. Remember that the panel should float freely; don't pin through it. If you don't have a pinner, use brads. After setting and filling the nail holes, the door is ready for finish.

Frameless cases have tongue-and-dado joints—I build ¾-in. birch plywood cases and join the side panels to the bottom and the top frame with tongue-and-dado joints (top photo, p. 75). This joint is strong, simple to make and self-aligning, which means you don't have to mess around trying to get panels flush. The two side panels are dadoed, and tongues in the top frame and bottom panel fit into these dadoes.

A ¼-in. plywood back panel is screwed to the case, and the exposed plies on the front edge of the case are edged with solid-birch banding.

Instead of a full top panel, my cabinets have ¾-in. poplar top frames. The frames require extra labor. But they make the cases easier to move around because they're a little lighter than cases with a solid top, and the frame acts as a handle. Also, an open top provides access to the cabinet and lets light in the cabinet, a real bonus when installing hardware. These frames are the first things I make. I assemble them with a biscuit joint. I make the frames bigger than necessary. Then when I cut up the birch-plywood panels, I trim all of the parts of the case so that all pieces are the same dimensions.

Because standard cabinets are 24 in. deep, I rip 4x8 sheets of plywood in half and trim the halves to a final width of 23½ in., providing two fresh edges without nicks. Next, I cut all panels to length, usually 30 in. for the side panels, because I set the cabinets on a separate 4½-in. high toekick structure. Widths of bottom panels vary with the kitchen design.

The tongue-and-dado joint is made on the table saw using a dado blade. I cut the dadoes first with a ¼-in. dado blade. The dadoes run perpendicular to the grain along the top and bottom edges of the side panels.

When I'm cutting with a dado blade, it helps to have a throat plate, the removable portion of the saw table that sits around the blade, for the ¼-in. dado. The throat plate supports the plywood's fragile veneer, reducing the risk of tearout.

The dado should go about halfway through the ¾-in. plywood. To adjust the depth of the dado, I place a scrap of the plywood flat on the saw table against the blade (top photo, p. 74). I raise the blade until it reaches halfway up the middle ply.

The next step is to adjust the fence to get the dado the correct distance from the edge of the plywood. I move the fence about ½ in. away from the blade and hold a piece of scrap plywood on edge against the fence over the blade. Then I adjust the fence so that the blade just pokes out a bit beyond the plywood (center photo, p. 74).

Now I check the setup by dadoing a scrap of plywood and holding another scrap on edge flush with the edge of the test piece. The inside edge of the dado should be barely visible.

The mating part to this groove is the tongue, which is made along opposite edges of the top frames and the bottom panels. I cut the tongues with a ⅝-in. dado blade with the saw arbor cranked slightly lower than it was when I dadoed the side panels. At this setting, the tongue should leave a small gap at the bottom of the dado to allow for glue runout. When changing blades, I leave the height setting alone so that no time is wasted making test cuts.

Although the dado is ¼ in., I start with a saw setting that will make a tongue slightly larger. I pass a panel through on edge (bottom photo, p. 74), then keep reducing this setting to pare down the tongue until it just slips into the dado. Before assembling the cases, I sand the panels. I take it easy when sanding the tongues to prevent changing the fit of the joint.

Use the back panel to square the cabinet—I assemble the case with glue. When the pieces are aligned, I shoot in one pin to hold them in position and then add four 1⅝-in. drywall screws to pull the side tight. The screws

Custom fixture is an accurate guide for plunge-routing mortises

A good loose-tenon joint depends on consistently sized, accurately placed mortises. I've devised a mortising fixture (drawing below) that guides my plunge router. With the fixture, I can cut consistently sized mortises in just the right spot so that stiles and rails line up. Once the fixture is set up, it takes about five seconds to cut a mortise. To make the fixture, you'll need about an hour.

Grooves in top of fixture house guide rails—The fixture's base is a piece of ¾-in. plywood. A pair of hardwood rails in the top of the plywood base guides the router. These guide rails are parallel and slightly closer together than the width of my router base.

I installed the rails in grooves in the plywood. Holding the same edge of the plywood against the saw fence each time I made a groove resulted in two parallel grooves. I widened the grooves little by little until the guide rails just dropped into the grooves. After gluing the rails in place, I shaved one down until the router dropped easily between the rails.

About 6 in. from one end of the fixture, I glued and nailed a stop block. Then, with a router between the rails and against the stop block, I routed a 6-in. long, ¾-in. slot in the plywood base. This slot is the one through which I lower a straight bit to cut mortises.

An adjustable stop block at the other end of the base limits the length of the mortise. This stop block is a 6-in. length of hardwood that's been pared down in width to slide between the rails. I cut a ¼-in. slot in the adjustable stop so that it can slide back and forth across a machine screw. The screw engages a threaded insert in the base; tightening the screw clamps the stop in place. The corners on the front edge of the stop block are nipped off. These cutoff corners catch sawdust. The front of the stop stays clean.

Fence on bottom of fixture positions workpiece—On the bottom of the plywood base, I installed a fence to which I clamp stock when routing mortises. The fence's position is critical. If it isn't parallel to the guide rails, mortises will come out cockeyed in the stock. So I set the fence in a groove parallel to the guide-rail grooves in the top of the fixture. I chose one reference edge, which I registered against the saw fence each time I grooved the base, ensuring that all grooves were parallel. I made the fence groove wider and wider until the fence, a 3½-in. wide, ¾-in. thick length of hardwood, just dropped into the groove.

Because I work mostly with ¾-in. and 1-in. stock, I located the fence so that a ⅜-in. wide mortise is centered in ¾-in. stock. Thicker stock has an offset mortise. Then, to square the fence to the base, I installed three square backing blocks behind the fence. If the fence isn't square to the base, mortises won't be parallel to the face of the stock.

Workpieces are clamped on the fence against an adjustable stop block (photo below). The stop block does two things: It positions workpieces in the fixture automatically, and it holds rail stock square in the fixture.

The stop block is slotted so that it can slide across a machine screw. The screw engages threaded T-nuts, which are similar to eyelets installed about 6 in. from both ends of the fence. Having two T-nuts allows me to move the stop block to the other side of the fence to make the second mortise in the stiles.

Next, I calibrated the fixture. I set my router in the fixture against the fixed stop block. Then I laid a scrap of wood 1⅝ in. wide beside the router. I butted the adjustable stop into the scrap and marked the stop's position on the guide rails. With a ⅜-in. straight bit in the plunge router, whenever the stop block is lined up with this mark, the router cuts a 2-in. long mortise. I glued an old tape rule to a guide rail and then screwed a plastic gauge to the adjustable stop to indicate the length of a mortise.

The last step was to figure out exactly where to clamp a workpiece in the fixture. I mortised a scrap in the fixture, removed the router and marked in the fixture's slot to show the end of the mortise nearest the fixed stop. Then I marked the fixture so that when I clamp on a workpiece, the mortise starts ⅜ in. from the end of the frame stock.—*P. L.*

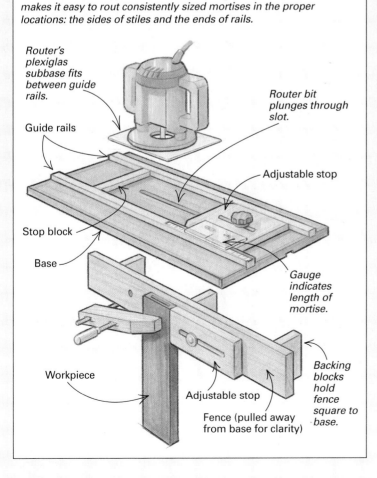

Router rides within rails and stops. *This mortising fixture makes it easy to rout consistently sized mortises in the proper locations: the sides of stiles and the ends of rails.*

Router's plexiglas subbase fits between guide rails.

Guide rails

Stop block

Base

Workpiece

Adjustable stop

Fence (pulled away from base for clarity)

Router bit plunges through slot.

Adjustable stop

Gauge indicates length of mortise.

Backing blocks hold fence square to base.

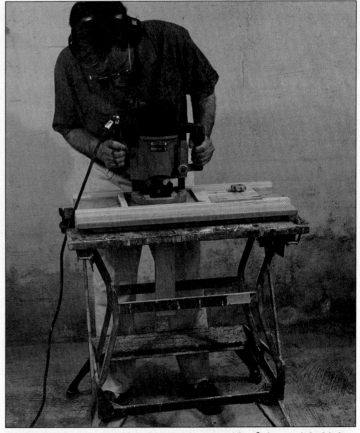

Using the fixture. A quick side-to-side pass with a ⅜-in. straight bit in a plunge router cuts a mortise whose length and width are limited by the fixture's rails and stops. The author uses a Workmate to clamp the fixture and the workpiece simultaneously.

Adjust the blade with a plywood scrap. The depth of the dado is ascertained by eye. Place a scrap of ¾-in. plywood atop the throat plate and next to the blade, and set it to cut halfway through the middle ply.

Dado is slightly more than ½ in. from edge of panel. Figure the distance from the edge of the panel to the dado with a piece of ¾-in. plywood. Move the fence until the dado blade just pokes out beyond the plywood.

Pass the panel through on edge to cut a tongue. Cut the tongues in the bottom panel and in the top frame with a dado blade set slightly lower than it was for dadoing side panels. This blade setting cuts a tongue that fits into the dado with a little clearance at the bottom of the dado for glue runout. Set up the saw fence so that the tongue is too fat, then pare it down with subsequent passes until the tongue just slips into the dado.

act as clamps. While the glue is still wet, I square the case by using one square corner of the back panel as a guide. I rack the case flush with the square corner of the back panel and pin it along both sides. Then I drive in some screws to hold the panel permanently and turn the case face up to apply the edging.

Edge the exposed plywood—The exposed edges of plywood cases are ugly. Beautifying these edges is a matter of applying hardwood edging. I rip ¼-in. thick edging from straight-grained, flat 1-in. stock. The side panels are edged first. I cut the edging to length, spread glue on both the plywood edge and the edging and then pin it in place with an air-driven pinner. Then I cut the crosspieces slightly long and flex them into place (bottom left photo, facing page). On narrow cases, I use a press fit because short pieces are too stiff to flex.

To trim the overhanging edging flush with the ¾-in. plywood, I use a router with a trimming bit (bottom right photo, facing page). Making several passes from right to left helps avoid splitting. The trimmer leaves a slightly proud edge that I take down with a sander or a plane. With a chisel I square the rounded corners left by the trimmer. After trimming, I use a belt sander to make all surfaces flush; then I use an orbital sander with 80-grit paper to round sharp corners. Eased corners make cases more comfortable to handle. Then I fill nail holes and sand all exposed surfaces with 120-grit paper.

Drawers are built like small cases—When making a drawer, I think of it as a minicase with ⅝-in. thick hardwood front, back and sides. When cutting drawer stock to length, I take into consideration clearance for the drawer slides; clearances vary depending on the type of drawer slides you use.

Although a dovetail is the ideal joint for a drawer, it's time-consuming to cut. As an alternative, I use the same tongue-and-dado joint that I used in the cabinet. The sides of the drawer are dadoed, and tongues in the front and

Simple drawer construction
Instead of dovetails, the drawer's front and back panels have tongues that fit into dadoes in the drawer's side panels.

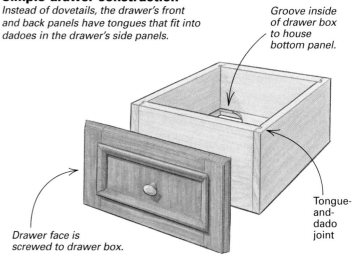

Groove inside of drawer box to house bottom panel.

Drawer face is screwed to drawer box.

Tongue-and-dado joint

the back panels fit into the dadoes (drawing above). I use a regular sawblade in place of the dado to make the dado, and then I make multiple passes with the regular blade to cut the tongues.

I also cut a groove close to the bottom edge of the stock. The groove houses the ¼-in. plywood drawer bottom. Glued in place, the bottom adds to the strength of the drawer and holds it square. I measure the diagonals and rack the drawer square. If a drawer won't stay square, I clamp it to pull or push it into square. Drawer faces are made like shortened door frames, and I screw the faces to the drawers after they're mounted in the cabinet. I close the drawer and clamp the drawer face to it. When the face is positioned, I reach through the top frame and drive a few screws through the drawer and into the face after I drill pilot holes. I check screws' lengths to be sure they won't punch through the face. □

Paul Levine of Sherman, Conn., is a cabinetmaker and the author of Making Kitchen Cabinets *(Taunton Press, 1988). His newest book,* Cabinets and Built-ins, *is from Rodale Press. Photos by the author except where noted.*

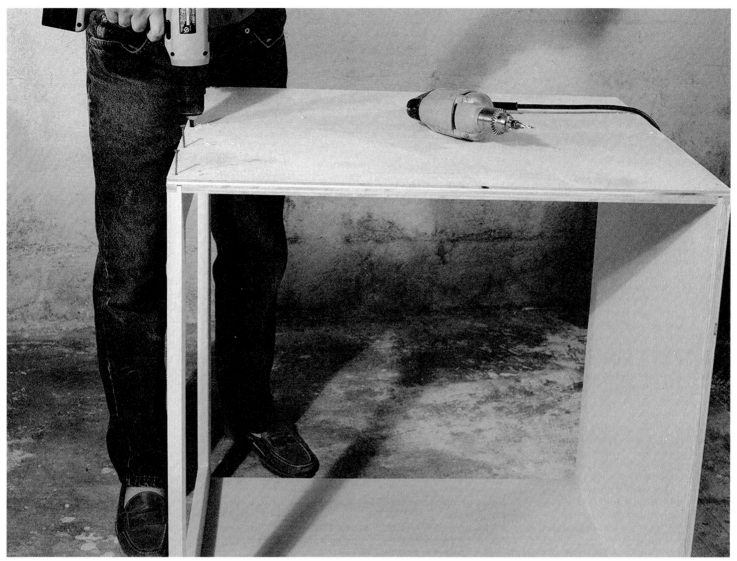

Cases are assembled with glue and screws. With the case lying on its side, the side panel is screwed to the top frame. Tongues in the top frame and the bottom panel interlock with dadoes in the side panel. Small gaps between the tongues and the dadoes allow for glue runout.

Hardwood edging covers the exposed plies on the front of the case. Traditional cabinets would have a face frame, but the cases featured here are frameless. Although full-overlay doors cover the cases when closed, opening doors reveals the edges of the case, so edging is required.

Here, edging is trimmed on the case's top frame. After the edging is glued and nailed in place, the overhanging edges are trimmed with a trimmer bit in a router. Edging tears out easily, so the first few passes should run right to left; the final pass runs left to right.

Site-Built Kitchen

Construct base cabinets with a carpenter's pragmatism and a cabinetmaker's precision

by Tony Simmonds

I built my first kitchen 11 years ago. It included 20 ft. of base cabinets, 14 ft. of uppers, 6 ft. of full-height pantry units, a 4-ft. by 6-ft. cooking island and a built-in computer desk. The job cost almost $7,000, and it was the biggest commission I had undertaken in my fledgling shop. When I finally pulled up to the job in a 24-ft. delivery truck to install all the parts, I was sweating more from apprehension than exertion.

I took a look around while the driver and his mate started bringing in the cabinets. Funny how narrow an alcove looks when your pantry units are standing beside it. And who put that window-sill there? Was this the same house I measured?

As I walked around I got more and more panicky. I felt like Alice, alternately crowding the ceilings and then shrinking to the floor. It didn't seem remotely possible that what I had put together on the level, unencumbered surface of my shop

Clean and simple. Waist-high drawers flank the stove in this site-built kitchen (photo above). The author made the edgebanded drawer fronts and doors out of a highly figured sheet of maple plywood. The cabinet carcases, also made of maple plywood, are edged with thin strips of solid wood.

floor could be reassembled here between these unaccommodatingly real, solid walls. The driver tapped my shoulder and pointed to one of the full-height units. It was lying on the floor next to its opening.

"Anything wrong?" I asked, with the sinking certainty that there was.

Don Watanabe, the site carpenter, was holding a level against the low ceiling over the cabinet's niche. The bubble was nowhere to be seen. Don smiled inscrutably. The converging lines of the

finished floor and the ceiling weren't even close to parallel.

"Cheat it," he said.

Take the shop along—Anyone who has built something in the shop for installation on a job site will recognize the scene. There are so many things to remember that it's nearly impossible to record all the data without dropping a detail here and there. And details can be expensive.

Three years ago, with my enthusiasm for plywood boxes flagging, I decided to get out of the full-time cabinet business and into remodeling. This has meant developing some different procedures for building cabinets and getting by with a no-frills complement of tools.

The heart of any cabinet shop is the table saw, and although I have learned to do a great deal with my old #1555 Rockwell radial-arm saw,

First the frame. The author assembled the base cabinets atop a frame of 2x4s toenailed to the wall and the subfloor.

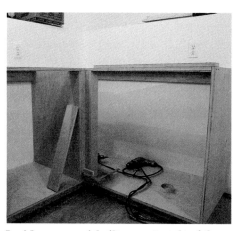

Inside corner. A built-up post made of three strips of plywood serves as an anchor for the cabinet-door hinges. The post is secured at the top by screws through the stretchers and at the other end by a couple of finish nails into the cabinet bottom.

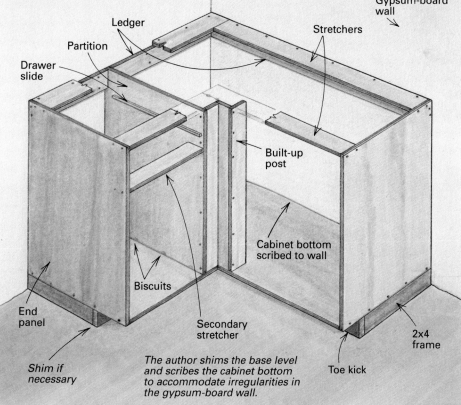

Cabinet components. *A site-built cabinet is a square piece of furniture built into a less-than-square environment, typically a wood-framed house. Ledgers screwed to the wall serve two functions: They anchor the end panels and the partitions, and they hold up the wall-side edge of the countertop.*

Gypsum-board wall

Ledger

Stretchers

Partition

Drawer slide

Built-up post

Cabinet bottom scribed to wall

Biscuits

End panel

Secondary stretcher

Shim if necessary

The author shims the base level and scribes the cabinet bottom to accommodate irregularities in the gypsum-board wall.

Toe kick

2x4 frame

---

when it comes to building a kitchen, the table saw is indispensable. Mine is a 10-in. saw, and I use a thin kerf, 80-tooth carbide-tipped alternating-top-bevel blade on it. This makes smooth cuts in plywood, even across the grain. I still take along the radial-arm saw, though—partly because it's mounted in an 8-ft. table, which I use for everything from workbench to router table to extension supports for the table saw.

I won't pretend there aren't times when I miss the resources of the fully equipped shop, but for me the disadvantages of on-site construction are outweighed by the rewards. Principal among them is that the clients can be involved with the process at every stage—from layout to drawer pulls. If the clients don't like something, they can change it. If they get an idea, they can act on it, and they can do so without feeling that they are causing the construction schedule to run backwards while the meter runs forward.

Maple-plywood cases—The installation I'll describe here was in a suite I helped my neighbors, Don and Shanti McDougall, build in their basement. By the time I got involved, the decisions still to be made centered on cabinet and counter materials and on door and drawer styles.

For the cases we settled on ¾-in. paint-grade maple plywood. The sink counter would be plastic laminate, and the food-prep area would be wood. Economy and expediency dictated that we buy the laminated beechwood counter ready-made. I reckoned I could do the laminate work without involving another subcontractor.

We all liked the idea of a waist-level band of drawers (photo facing page). To these we added two deep bins on drawer slides next to the stove for pots and pans (photo p. 78). The rest of the bases would be simple cupboards with hinged doors. Drawer fronts and doors were to be maple plywood, just like the cases.

With these questions resolved, I set about dimensioning the basic elements of the cabinets—the partitions, the floors and the door and drawer fronts. They were all going to be the same material, so the first thing I did was sort the sheets, selecting one with interesting color and figure for the doors. Then I had to figure out how to cut everything economically.

Paint-by-numbers layout—One thing I like about building cabinets on site is that I can usually pencil a full-size layout on the floor and on the walls too, if necessary. Then the job becomes almost like a paint-by-numbers kit: cut the pieces and put them where they go in the picture.

I begin a layout by marking the length and the height of the last piece—the countertop—and work backwards. Before I settle on countertop dimensions, I make sure I know everything there is to know about the appliances that have to fit in and around the countertop. If I don't have an appliance on hand, I find it at a showroom and take very careful measurements. This is critical—fridges don't trim easily.

For this job the counter is 36 in. high and 24 in. deep. I allow an overhang of at least ½ in. between the countertop and the face of the cabi-

nets (usually the door or the drawer face). With a smaller overhang, drips from the counter will run down the door front instead of onto the floor where they belong. At all costs avoid the sheer, modernist cliff, zero-overhang look. This style directs the drips down the inside of the door.

A cabinet end that is open to view should also have a ½-in. countertop overhang. But where a freestanding range (yup, they're still out there) has to be slotted between two runs of cabinets as in this case, I allow ¼-in. overall clearance between the finished ends of the countertops and another ¼ in. between the finished ends of the cabinets. This doesn't leave a great deal of space for jimmying a heavy stove into position, but face it: It's going to get dirty in there. The narrower the gap, the better.

The other overhang, between the door face and the toe kick at the bottom of the cabinet, is usually about 3 in. Remember to allow for the thickness of the finish material on the toe kick.

Pay particular attention to inside corners. One typical treatment is installing piano hinges between two doors at right angles to each other. This allows the doors to be opened and closed simultaneously. But what about the drawers above them? They need space to pass each other, and that space has to allow for any handle projection. I've found that a 1½-in. space between the inside corner and the beginning of the drawer allows for a wide range of handle choices.

Framing cabinets in place—The first step in building the cabinets (top photo, above) is to establish a level base for them. For this kitchen I had to get ⅛-in. vinyl-tile flooring over ⅜-in. underlayment, so I decided to set kiln-dried spruce 2x4s on edge directly on the subfloor. For a higher toe kick, or to allow for thicker finish flooring, I add furring strips to the tops of the 2x4s.

With pieces cut and assembled, I set the completed frame on the layout lines. Then I check for level. If the high point is at the wall, I screw the back to a level line, then shim up the front as necessary and toe-screw the frame to the subfloor. If the floor slopes down from the middle of the room to the wall, I raise the back accordingly and fasten it to the wall like a ledger, shimming under it if necessary.

With a solid, level base frame in place, the next step is to cut the cabinet bottoms. One side of the kitchen shown here has a run of less than 4 ft., so I cut the bottom from one piece of ¾-in. plywood. When I need to join two or more pieces to make the bottom, as I did on the other side, I use a plate joiner and glue the pieces together as I lay them.

One advantage of site-built base cabinets is that the walls double as the backs of the cabinets, saving on the cost of a plywood back. On the other hand, the back edge of the cabinet bottom has to be scribed to the uneven plane of the wall (drawing p. 77). This joint is practical rather than aesthetic, so I leave a gap that can be easily caulked, and I screw the bottom to the base. If screws are counterbored, they can be plugged later, but I don't plug them at this point in case I need to make minor adjustments after the doors are hung.

Next I cut the four cabinet end panels and the three partitions. I planned to flush-fit the doors and the drawer fronts, and because there was no back to allow for, the widths of all the end panels and the partitions were the same. If the bottom of the cabinet has been heavily scribed to accommodate a bulge in the wall, the partition or the end panel may have to be cut down correspondingly. As for height, the end panels overlap both the cabinet bottom and the top stretchers, so they're two thicknesses of plywood longer than the partitions. There's no reason you couldn't run the cabinet ends all the way to the floor, but you'd need to notch them for the toe kick, and you'd need a 35¼-in. long panel. I generally cut the longest panels at 31⅞ in. That way I can get three panels out of an 8-ft. length of plywood.

This is a good time to put at least some of the hardware on the cabinet end panels and partitions. Mechanical drawer slides and European-style hinge-mounting plates go on easier with end panels and partitions layed flat on the bench. For this job I used ½-in. by ½-in. wooden drawer slides screwed to the plywood.

Before I install the end panels and the partitions, I cut some strips of plywood about 3 in. wide for the ledgers and the stretchers. These plywood strips usually come from the offcuts of the cabinet pieces.

Next I select one partition and check that it's square and correctly dimensioned. Standing it upright on the cabinet bottom and flat against the wall, I pencil a line on the wall along the

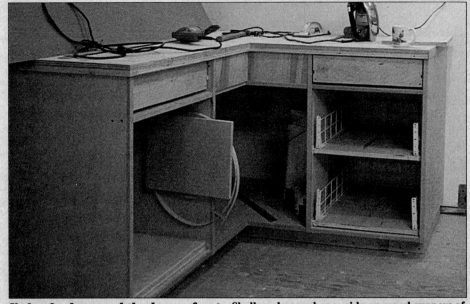

Under the doors and the drawer fronts. Shallow drawer boxes ride on wood runners affixed to the cabinet partitions and end panels. The lower drawers on the sink-side base cabinets are commercial bins that use roller hardware.

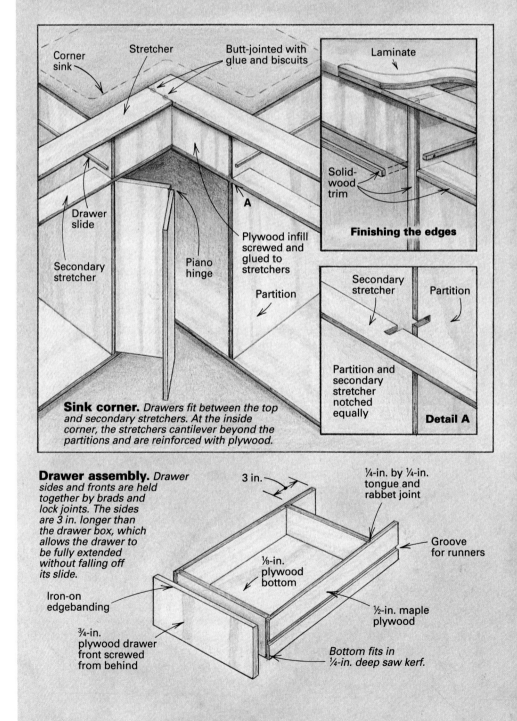

Corner sink

Stretcher

Butt-jointed with glue and biscuits

Laminate

Drawer slide

Solid-wood trim

Finishing the edges

A

Secondary stretcher

Piano hinge

Plywood infill screwed and glued to stretchers

Partition

Secondary stretcher

Partition

Partition and secondary stretcher notched equally

Detail A

Sink corner. *Drawers fit between the top and secondary stretchers. At the inside corner, the stretchers cantilever beyond the partitions and are reinforced with plywood.*

Drawer assembly. *Drawer sides and fronts are held together by brads and lock joints. The sides are 3 in. longer than the drawer box, which allows the drawer to be fully extended without falling off its slide.*

3 in.

¼-in. by ¼-in. tongue and rabbet joint

Iron-on edgebanding

⅛-in. plywood bottom

Groove for runners

½-in. maple plywood

¾-in. plywood drawer front screwed from behind

Bottom fits in ¼-in. deep saw kerf.

partition's top edge. I slide the partition along the bottom of the cabinet, marking the wall as I go. Now I can set the ledger to a level line.

I mark the position of the partitions on the front edge of the cabinet bottom and extend the lines across the cabinet bottom with a framing square. Then I use the partition, resting on the cabinet floor and flat against the wall, as a big square to draw plumb lines on the wall that mark the vertical lines of the partitions and the end panels.

Ledgers go between partitions—I join the partitions to the floor with biscuits, cutting the slots with a plate joiner. If there's a shelf between two partitions, I'll cut it now and use it to guide the plate joiner (drawing below). Otherwise, a spare piece of plywood can be clamped or tacked to the layout line as a guide.

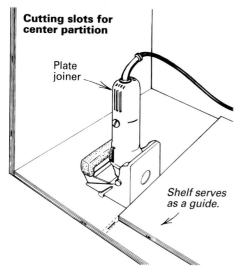

Cutting slots for center partition

Plate joiner

Shelf serves as a guide.

Once I have the slots cut for the partition biscuits, I can assemble the pieces. Beginning in one corner, I cut the ledger long enough to take me from the corner to the edge of the first partition. I screw the ledger to the wall, drop the partition onto its biscuits and run a screw through the partition into the end of the ledger. Then I install the next length of ledger and partition and so on until I get to the end panel.

The stretchers are screwed to the end panels and the partitions. To keep things square and plumb while installing the stretchers, brace the end panel temporarily by pipe-clamping a piece of plywood about the size of your cabinet door in the opening the door will occupy.

The back stretchers intersect at the corner of the walls. Make the butt joint there with glued biscuits or by screwing a piece of plywood across the joint from underneath. If you screw plywood across this joint, make sure it won't interfere with the door or the drawer.

In this kitchen I wanted to emphasize the division between the band of drawers and the doors underneath them, so I installed a secondary stretcher between them. Each secondary stretcher is screwed in place on the ends and half-notched into the front edge of any partition that it intersects (detail A, facing page).

To support the corner sink, I cantilevered the stretchers beyond the partitions and attached them to each other with a glued biscuit. I filled the spaces between the top and secondary

stretchers with plywood, which acts like the webs of two short trusses. The corner is solid.

The other inside corner required a post made out of a couple of filler pieces to create a jamb for the cabinet-door hinges and clearance for the drawer (bottom photo, p. 77). We did without a lazy Susan or a revolving-shelf fitting for this corner. If you're using one, make sure the corner post will accommodate its mounting brackets.

Mounting shelves and slides—I like to do all the work I can on the interior fittings of the cabinets before installing the countertop. There's more light in there without the roof, and countertops are susceptible to damage through misuse as workbenches.

Adjustable shelves used to be considered a luxury in a kitchen cabinet. Now they're practically de rigeur. I use the little spade-shaped nickel-plated steel shelf supports with a ⅜-in. long shaft that can be inserted into a 7mm hole. I make a template with holes on 2-in. centers out of a strip of plywood as wide as the shelf, and I clamp it against the partitions and the end panels to guide my drill (drawing below).

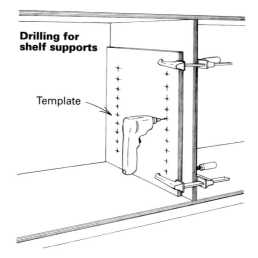

Drilling for shelf supports

Template

To control the depth of the holes for the supports, I make a depth gauge out of a short length of dowel. I drill the appropriate-diameter hole in the dowel and slip it over the bit. I use this depth gauge to avoid drilling through an exposed surface. Even where two sets of holes in a partition line up opposite each other, I drill from both sides using the depth gauge to avoid the tearout that occurs when a bit exits the back of the work.

When I finished with the template on this job, I ripped it in two and screwed each half to the inside corners where I would need shelf support, but there was no partition to provide it.

If you're using drawer slides, and you didn't mount them before installing the partitions and the end panels, you can make the job easier by using a plywood spacer. Shove it against the underside of the stretcher, butt your slide to it and hold the slide steady while running in the screws.

Doors, drawers and counters—The door blanks I cut earlier now had to be trimmed to size and have their drawer fronts separated from them. The grain pattern of the sheet I had selected made it important to do this carefully to pre-

serve the flow of the intricate figure across the front of the cabinets, as well as vertically from door to drawer. I made sure I had a helper on hand to assist with the delicate table-saw cuts.

All four edges of the doors and the drawer fronts are bound with hot-melt glue veneer strips. This edgetape is available in several wood species and is easy to apply with a household iron (medium setting—no steam). It never fails to amuse a client if they happen to come in and see me in my apron doing the ironing.

I made the drawers for this job out of ½-in. maple plywood (bottom drawing, facing page). I let the sides run 3 in. long to allow the drawer to extend all the way without falling off its runners. The width of the drawer should equal the face-to-face distance of the runners plus ½ in. The fronts and backs of the drawers are joined to the sides with a tongue-and-groove joint (called a drawer-lock joint) and glue and brads. For drawers of this size, I use ⅛-in. plywood bottoms, which fit in a regular saw kerf. To cut the ¼-in. deep grooves for the runners, I run the assembled box over a ½-in. dado head with a plastic-laminate spacer added between the blades to make the grooves slightly larger. The runners are ½ in. wide, so the laminate provides the necessary clearance. I take care when assembling the drawers not to put any nails where the groove will be.

So-called European-style concealed cabinet hinges, with their several adjustments, have made hanging cabinet doors a snap. About the only thing you can do wrong is make the doors too big. I cut them to be ³⁄₁₆ in. shorter and narrower than their openings. The edgebanding adds ¹⁄₁₆ in. to that, leaving a ¹⁄₁₆-in. gap all around in the finished installation. The doors stop against a continuous strip of wood that is affixed to the underside of the stretcher. A continuous strip looks more like a trim piece than a little stop block, and it's easier to install. The edging I used for these cabinets was cut from a single piece of Douglas fir, which yielded a particularly crisp and pleasing pattern in its edge grain. The vertical edges are finished with ⅜-in. thick strips, and the horizontal edges are capped with ⁵⁄₁₆-in. strips, making for a stepped intersection that is more practical and more pleasing than is a flush one.

I hung all the doors and adjusted them, then I fastened the drawer fronts to their boxes with screws driven from inside the drawer. Where two or more drawer fronts are stacked on top of each other, as on the left-hand side of the range here, I install the bottom one first and then use a spacer (two thicknesses of edgetape is about right) to position the one above it.

I attached the wood counter to the stretchers with #8 wood screws driven into pilot holes for #10 screws. The oversized shank holes allow seasonal expansion and contraction of the countertop without splitting the wood. The countertop on the sink side of the range is plastic laminate installed over a substrate of ¾-in. AC plywood. We added a tiled backsplash with green grout to pick up the color of the deep-green laminate. □

Tony Simmonds is a designer and builder in Vancouver, B. C., Canada. Photos by the author except where noted.

Installing Kitchen Cabinets

How to fit and fasten cabinets to wavy walls and floors

by Tom Law

Well, there you are, just walking into a new kitchen with freshly painted drywall. Or maybe you're remodeling, and you've spent the last few days gutting the kitchen. But now you've got a clean slate to work with. The kitchen cabinets are in cardboard boxes, and all you have to do is unpack them and fasten them to the wall, right? Easy, tiger.

Kitchen cabinets are like carry-out food: A lot can go wrong with the order, and you don't want to be five miles down the road when you discover that something's missing. Before you begin installing cabinets, check all the boxes. Make sure you have everything you need and that the cabinets are what the customer ordered.

Take a close look at the walls and the floor—they're probably not as flat as they appear. You'll have to compensate for any imperfections because the cabinets take precedence. You don't distort a straight cabinet to fit a crooked wall.

Here, I'll discuss the methods I use to install cabinets when conditions are less than perfect, and believe me, they usually are.

Know the room conditions—Every installation begins with a check of the floor and the walls for the carpenter's guiding principles: plumb and level, straight and square. I use a straightedge and a level to see how the floor goes. The goal is to locate high and low spots because one of these spots will be the starting point for the cabinet layout, ultimately determining the height of the countertop.

I also use the straightedge to check the walls for straight and plumb. If there is a corner, I check it for square. Although serious flaws are uncommon, minor problems like crooked studs or spackle buildup often appear.

Marking the wall and the floor—To get over the fidgets of starting the job, I mark the cabinet layout on the wall. Marking the layout helps me visualize the finished job.

To begin with, I decide whether to use the high or low spot on the floor for my starting point. Choosing the high spot probably means that only one base cabinet will sit directly on the floor; all the others will be shimmed up. Using the low spot means that most of the cabinets will have to be scribed to fit the irregularities of the floor (more about scribing later). It's easier to use the high spot because it's easier to shim up than to cut off, but the determining factor is countertop height. Usually a countertop is 3 ft. from the floor.

Marking the base-cabinet line. Starting from the high or low spot on the floor, the height of the base cabinets is marked on the wall, then the mark is transferred around the room with a water level. The line is also a reference point for laying out the upper cabinets.

Countertops themselves are normally 1½ in. thick, so the base cabinets are 34½ in. high. I mark this height on the wall above either the high or the low spot on the floor, whichever I've chosen as the starting point. Then I transfer that mark around the walls using a water level (photo above). I use the water level to mark the cabinet height at each corner, then I strike a chalkline between the marks (for more on water levels, see *FHB* #85, pp. 58-60). If you don't have a water level, a conventional spirit level and a straightedge will do.

After the base-cabinet line is marked on the wall, I mark the location of the individual cabinets. I usually don't mark full plumb lines (the vertical lines) for each cabinet; I just make check marks along the base-cabinet line to indicate the width of each cabinet.

The face-frame stiles on most cabinets project beyond the sides ⅟₃₂ in. to ¼ in., which allows the stiles of two cabinets to be joined tightly without the sides of the cabinets bumping together. I mark each cabinet's actual size (its width from stile to stile) on the wall and then subtract the amount the stiles protrude to locate the back of the cabinet accurately.

I also use the base-cabinet line as a reference for laying out the upper cabinets. The space between the upper cabinets and the countertop is usually between 16 in. and 18 in. When measuring up from the base-cabinet line, I add 1½ in. for the countertop. Then I mark the wall to indicate the bottom of the upper cabinets. I double check to see that the top of the upper cabinets is the same height as the top of any full-length cabinet, like a broom closet or a pantry unit. If it isn't, I adjust the layout of the upper cabinets.

Next, I mark the location of each upper cabinet, again with either check marks or full-length lines. Most of the time the upper cabinets are the same width as the base cabinets below them, and their edges align vertically. Cabinets must line up where an appliance, such as a refrigerator, protrudes into the upper-cabinet space. And by the way, you shouldn't add anything to the space indicated on the plans for an appliance. A 30-in. stove or refrigerator as called out on the plan will fit a 30-in. opening.

Some cabinets, such as those over refrigerators and stoves, don't come down as low as the other upper cabinets. And some cabinets, such as desk units, sit lower than the other base cabinets. I measure these cabinets and mark their locations.

Next I find the studs and mark their locations on the wall because I'll be fastening the cabinets to the studs. I mark stud locations with straight lines. Studs can be sounded out (where you tap the wall and listen for the higher pitch that occurs when you strike a stud) and probed for with a hammer and a nail, or they can be located with an electronic stud finder. If you use the hammer-and-nail approach, be sure to punch the holes where they'll be covered by cabinets.

It's OK to fasten a base cabinet to only one stud. Upper cabinets, however, are better off attached to two studs. Sometimes a cabinet isn't wide enough to catch two studs. I either attach narrow cabinets to their neighbors, or I might add blocking in the wall where it will be covered by a cabinet. I use a reciprocating saw to cut a hole in the drywall, then I insert a glue-covered piece of 1x that will span the hole. This block is the backing that I'll attach the cabinet to, so I make sure the hole is in the right place behind the cabinet.

Which cabinets come first?—The most important consideration when deciding which cabinets to set first, the uppers or the bases, is comfort. Some manufacturers suggest hanging the upper ones first because you can stand closer to the wall when the base cabinets aren't in the way. If you hang the upper cabinets first, it's sometimes recommended that you nail a 1x2 ledger strip on the wall to support the upper cabinets while you fasten them to the wall. It's a good idea if the backsplash will later cover the nail holes. But you wouldn't want to nail a ledger strip on a finished wall.

There are lots of ways to hold upper cabinets in place as you install them. You can buy or make various jacks and props, but it's been my experience that when hanging upper cabinets first, it's better to have two people doing the work—one holding, one fastening.

When I work alone, I find it awkward to hang upper cabinets first. By installing the base cabinets first, I can use them to support the upper cabinets (more on this method later). Plus the base cabinets are more complicated because they have to be fitted to both the wall and the floor, so I start with them.

Start from a corner—It's much easier to start in a corner and work out of it than to put yourself in one. Most corner cabinets have their backs cut on a 45° angle, so setting them into an out-of-square corner is easy. If the cabinet has a square

Shimming a cabinet. Shims are used to level a cabinet, but they also bring cabinets that sit in low spots of the floor up to the proper height. Here, the end cabinet of a peninsula is leveled.

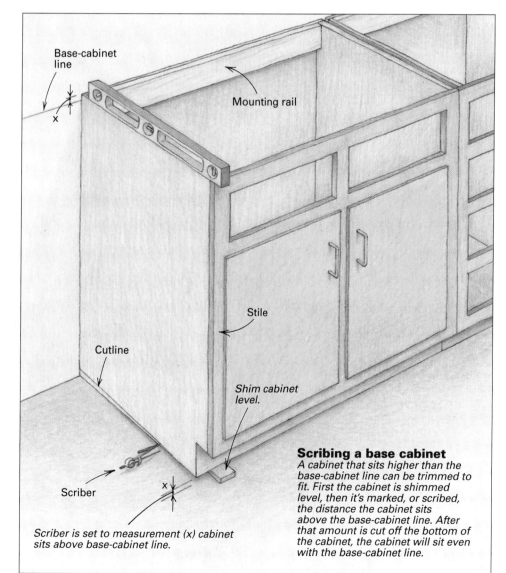

Base-cabinet line

Mounting rail

Stile

Cutline

Shim cabinet level.

Scriber

Scriber is set to measurement (x) cabinet sits above base-cabinet line.

Scribing a base cabinet
A cabinet that sits higher than the base-cabinet line can be trimmed to fit. First the cabinet is shimmed level, then it's marked, or scribed, the distance the cabinet sits above the base-cabinet line. After that amount is cut off the bottom of the cabinet, the cabinet will sit even with the base-cabinet line.

Fitting an end panel. Some cabinets have a separate end panel that should be scribed to fit tightly against the wall. With the panel clamped in place, the author uses a pocketknife to hold a strip of wood for scribing. The wood strip, like a scriber or compass, holds the pencil a set distance from the wall. The scribe mark is made on masking tape.

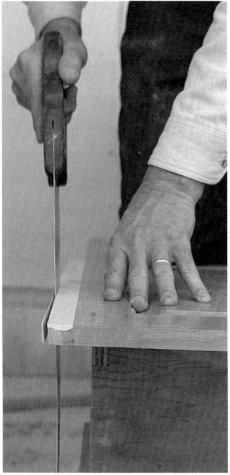

Cutting the end panel. The author uses a handsaw to get a clean cut along the scribe line. A slight back cut ensures that the face of the end panel will fit tight to the wall.

back, spackle buildup will probably have to be sanded down, but there are times when the only thing to do is cut away the drywall or plaster to get a square-back unit in place.

Because most corner cabinets have cutaway backs, they tend to shift around and are difficult to set in place. One way to shore up corner cabinets is to attach cabinets to each side and then push all three into place as a unit.

Another thing about corner cabinets with cutaway backs is that they often require a ledger strip along the wall to support the countertop. I nail a piece of 1x stock along the base-cabinet line to support the countertop in the corner.

Scribing a cabinet—When a base cabinet—corner or otherwise—is installed, it must be set level and plumb. If the floor isn't level, there are two ways to get that base cabinet level and plumb—shim it or scribe it. Shimming is much easier; I just slip shims under the cabinet until it's level and at the proper height (photo p. 81). When the top is level, I check all the sides; as long as the cabinet is square, the sides should be plumb no matter how I place the level. Exposed shims and gaps are often covered by a vinyl base; sometimes there's a separate toe-kick board that's scribed to fit the contours of the floor. If I'm installing base cabinets over a wood floor, I hide the shims and the gaps with shoe molding.

If the top of the cabinet is above the layout line even before I shim it, scribing is necessary. To scribe a cabinet to the floor, I bring the cabinet as close as I can to where it belongs in the kitchen, then shim it level. I set my scriber (or pencil compass) to the amount the cabinet extends above the line and scribe the cabinet at the floor (drawing p. 81). (For more on scribing, see *FHB* #77, p. 61.) I cut the bottom of the cabinet at the scribe line. When I replace the cabinet, it sits level with the base-cabinet line.

When the side of a cabinet is exposed, it must fit perfectly against the wall. The side panels of many cabinets project beyond the back panels. These cabinets are easy to scribe to a wall. First, I level the cabinet, then set the scriber to the widest space between the cabinet and the wall and scribe both sides. I remove the cabinet, cut the sides to the scribe lines, then reinstall it. In some kitchens a decorative end panel is used to dress up the exposed side of a cabinet. Such panels are usually slightly oversized so that they can be scribed to the wall (photos left). If the cabinet has a flush back, however, scribing is impossible, so straightening the wall or shimming the back and covering the gap with molding is the only choice.

Installation information—Now that I've talked about laying out and fitting cabinets to the floor and the wall, here's how I go about installing a kitchen. First I put the corner cabinet in place, shim it level with the base-cabinet line and, if necessary, scribe the cabinet to fit. Then I fasten the cabinet to the wall by driving screws through the mounting rail into the wall studs. The mounting rail is a horizontal piece of wood at the back of the cabinet.

Screws need to bite into studs at least ¾ in., so I use 2½-in. or 3-in. long drywall screws. But you may prefer to use wood screws, which have thicker shanks, or use the screws supplied by the manufacturer. If there's a gap between the mounting rail and the wall right where I want to run a screw, I slip a shim into the gap to keep the back of the cabinet from distorting when I put in the screw.

After the first cabinet is in place, I bring the second one to it, level it, get the face frames flush by lining up the top and the bottom of the cabinet's stiles, then I clamp the stiles together.

When the stiles are flush and tight with each other, I fasten them with screws (top left photo, facing page). I always drill pilot holes and countersink the screws. Usually two screws in each stile are sufficient. When the doors are closed, the screws are hidden, but I still try to make them inconspicuous when the doors are open by putting the screws close to the hinges. Once the adjoining stiles are screwed together, I screw the cabinet to the wall.

I install each succeeding base cabinet the same way—level it, shim or scribe as required, fasten the stiles and then screw it to the wall. As the run of cabinets grows, I put a straightedge across the front of the cabinets to make sure they're in line (top middle photo, facing page). I make any adjustments at the wall by tightening or loosening screws and adding shims.

Installing a sink base—Sink base cabinets with back panels may be more difficult to install because they might have to be bored for plumbing and electrical lines. If the cabinets on each side of the sink base are in position—even temporarily—I use them as reference points from which to measure the locations of pipes and wires. If the surrounding cabinets aren't in place, I mark the sink base-cabinet layout full size on both the wall and the floor. Then I can measure the pipe and wire locations from the layout lines.

If I drill holes in the back of the cabinet from behind, I complete them from the finished side to avoid tearing out the veneer. A little tearout isn't a big deal because the plumber usually puts a finish plate around the opening that covers a rough cut.

Some sink base cabinets have no back panel; obviously it won't be necessary to drill holes if the pipes and the wires come through the wall. But sometimes they come up through the floor. And that's when the layout lines on the floor come in handy.

Installing between walls—When a run of base cabinets fits between walls, the dimensions may work out, and the cabinets will fit exactly. But more often than not, the cabinets will require some fitting.

If the total dimension of the cabinets is just slightly more than the space to be filled, I put all the cabinets in except the last one, and I leave the next-to-last cabinet unattached; that is, I don't screw it to the wall yet. I measure the space left for the last cabinet. Then I remove the next-to-last one and put the last one back in plumb and level. I scribe it to fit the return wall. The amount of material to be scribed off the last cabinet's stile will be determined by the space required for the next-to-last cabinet when it's replaced.

Once all the scribing and trimming is complete, I put the last cabinet in place, then push the next-to-last cabinet in place with a pry bar. I use wax paper between the stiles to help the cabinet slide in without marring the finish.

Installing filler and backer strips—When a run of cabinets doesn't quite fill the space between walls, filler strips are used. A filler strip is simply a board of the same kind of wood and finish as the cabinets, and it gets screwed to a cabinet's stile to fill a gap. Sometimes cabinets can be ordered with wider stiles to make up the difference, but fillers are more common.

To scribe a filler strip, I first screw it onto the cabinet stile, move the cabinet as close as possible to its final position, then I scribe, using the widest gap as the amount to cut off. I almost al-ways leave a filler strip on a cabinet and cut the strip in place.

Backer strips are frequently installed at inside corners to keep cabinets as far enough apart so that drawers or drawer handles don't bump into each other. Because the cabinets have to be separated by the thickness of the drawer front and the hardware, fastening a backer strip to the abutting cabinet will increase the clearance (top right photo, below). We'll run into an inside corner later when I talk about peninsulas. But right now, I've still got to hang the upper cabinets.

Installing upper cabinets—Like the base cabinets, upper cabinets should be installed level and plumb, with sides parallel and stiles screwed together. All of the cabinets should be fastened to the wall using the same screws as those used for the base cabinets. I like to drive two screws in the top mounting rail and two into the bottom mounting rail. I fill gaps between the wall and the cabinet with shims as needed.

When hanging big, heavy upper cabinets, I lighten the load by removing all doors and shelves, and I reinstall whatever I've removed when all the cabinets are set. Removing the doors before hanging the cabinets also makes it easier to clamp the stiles together before driving the screws.

Instead of holding the cabinets in place as I try to fasten them to the wall, I typically use some plywood props (drawing below) or adjustable cabinet jacks (bottom photo, below). I made two different-size props from ¾-in plywood; one prop is 17¼ in. high for a 16-in. spacing between upper and base cabinets; the other is 19¼ in. high for an 18-in. spacing (16 in. and 18 in. are the two most popular spacings between upper cabinets and base cabinets). The finish space between upper and base cabinets is 16 in. or 18 in.; the additional 1¼ in. on each prop

Joining cabinets. **Cabinet stiles are clamped flush and joined with wood screws before the cabinets are installed. Two wood screws hold the cabinets together, one near each hinge.**

Aligning cabinets. **A straightedge placed along a run of cabinets shows which cabinets must move in or out. Here, a cabinet is pried away from the wall and shimmed out.**

Fastening a backer strip. **This strip of wood acts as a spacer to hold the corner cabinets far enough apart so that their drawers don't bump into each other.**

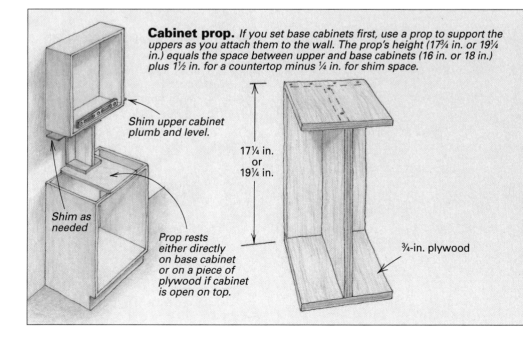

Cabinet prop. *If you set base cabinets first, use a prop to support the uppers as you attach them to the wall. The prop's height (17¾ in. or 19¼ in.) equals the space between upper and base cabinets (16 in. or 18 in.) plus 1½ in. for a countertop minus ¼ in. for shim space.*

Shim upper cabinet plumb and level.

17¼ in. or 19¼ in.

Shim as needed

Prop rests either directly on base cabinet or on a piece of plywood if cabinet is open on top.

¾-in. plywood

Cabinet jacks **consist of square steel tubes that slide inside each other; a cabinet sits in cushioned angle iron (see *FHB* #52, p. 98).**

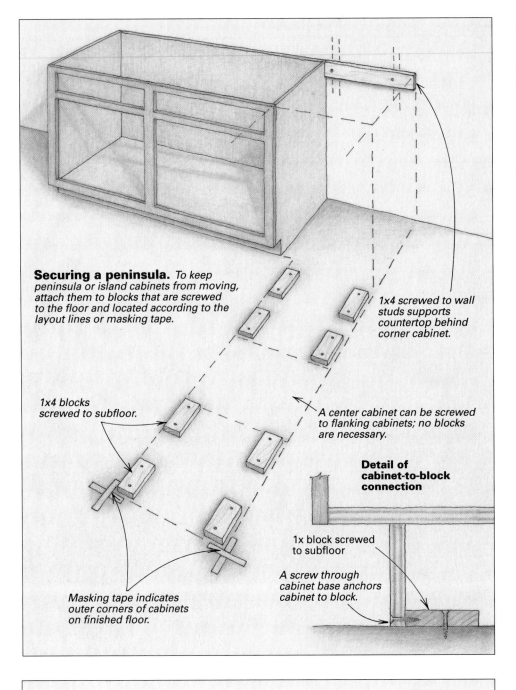

Securing a peninsula. *To keep peninsula or island cabinets from moving, attach them to blocks that are screwed to the floor and located according to the layout lines or masking tape.*

1x4 blocks screwed to subfloor.

Masking tape indicates outer corners of cabinets on finished floor.

1x4 screwed to wall studs supports countertop behind corner cabinet.

A center cabinet can be screwed to flanking cabinets; no blocks are necessary.

Detail of cabinet-to-block connection

1x block screwed to subfloor

A screw through cabinet base anchors cabinet to block.

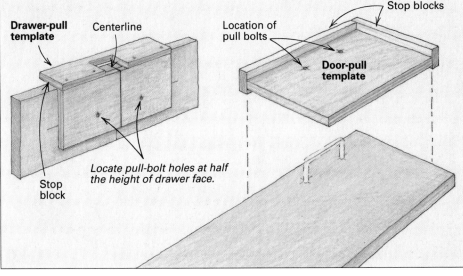

Using hardware templates. *Both templates have stop blocks that register against the edges of drawers and doors. The drawer-pull template has a centerline that you align with the centerline of the drawer face, and the door-pull template is self-aligning and reversible for use on a right- or left-hand door.*

Drawer-pull template

Centerline

Stop block

Locate pull-bolt holes at half the height of drawer face.

Stop blocks

Location of pull bolts

Door-pull template

makes up for the countertop that's not yet in place. The missing ¼ in. is shim space. I put a prop on a base cabinet and rest an upper cabinet on the prop. I use long shims to adjust the height of the upper cabinet to the layout line. (Some base cabinets are open on top, so I lay a piece of plywood on top of these cabinets and use the shorter props.)

Just as I installed the base cabinets, I start with a corner cabinet and work my way out. Each succeeding cabinet is put into place on the plywood prop and shimmed level. Then I clamp and screw the stiles together. Finally I screw the cabinet to the wall and remove the prop.

The fronts of the upper cabinets should also be checked with a straightedge and adjusted at the wall line, again either by tightening screws or backing them out and adding shims.

Islands and peninsulas—When the kitchen plan includes an island or a peninsula, I make a full-size layout on the floor and check the squareness of the corner with the old 3-4-5 triangle. If the finish floor isn't down yet, I snap chalklines. But if the finish floor is in place, I don't want chalk everywhere, so I use masking tape to show where the cabinets go.

An island or a peninsula should be secured to the floor, and I do it by screwing 1x blocks to the floor, then placing the cabinets over the blocks and screwing the cabinets to the blocks (top drawing, left).

Using my layout lines, I measure in from the edge of the masking tape or chalkline (which represents the outside of the cabinet) and mark the thickness of the cabinet's base. The new marks indicate where to screw the blocks down. Usually I just use a 6-in. to 8-in. block of 1x4 in each corner. Before I screw the cabinet to the blocks, I shim or scribe the cabinet so that it's plumb, level and at the same height as the other cabinets. When an island or a peninsula cabinet is placed over the blocks, it can't be shifted side to side, and when the screws go through the cabinet into the blocks, it can't be lifted either.

Hardware and handles—After I've replaced all the doors and the drawers, I install the hardware. If the holes for the pulls have been predrilled, it's easy enough to screw the hardware on. But if I need to drill the holes myself, and there are a lot of holes to drill, it's best to make a template (bottom drawing, left). I use a piece of plywood and glue a stop block at its edge, which holds the template in place on the door or the drawer.

I sometimes use masking tape to mark the hole centers. Masking tape makes pencil marks more visible, but I double check the marks by holding the handle up to them. I use a sharp scratch awl or punch to mark the hole, then drill it through. The center punch keeps the drill bit from wandering. □

Tom Law lives in Westminster, Md., and is a consulting editor for Fine Homebuilding. *His video on installing kitchen cabinets is available from the Taunton Press. Photos by Rich Ziegner.*

Installing European cabinets

by Tom Santarsiero

Cabinetry manufactured in Europe brought both a new look and a new installation system to the United States. European cabinets are frameless—they have no face frame—and the shelf pins, the hardware mounting screws and the dowels that join the carcases are drilled on 32-mm centers. Although many American cabinet manufacturers have incorporated the European look and construction system into their lines, few have fully incorporated its installation system.

European cabinetry has its own suspension and support hardware that makes installing cabinets fast and efficient, even if you work alone. Upper cabinets are hung from a steel rail that you screw to the wall studs. Base cabinets stand on adjustable leveling legs. Thanks to this hardware, plumbing and leveling cabinets are much simpler.

When laying out a European kitchen, I snap three level lines on the walls. One line indicates the top of the base cabinet; one line indicates the bottom of the upper cabinets, and the third line is for the upper cabinets' hanging rail. The height of this rail varies from brand to brand.

The hanging rail is a length of steel about 1¼ in. wide with an offset bend along the top edge. I predrill ¼-in. holes at 5 cm o. c. (about 2 in. o. c.; European cabinetry is all metric). I screw the rail to the wall through these holes with #14 2½-in. pan-head screws.

I install the upper cabinets first. They hang on the channel in the hanging rail via a pair of adjustable hooks (top two photos, right) that protrude from the back of each cabinet. Two set screws on each hook adjust the wall cabinets. One screw moves the cabinet in and out; the other moves the cabinet up and down. With this system, one person can easily hang and adjust wall cabinets.

When the hanging rail is above the cabinets, crown molding conceals it. If the hanging rail runs behind the cabinets, I notch the back of the cabinets to fit over the rail. However, end cabinets with visible side panels aren't notched; the hanging rail stops against the inside edge of a visible side panel.

Once the upper cabinets are aligned, I bolt them together using joining bolts supplied by the manufacturer. Most European cabinets have partially bored holes inside along the front of the side panels. I clamp the cabinets together, finish drilling the holes and then pass the bolts through. The bolts are similar to small carriage bolts with a threaded cap or socket. All of the European cabinets I've seen come with these bolts. If the cabinets you're installing come without bolts, you can use short drywall screws.

Base cabinets have leveling legs that slip into plastic sockets on the bottom of the cabinet. The legs usually come with each cabinet, along with caps that cover adjustment access holes in the cabinet floor. To level and plumb a cabinet, I either use the access holes to turn the legs with a screwdriver (bottom photo, right), or I turn the legs by hand.

Hanging an upper cabinet. A hanging rail screwed to the studs supports upper cabinets that have adjustable leveling hooks. This system allows one person to install cabinets.

Adjusting the leg. You don't have to shim or scribe European cabinets because they rest on legs that are adjusted up or down with a screwdriver. The toe kick clips onto the legs; the clips are also adjustable.

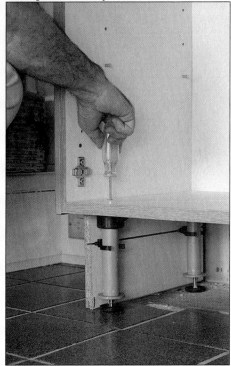

Europeans don't fasten base cabinets to the wall. The thinking is that because base cabinets are joined together and attached to countertops and appliances, the cabinets won't move. Also, Europeans take their cabinets with them when they move, so fewer screws going in during installation means fewer screws to take out on moving day.

I like to be sure that my cabinets will stay put, so I fasten them to the wall. How I fasten them depends on the brand of cabinet I'm installing. True European cabinets are a bit shallower than the typical 2-ft. deep face-frame cabinet. When I install European cabinets, I space them away from the wall slightly so that they'll be the right depth for a conventional countertop. Some manufacturers supply special particleboard blocks with their cabinets that are screwed to the wall and to the cabinet, serving as both a spacer block and a rigid means of attachment.

If the manufacturer doesn't supply blocking, I screw a 2x4 cleat to the wall at the level line and fasten the cabinets to the cleat. I use a length of predrilled metal angle inside each cabinet to keep the wall-mounting screws from pulling through the back panel.

Toe-kick material, usually particleboard covered with plastic laminate or veneer to match the cabinets, comes in long lengths about 7 in. wide. I rip it to the proper width. If the finish flooring is not in place, I rip the toe kick narrow enough to accommodate the flooring. Or better yet, I cut and install the toe kick after the flooring has been installed. A vinyl sealer strip (similar to weatherstripping) comes either attached or loose to seal the bottom edge of the toe kick to the floor.

After cutting the toe kick to length, I join inside and outside corners with plastic end caps. If corners join at angles other than 90°, I miter the toe kicks and glue the joints. The toe kick is grooved on the back to accept knock-in clips that grip the leveling legs. To install the clips, I lay the toe kick face down on the floor in front of and aligned with the cabinets, and then I mark the location of every other leg and pop in the clips. The clips consist of a T-shaped knock-in and a U-shaped clip that slides over the knock-in. This combination allows some side-to-side adjustment of the toe kick once it's pressed onto the legs. End caps then snap onto the kick ends.

Island and peninsula cabinets are freestanding and are likely to tip and sway. To anchor these cabinets to the floor, I make L-shaped plywood brackets. The vertical side of the L is about two-thirds the height of the toe kick. I use these brackets in pairs, usually two pairs per cabinet. I screw one bracket to the floor and the other to the bottom of the cabinet, installing them so that the vertical faces of the brackets ride against each other. Then I set the cabinets in place, level them, join them and screw the brackets together.

—Tom Santarsiero is a cabinetmaker and president of The Kitchen Design Center in Montclair, N. J.

Choosing Kitchen Countertops

Plastic, tile, wood, stone or steel? The choice is easier if you know the pros, cons and costs

by Kevin Ireton

Early in this century, the mineral mica was commonly used as an electrical insulator in small motors and appliances. But mica is fragile, and if it broke, your appliance shorted out. In 1913, Hebert Faber and Daniel O'Conor, working for the Westinghouse Corporation, started looking for a more durable insulator. By soaking canvas in synthetic resins, Faber and O'Conor made thin sheets of material that wouldn't conduct electricity. Westinghouse wasn't interested in their experiments, so Faber and O'Conor quit and started their own company. Because the new product was a substitute for mica, the two inventors decided to call it Formica.

Within a few years, Faber and O'Conor discovered that their thin, tough insulator, which they manufactured in large sheets, made a durable work surface, so they covered the tables with it at their plant in Cincinnati, Ohio. Before long, Formica was covering restaurant counters and bar tops all over Cincinnati. Seventy years later, the modern version of Faber and O'Conor's invention, high-pressure plastic laminate, covers more residential kitchen counters than any other material.

Despite the prevalence of plastic-laminate counters, however, there are plenty of other choices for your culinary workbenches. According to a recent survey conducted by the National Kitchen and Bath Association (NKBA), kitchen designers report that 30% of their kitchens now feature solid-surface countertops, such as Corian, Avonite, Fountainhead, etc. But you can also have tile, wood, stone, metal or even concrete countertops (see sidebar p. 88). All of these materials can make a serviceable surface, and deciding which to use will likely boil down to personal preference and price. Still, each material has its advantages and disadvantages.

Questions to ask—"Can I cut on it?" That's the first thing Bill Peterson's customers ask when he suggests a certain countertop. Peterson is a kitchen designer in southern California who also teaches kitchen design at the University of California at Los Angeles (UCLA). Peterson's reply: "Would you cut on your dining-room table?" Even people who never cook want to know if they can cut on their countertop and if they can set hot pans on it. Both issues, of course, disappear with the investment of a few dollars in a cutting board and a trivet. If you spring for a marble pastry board, you've answered the principal needs of food preparaton, and you can select a counter based solely on looks and cost.

Aside from looks and cost—issues that vary considerably depending on who is looking and buying—there are several other qualities by which a countertop material is judged. Homeowners who are selecting a countertop always want to know if the material is easy to clean. Will the counter resist scratches, stains, water and heat? If the countertop is scratched, chipped or burned, can it be repaired? In general, seams in the countertop surface are considered a detriment because they not only look bad but also

Laminate layers. **Plastic laminate is made with kraft paper topped by decorative paper, combined with melamine and plastic resins under intense heat and pressure. The foil, curled back in the photo below, smooths the surface in the process but isn't part of the final sandwich.**

collect dirt. So homeowners need to know if the material they want comes in pieces large enough to avoid seams in their counter. And if seams are necessary, the homeowner will also need to know how they will look.

High-pressure plastic laminate—Available from lots of companies, today's plastic laminate is made with several layers of kraft paper and a layer of decorative paper combined with melamine (a clear plastic) and phenolic resins under intense heat and pressure (photo below). The resulting sandwich is about $\frac{1}{16}$ in. thick and is bonded with contact cement to a substrate of particleboard (preferably) or plywood to make a countertop. (For more on making plastic-laminate countertops, see pp. 106-111.)

Plastic laminate is inexpensive, comparatively speaking (see sidebar p. 90), and it comes in hundreds of colors and patterns. The largest laminate manufacturer in the country, Ralph Wilson Plastics Company, offers its Wilsonart laminates in 234 colors, plus 15 textures and finishes. Plastic laminate is easy to clean. It resists stains very well, though it's not stain-proof. Plastic laminate comes in sheets up to 5 ft. wide by 12 ft. long. Any surface bigger than that requires a seam. A good fabricator can make a seam that's unobtrusive but not invisible.

Water won't harm plastic laminate, but water can wreak havoc with the particleboard underneath the laminate. That's why some fabricators argue that seams in laminate should be kept away from sinks. (Other fabricators splice laminate in the middle of a sink so that the visible seam will be shorter and less conspicuous.) It's also good insurance to seal the particleboard edges of a sink cutout with silicone or urethane caulks.

Plastic laminate scratches easily. You can't cut on it, for instance, without marking it. The layer of decorative paper is pretty thin, too, so you don't have to scratch very deep to expose the dark kraft paper beneath. Keep in mind that plastic

Integral sinks. Made of DuPont's Corian, this counter and double-bowl sink are joined with seam adhesive. Hence, there is no rim around the sink where food and water can collect. Also, you can rout a drain board right into a solid-surface counter like this one.

laminate with a matte finish will not scratch as easily nor show scratches as readily as one with a high-gloss finish. Another problem with a plastic-laminate counter is that you can't set hot pans on it without scorching the surface.

Avoiding the dark seam—A common objection to the appearance of plastic-laminate counters is the dark seam line at the front edge when laminate is also used for the nosing. This type of nosing is called a self edge, and the dark line is the exposed kraft paper of the surface laminate. There are ways to avoid this dark line: For one, you can use a wood nosing instead of laminate.

Another alternative is to select a postformed laminate counter. With this type of counter, a single piece of laminate forms the nosing, the surface and the backsplash. The term postformed comes from the process by which the laminate is heated and bent to create the bullnose at the front of the counter and the cove at the back. But postformed counters require a slightly thinner laminate, so their color selection is limited. And postformed counters must be fabricated by a specialty shop.

Another way of avoiding the dark seam of standard-laminate counters is to use a solid-color laminate, made without kraft paper, where the surface color runs all the way through. Unfortunately, solid-color laminates cost three times as much as standard laminates. Many fabricators

Bevel-edge moldings. Offered by the makers of Wilsonart laminates, the edge moldings shown below eliminate the seam typically seen at the front edge of plastic-laminate counters and make the counter appear monolithic.

Photo courtesy of Ralph Wilson Plastics

Photo courtesy of Ralph Wilson Plastics

The cutting edge. Solid-surface fabricators are still searching for the limits of the materials' design possibilities. The Fountainhead counter below sports a floral inlay and a spiral-edge nosing.

Photo courtesy of Nevamar

Top photo: Courtesy of DuPont

don't like the solid-color laminates because they are brittle and will crack easily. Also, sheets of solid-color laminate come in smaller sizes than standard laminate, which can mean more seams. And while manufacturers argue that scratches don't show as much because the color runs through, solid-color laminates scratch more easily than standard laminates do. And the scratches will show when they fill with dirt.

Perhaps the best alternative for avoiding the dark line is to use a bevel-edge molding. Available from Ralph Wilson Plastics Company and from fabricators around the country, bevel-edge molding is a ¼-in. by 1½-in. strip of medium-density fiberboard with laminate on its face (top left photo, bottom of page 87). Along the top, the bevel-edge molding has a narrow piece of laminate set at a 45° bevel and mitered to the face laminate so that no dark kraft paper shows. Wilsonart's version, which is called Perma-Edge, has a tongue that fits into a slot you cut in the edge of the countertop substrate. The resulting nosing makes the counter appear monolithic (bottom left photo, p. 87) because the beveled strip of laminate is mitered to both the surface laminate and the nosing laminate.

Solid-surface materials—DuPont developed Corian, the first solid-surface countertop material, in the late 1960s. But developing the product was the easy part. At that time, there was no market for Corian because plastic laminate dominated the countertop market. DuPont spent 15 years setting up distribution, training fabricators and wooing the public. DuPont's persistence paid off. At least a half-dozen companies now manufacture solid-surface materials, and their products are second only to plastic laminate in the number of kitchen countertops they cover. Many people consider solid surface the finest countertop material available because it is repairable.

Solid-surface materials are essentially cast plastic—acrylic, polyester or a combination of the two. Each manufacturer has a different formula for solid-surface material, and each claims that its material is the best. Sorting these claims is beyond this article's scope. But today each major manufacturer of solid-surface material offers a warranty of 10 years or more on their product.

Solid-surface materials are waterproof and resist scratches, stains and heat. These things can damage the material, but you have to work at it. And because solid-surface counters are homogeneous—the same material throughout—you can sand out blemishes. Chips can be repaired with seam adhesive, which is a liquid version of the countertop material. With solid-surface materials, you could even patch a damaged section.

Solid-surface materials come in many colors and patterns, though nothing like the variety found in laminates. Corian is available in over two dozen varieties, for instance, and Avonite in even more. Sheets of solid-surface material come in 30-in. and 36-in. widths and in lengths up to 12 ft. Because solid-surface material is synthetic, the techniques for joining pieces result in a chemical bond and a virtually invisible seam.

Manufacturers of solid-surface countertops also offer the option of matching sinks, cast from the

Concrete countertops

For seven years, architect Rob Thallon has been building a home for himself in the forested hills south of Eugene, Oregon. When the time came for kitchen countertops, Thallon wanted a material that was monolithic, durable, cheap and fireproof. Concrete fit the requirements.

Thallon doesn't like toe kicks, so his cabinets don't have them. Consequently, he wanted the counter to cantilever 4 in. beyond the cabinets so that you could walk up to the counter and have space for your toes. Laying plywood on top of the cabinets would have been the easy way to support the cantilever, but he didn't want plywood showing above the face frames. Instead, 4-in. strips of plywood were positioned in front of the cabinets as temporary forms, supported by legs down to the floor.

Thallon screwed 2-in. wide strips of wood to the front of these forms, which created a lip to hold the concrete. Tiny chamfer strips were attached inside the 2-in. lip to give some shape to the concrete nosing.

He lined the bottom of his forms with 15-lb. builder's felt and coated the front lip with form oil. Lengths of #3 rebar help to support the 4-in. cantilever.

Next, Thallon went out and spent $32 on cement, sand and pea gravel. Keeping the mix pretty stiff, he placed, screeded and troweled the concrete. Then he waited a couple of hours and unscrewed the 2-in. lip at the front. This gave him the chance to rub out any defects.

Several days later, Thallon decided that he didn't like the sandy look of the concrete surface. The counters were still pretty green, so he went over them with a Carborundum stone and literally rubbed away the cream in some areas, exposing the aggregate. This action gave the counters a rich, variegated texture.

Thallon left the supports for the 4-in. cantilever in place for two weeks. Then he gave the counters a few coats of concrete floor sealer. The counters have been in place for several years now, and Thallon happily reports that they're easy to clean, suffer spills without staining and tolerate hot pots without burning. —*K. I.*

This homemade countertop cost $32.

same material (top photo, p. 87). However, sinks are not usually available in as many colors and patterns as the counters themselves.

Although solid-surface materials are harder than wood, they can be worked with carbide-tipped woodworking tools. Consequently, an enormous variety of nosing profiles, accent strips and inlays are possible (bottom right photo, p. 87). You can also rout a drain board right into a solid-surface countertop.

Despite the relative ease with which solid-surface materials can be worked, many manufacturers will warrant their countertops only if they're installed by a certified fabricator. In fact, sometimes you can't even buy the material unless you've been certified at a manufacturer's training workshop.

The disadvantage commonly attributed to solid-surface material is its high cost: It's three to five times as expensive as plastic laminate.

Ceramic tile—By itself, ceramic tile would make a great countertop. Tile is highly resistant to heat, water and stains. It will scratch but not easily. Although it's generally more expensive than plastic laminate, it's typically less expensive than solid-surface material. Given the range of sizes, shapes, colors and patterns, tile offers an even greater visual variety than plastic laminate. But the problem with tile countertops, at least in the past, hasn't been the tile, it has been the grout.

Grout has a reputation for staining, cracking and mildewing. But advances in grout technology, such as latex admixtures and acrylic sealers, have improved the situation. The biggest advance, however, is the advent of epoxy grout, which is extremely hard and flexible at the same time. Epoxy grout is also highly stain resistant. But expoxy grout costs about three times as much as standard grout and is harder to use because working time and cleanup time are very short. Still, epoxy grout is the best way to treat a tile countertop (bottom photo, facing page).

Ceramic tile is categorized in a confusing variety of ways: by permeability (how waterproof it is); by finish (glazed or unglazed); by where it's used (wall tile or floor tile); by size (pavers or mosaic). Just about any tile can be used for countertops, but common sense suggests that a glazed, highly waterproof tile would be best.

When choosing tile for a countertop, keep in mind that, like plastic laminate, bright colors and high-gloss finishes scratch more easily, and the scratches show. Matte finishes are better suited to countertops. With tile you have a choice of either tile nosing or wood nosing. If you opt for wood, seal the backside thoroughly ahead of time to ensure against water damage.

Probably more so than with any other countertop material, a good installation is crucial with tile. Tiles crack and pop if the substrate flexes. The best way to tile a countertop is the mortar-bed method. But unless you live in California or the Southwest, you may have trouble finding a tilesetter who knows how to do a mortar-bed installation. Atop a plywood substrate, the tilesetter puts down a 1-in. thick or so layer of portland cement as a base for the tile. Tiles are then adhered to this base with thin-set adhesive. This method is

Scars add character. After Phil Sollman installed his maple counters (above) and finished them with mineral oil, he inaugurated the counters with a meat cleaver. Years later, scars from chopping and stains from cast-iron pots give the counter a beautiful patina.

expensive and time-consuming, but tiles set in this fashion tend to stay put (for more on mortar-bed countertops, see *FHB* #25, pp. 32-37).

The next-best installation is the thin-set method, in which a ½-in. thick cement backer board is screwed down on top of the plywood substrate as a substitute for the mortar bed. Setting tiles directly onto a ¾-in. thick plywood substrate is the least-effective method of tiling a countertop. Such a counter is more likely to flex and is more susceptible to water damage.

Wooden countertops—"I wanted a functional countertop, not a precious object. I didn't want to be afraid of using the counter," says Phil Sollman, a woodworker in Pennsylvania. So he hacked up his maple counters with a cleaver as soon as he finished installing them.

Sollman oiled his counters initially with mineral oil, which he reapplies once a year. The counters (photo above) get wiped every day with a

Use epoxy grout. The chief complaint with ceramic-tile countertops has been that food spills stain the grout. But epoxy grout (below) is highly resistant to staining.

dish rag, and only fruit and vegetables are cut on the counters. Meat and cheese are cut on a separate cutting board. This segregation reduces the risk of contaminating the countertops with salmonella bacteria and other undesirables.

With the exception of two stainless-steel wings on either side of the sink, all the counters in Sollman's kitchen are maple. The one thing Sollman would do differently next time is seal most of the counters with urethane and have only one area with an oil finish for chopping. The sealed counters would be easier to clean.

After 10 years, Sollman's counters show lots of cuts and stains—wet cast-iron pans, in particular, leave conspicuous black rings. But the scars lend character to the counters.

Wood is the only counter material that you can cut on without harming your knives. Hard maple is the traditional choice because it stands up well to the cutting and is less porous than other woods. Traditional chopping blocks in a butcher shop were made 12 in. to 16 in. thick with the end grain of the wood up. Athough still manufactured, such blocks cannot be used commercially in many places because the absorbent end grain runs a high risk of contaminating food.

Sollman's counters were made by Bally Block (P. O. Box 188, Bally, Pa. 19503; 215-845-7511), the largest manufacturer of wood countertops in the country. Although they make chopping blocks and red-oak countertops, Bally's mainstay is 1½-in. thick hard-maple countertops, glued up from narrow strips with the edge-grain up—edge grain is tougher and less porous than face grain. Ballys uses an electronically cured urea-resin glue, and these days they seal all their counters with a nontoxic acrylic finish, on which you can cut. When it comes time to refinish the counter, the folks at Ballys recommend tung oil instead of mineral oil because tung oil dries more thoroughly and hence is easier to clean.

According to Jim Reichart, vice-president at Bally Block, the people who say it's risky to set a sink in a wooden countertop are right. If you decide to do it, Reichart says, be sure the countertop and the edges of the sink cutout are both sealed thoroughly.

Stone—Many kitchen designers dismiss marble as too soft and too porous for kitchen countertops. Marble is okay in a bathroom, they say, where it won't suffer as much abuse as in the kitchen. Marble is also fine in a section of the kitchen where all you want to do on it is roll out pastry dough. But then again, like wood, marble can bear its scars gracefully, improving with age and wear. So if you love marble, don't dismiss it out of hand. Get some prices, and if posssible, talk to people who have marble countertops in their kitchen.

These days, the prestige countertop in designer kitchens is granite (bottom photo, facing page), and for good reason. Granite can easily tolerate a hot pan. According to Kelly Dellacroce at Connecticut Stone Supplies (311 Post Road, Orange, Conn. 06477; 203-795-9767), granite is second only to diamond in hardness, so you can't scratch or scar it easily. Hot oil is about the only thing that will stain granite. And granite's cold, polished surface is great for rolling out pastry dough.

Much of the granite quarried in North America goes into headstones, monuments and building facades. The wildly colored and richly veined granite often chosen for countertops comes primarily from South America and India. And as with many natural materials, there is a tremendous variety of colors and patterns, with no two pieces the same. If you want granite counters, you should definitely visit a stone yard and select your granite personally.

On the downside, granite is typically the most expensive choice for a countertop. Shop around, though, because some yards run specials or have remnants that can make granite competitive with solid-surface materials. Granite is also brittle and heavy. At 12 lb. per sq. ft. for ¾-in. material, it is twice as heavy as 1½-in. thick maple or ¾-in. solid-surface material. Consequently, granite is only available in pieces up to about 4 ft. or 5 ft. wide by 8 ft. or 9 ft. long, which means there will be seams in most kitchens.

Granite can be worked somewhat like solid-surface material but requires diamond tools. Strips of granite can be laminated with epoxy to the edge of a counter to make the slab look thicker. Molding profiles can then be cut into this edge. Weak spots (around a sink cutout or a natural flaw in the granite) can be reinforced from underneath by routing a channel in the granite and inserting a length of rebar embedded in epoxy. Although some builders tackle this work themselves, given the cost of the granite and of the diamond tools, fabricating granite countertops is best left to the experts.

If you like the look of granite but can't afford it, consider granite tiles. They come in 1-ft. squares and in some places are even available in 2-ft. squares. Granite tiles cost around $9 per sq. ft.

Stainless steel—"Stainless steel is the finest countertop material available," says Bill Peterson. "Once you get it into a person's kitchen, you can never get it out. Of course, you usually can't get it in." Stainless-steel countertops will not stain, will stand up to heat and are easy to clean. This is why commercial kitchens and hospitals use stainless-steel counters almost exclusively.

Most people object to stainless-steel counters because they look cold, industrial and clinical. Nobody wants their kitchen to look like a hospital operating room. But other elements in a kitchen can warm up the look of stainless-steel counters (top photo, facing page).

According to Jim Hansett, a steel fabricator in Portland, Oregon, grades of stainless steel vary considerably. If you decide to have stainless-steel counters made for your kitchen, Hansett says, hold out for 16-ga. or thicker, 300-series stainless steel (this advice holds true for sinks as well). Anything thinner than 16 ga. will dent too easily. Stainless-steel alloy is graded according to the amount of molybdenum, chromium and nickel it contains. The stainless-steel sinks that you commonly find in home centers are 400-series stainless steel, which will stain, rust and not hold up as well as 300-series stainless steel.

Stainless-steel counters are typically set on a ¾-in. plywood or particleboard substrate. The substrate should end flush with the cabinets to allow room for the nosing, which supports itself, thanks to the strength of bent steel. Even with stainless-steel counters, you have a choice of nosing profiles. A marine edge, for instance, turns up in front, levels off and then turns down to prevent water from spilling onto the floor. A good fabricator can weld, grind and polish a nearly invisible seam. You can also have a custom sink welded directly into your counter.

Mixing materials—No countertop material is perfect, so a combination of materials may make the most sense for your counters. Consider a stainless-steel sink, like Sollman's (top photo, p. 89), with wings on either side. Install tile or granite counters near the stove where you can rest hot pans on them. Or inset a piece of granite or a section of tile into your solid-surface counter. Wooden cutting boards can be inset, too, but they're best made removable so that you can clean them easily. Pull-out cutting boards are an-

---

Comparing countertop costs

Lots of variables affect the cost of a countertop—the type of backsplash and edge treatment, for instance, or the number of cutouts for sinks or cooktops. When I asked various dealers and fabricators about cost, some quoted prices per running foot, others quoted square-foot prices. Some gave me uninstalled cost, others installed.

In the end I decided to bid a typical counter (drawing below): L-shaped, with a self-edge and a 4-in. backsplash of the same material, a 36-in. sink cutout in one leg and a 30-in. cutout for a cooktop in the other. I asked three kitchen dealers in the Northeast to give me an installed price for this particular countertop in each of six different materials. For each material I made as conventional a choice as possible: standard laminate, ½-in. Corian, medium-priced domestic tile with portland-cement grout, edge-grain maple, medium-priced granite and 16-ga. stainless steel. I took the average prices from the three dealers; those are the figures listed in the chart.

These are probably the highest prices you could pay; you can reduce costs greatly by fabricating your own counters or by dealing directly with a fabricator and installing the counters —K. I.

Material	Total cost	Cost per running ft.
Plastic laminate	$792	$46.59
Solid surface	$2,915	$171.47
Tile	$967	$56.88
Wood	$1,586	$93.29
Stainless steel	$3,592	$211.29
Granite	$4,253	$250.18

11 ft.

8 ft.

Not so clinical. Stainless-steel counters are durable and sanitary, which is why restaurants and hospitals use them almost exclusively. In the kitchen above, wood cabinets keep the stainless-steel from looking too cold and clinical. Note the granite pastry board at the far end of the kitchen.

Granite counters. Extremely hard and highly stain resistant, granite counters are typically the most expensive choice you can make. And if you want granite counters, you should visit the stone yard and select the granite yourself because no two pieces of granite are exactly alike.

other option. Integrating different materials may be a challenge aesthetically, but from a functional standpoint, it makes good sense.

Except for the occasional splash of water or collision with a toaster oven, a backsplash isn't subjected to much abuse, nothing like a countertop. So any of the materials discussed in this article will work fine as a backsplash. Here again, mixing materials makes sense. Lots of people who wouldn't consider ceramic tile on a countertop choose tile for their backsplash. As Peterson puts it: "Ten dollars a piece for hand-painted 4x4 tiles may sound expensive, but spread 20 of them around a backsplash, and suddenly $200 worth of pizzazz is mighty cheap." ☐

Kevin Ireton is the editor of Fine Homebuilding. *Photos by the author except where noted.*

Good books about kitchens
For more information about countertops in particular, and about kitchens in general, consult the following books, both of which were helpful in the writing of this article: *This Old House Kitchens: A Guide to Design and Renovation* by Steve Thomas and Philip Langdon, Little Brown and Co., 1992, 273 pp. hardcover, $40. *Complete Book of Kitchen Designs* by Ellen Rand, Florence Perchuk and the editors of Consumer Reports Books, Consumer Reports Books, 1991, 240 pp. softcover, $16.95.

Bottom photo: Brian Vanden Brink

Making a Solid-Surface Countertop

Synthetic materials can be worked like wood and polished like stone

by Sven Hanson

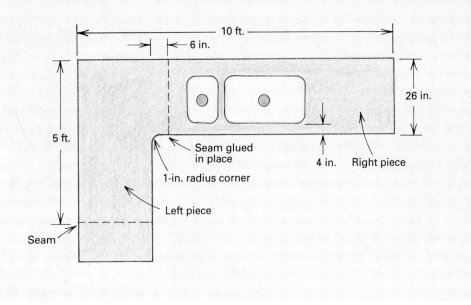

Seams, edges and corners. *Like plywood, solid-surface material comes in wide panels that have to be ripped to the correct width. But unlike plywood, they can be assembled with nearly invisible seams. To build the L-shaped counter shown below, the author used three pieces. Because the counter was too unwieldy to preassemble, he made it in two sections that were then assembled on site.*

10 ft.

6 in.

26 in.

5 ft.

Seam glued in place

1-in. radius corner

4 in.   Right piece

Left piece

Seam

Built-up nosing

The thick, rounded nosing of a solid-surface countertop is built up from ½-in. thick strips of the countertop material.

Countertop
Nosing

½ in.   1 in.   ½ in.

Flat style   Vertical style

Inside corner block

Inside corners are radiused and reinforced with blocks.

Minimum
1-in. radius

Twenty years ago DuPont introduced Corian, the first solid-surface countertop material, to the building community. It was received with a chorus of yawns. On the one hand, it looked like stone but wasn't the real thing. On the other, it resembled plastic laminate while costing three to four times more money.

But this neither fish-nor-fowl quality of the material doesn't tell the whole story. The most desirable aspects of solid-surface material are its workability and durability. Unlike laminate, the color and pattern of solid-surface countertops go all the way through the material, which means it lasts longer and can be repaired easily. The material is almost as dense as stone—in the range of 100 lb. per cu. ft. But unlike stone, it can be glued up with imperceptible seams and cut and shaped with carbide woodworking tools. And as more colors and patterns have come on the market, the once-reluctant public has em-

Finishing up. **Once sanded and buffed, the seam (left of sink) is nearly invisible.**

braced solid-surface countertops in a big way.

Corian, which is made of acrylic plastic mixed with a powdered clay filler called aluminum trihydrate (ATH), now has competition. Other brands of solid-surface material, such as Avonite, Surell and Gibralter (see Sources of supply), are made of polyester resin and the same ATH filler and color-fast pigments. The working properties of the materials, however, are the same. And even the distributors say that, once installed, the main difference between brands is pattern.

All of the manufacturers offer seminars on working with their material, and you typically need to take a course before you can buy the goods. That's because manufacturers are understandably nervous about bad fabrication practices infecting the reputation of their products.

When I started building solid-surface kitchens, I liked the patterns and colors of Avonite's materials. So three years ago I took their one-day cer-

Drawings: Maria Meleschnig

Cutting down to size. Solid-surface materials come in big sheets that have to be ripped to width using a table saw with a special solid-surface blade. Sprinkling the saw's table with cornstarch makes it easier to slide the sheet. A dust mask is essential for working the material.

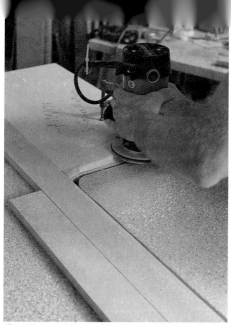

Cutting guide. Inside corners have to be radiused to reduce stress. This MDF cutting guide has a radiused wood insert at its corner.

Collar and bit. A metal sleeve called a collar, or template guide, rides along the edge of the cutting guide and separates the guide from the ½-in. straight-flute bit.

Mirror jig. A slot down the center of the mirror jig guides the router's collar as abutting pieces of counter are jointed simultaneously.

Edge treatment. Prior to glue up, mating edges are cleaned up with a sanding block. This block is made with a sticky-backed disk stuck to a hunk of plywood.

tification class. It cost $50, most of which I made back in doughnuts, soft drinks and router tricks.

Since that introduction to the material, I've made a lot of kitchen counters and lavatory tops, and I've taken Avonite's advanced class. I've found the material to be surprisingly workable, and mistakes are pretty easy to fix, which is no small consideration when the material costs $15 per sq. ft. and up. This article is about the basics, and I'll focus on a typical kitchen counter to illustrate the tools and the techniques for working solid-surface materials. To see what you can do with these materials once you've mastered the basics, check out *FHB # 84*, pp. 90, 91.

Start at the corner—Most counters have a dogleg in them where they turn a 90° inside corner—at least it looks like a 90° corner. Veteran installers have learned the hard way always to check for square and to adjust according to

what's really there because solid-surface counters are tough to trim in the field.

If the counter's shape is complicated, I make a full-size template. I prefer ½-in. medium-density fiberboard (MDF) for template material, but cardboard will do in a pinch. If you use cardboard, though, and need to collapse the template for transport, cut it into segments with a chevron or zigzag pattern; don't fold it. The segments can be reassembled only one way and won't lose the ¼ in. or more of length that folding can cause. If I'm replacing an old countertop, I sometimes use it as a template.

I start a job back in the shop by deciding the most efficient way to use the materials. Economy, maneuverability and color matching all are important. For example, the project illustrated here had a 10-ft. long counter intersected by a shorter countertop (drawing facing page). Avonite sheets are ½ in. or ¾ in. thick and come in 5-ft. or

10-ft. lengths that are either 30 in. or 36 in. wide. For a minimum order of 25 sheets, you can get ¼-in. thick material. I use ½-in. material for counters because it costs 30% less than ¾-in. thick stock. When supported every 18 in., it's plenty strong, and adding a built-up edge, or nosing, can easily make ½-in. thick material look as though it's 1½ in. thick.

I bought a 10-footer and a 5-footer for this job, both 36 in. wide. The extra width costs more but gives me matching material for backsplashes and built-up edges. I cut down the 10-ft. sheet to 85 in. (the right piece) and glued part of its offcut onto the 5-ft. sheet (the left piece) to make it the correct length. This way I made two manageable pieces by making an extra seam. I later joined the two pieces in place, making one L-shaped counter, but I'm getting ahead of the story.

Before making any cuts, I studied the color and pattern of the two sheets. Each batch of material

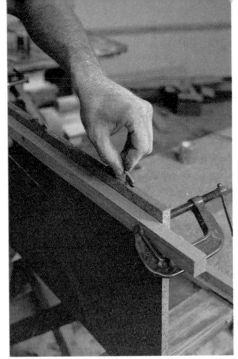

Fill, then clamp. During glue up, adjoining pieces are kept ⅛ in. apart while glue is drizzled into the gap. Then the pieces are put together, and spring clamps are applied on 3-in. centers to the 1x clamping blocks.

Plastic biscuits. Butt seams between mating pieces are aligned and strengthened with biscuit joints. Note the gray glue, custom mixed to match the material.

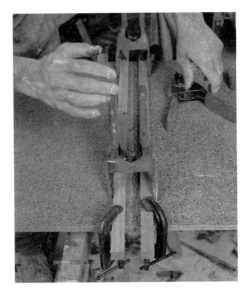

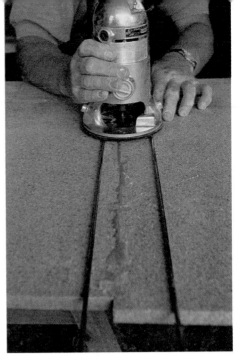

Ski time. Cured glue squeeze-out is cut away with a straight-flute bit and a router riding on slippery tracks, such as these bronze brazing rods. The process is called skiing.

is slightly different, so it's important to get sheets from the same run if they are going to be joined together. The pattern can even change from one end of the sheet to the other.

Ripping with cornstarch—This counter is 26 in. wide, and with my first cut I ripped the 10-ft. piece down to 26½ in. (top left photo, p. 93). Then I removed ½ in. from the other side to get rid of the factory edge, which is usually a bit rounded and sometimes chipped. Rather than fuss with the factory edge, I've found it more efficient just to eliminate it.

To minimize scratching, I saw the sheets face up, with a blade specially made for solid-surface materials (Golden Eagle Model G1060S, DML, 1350 So. 15th St., Louisville, Ky. 40210; 800-242-7003). The blade's teeth have equally beveled top corners, resembling little coffins (this tooth configuration is called a triple-chip grind, or TCG). It makes a nearly chip-free cut on both top and bottom surfaces and works equally well on other plastics.

To help slide the unwieldy sheets across the saw, I dust the top of the table with cornstarch. Cornstarch is cheap, available, biodegradable and won't contaminate the saw or the material.

Next I lopped off the 10-ft. sheet to get a piece 85 in. long. I used a circular saw to make the rough cut, then jointed the edges with a router to get rid of the saw marks because each line in a saw kerf is a potential starting point for a stress-induced crack. Leaving the tooth marks voids the warranty on the material. By the way, you shouldn't cut solid-surface material with a jigsaw. Its up-and-down action can cause fractures.

Note in the plan drawing of the counter that the inside corner is radiused (minimum 1 in.) and that the seam is 6 in. from the corner. These two details, which help relieve stress at the corner, require the left piece of the counter to look a little like an L. To cut the piece, I used a shop-built cutting guide (top right photo, p. 93) that

steers the router down the counter, around the corner and off the narrow end where the joint will go. I use a ½-in. dia., two-flute bit to make this cut. A ¾-in. collar, or template guide, affixed to the router's base rides against the cutting guide (bottom left photo, p. 93).

Solid-surface materials put heavy loads on a router and the bit. Manufacturers of solid-surface materials recommend 3-hp routers and bits with ½-in. shanks. I use the recommended ½-in. shanked bits, but my 1½-hp router has proved to be plenty powerful.

Joining two pieces—Inconspicuous seams between mating pieces are easy to make if the pieces fit together tightly. And the key to tight seams is the mirror jig (bottom middle photo, p. 93). My version is a 12-in. by 48-in. by ¾-in. scrap of veneered particleboard with a ¾-in. by 40-in. slot down the middle. I clamp abutting sections of counter to the jig, with their leading edges in correct alignment, so that my router bit cuts both their mating edges simultaneously. I support the pieces during the cut on a couple of 2x4s laid flat across a pair of sawhorses.

When I dry-fit pieces together, two tests determine a good seam. If a line can't be seen easily, I'm ready. If I see a gap, but the corner of a dollar bill won't fit into it, I'm still ready; otherwise, I must lightly recut the joint.

Before joining the pieces, I lay out marks for #20 clear plastic biscuit splines. Avonite is the only company I know of that requires them, but I use the biscuits no matter which brand of material I'm working with because the biscuits help align mating pieces. I place one 3 in. from each edge and add a third in the middle.

Using a square sanding block with 120-grit PSA (pressure-sensitive adhesive) sandpaper stuck to it, I give the edge, the top and the underside of the seam two firm swipes each (bottom right photo, p. 93). The possibilities of rounding the corners are outweighed by the probability that I'll knock down some extra plastic that might have held the seam open. Finally, I clean each edge and biscuit slot with a dust-free, colorless rag soaked with denatured alcohol.

Glue up—Before I mix a glue batch, I use hot-melt glue to attach 1x1 scraps to the face of the sheets on both sides of the seams about ½ in. from the edge. The scraps will supply clamping points for spring clamps. I use a medium-strength (clear or milky white) hot-melt glue, which can take plenty of spring-clamp pressure but can be peeled off without pulling up chips. The glue will usually lift away easily from the counter. If it needs coaxing, I pour some denatured alcohol on it and pry it off with a wide chisel.

Solid-surface glues come in two speeds: fast and slow. Both require a catalyst, and both have to be liquid to make a good seam. The fast glue has a pot life of about seven to 10 minutes before it turns to marmalade. The glued-up pieces are ready to work in about an hour. Slow glue has a slightly longer pot life of about 12 minutes, and pieces glued up with slow glue are ready to work in about eight hours.

The slow glue is a lot less expensive than the fast stuff. It's also more relaxing to use. I typically prepare all the pieces that need gluing, mix a big batch at the end of the day, assemble the parts and let them cure overnight.

Right photo, this page: Sven Hanson

Fast glues are available in different colors; you should use the one that matches the material at hand. For slow glues, I keep a range of Avonite glue pigments around so that I can mix colors as necessary. I go easy on the pigments because glues should be translucent, not opaque.

When I've got the color right, I stir in the recommended amount of catalyst. I've found that adding more catalyst just decreases the pot life of the glue without speeding the cure time.

Using a 1/8-in. bronze brazing rod, I shove glue into the biscuit slots and spread it along the edges. (I use brazing rods because they fit, and I have them handy.) Then I dunk the clear plastic biscuits (no wood, please) and stuff them into the slots (left photo, facing page).

With the pieces on my 2x4 workbench, topside up, I push them together within 1/8 in. and pour the rest of the glue into the gap. Then I align the front and back edges and apply the spring clamps to the clamping blocks every couple of inches. I should see a continuous bead of squeeze-out (middle photos, facing page). Like epoxies, these glues must have dimension. Too much pressure will cause a glue-starved seam, so spring clamps are the right choice for the job: They don't clamp so tightly as to squeeze out all of the glue. I let the squeeze-out cure rather than trying to remove it while it's still soft. Premature removal can lift the glue out of the joint.

I remove the cured squeeze-out with the router (right photo, facing page). Called skiing, this method requires a router with a straight bit and a couple of thin runners for the router to ride on (I use bronze brazing rods).

When I've removed the glue from the bottom of the counter, I glue a seam block over the seam. Seam blocks are 4-in. wide strips of the counter material that run the depth of the counter, minus any built-up edges.

Rounded edges and corner blocks—A thick, rounded nosing on a solid-surface countertop gives the counter visual weight. To make the nosing, I rip two 1-in. wide strips of edging stock from the cutoffs. Then with my sandpaper block, I lightly sand all faces, edges and ends of the strips.

There are two ways to apply the edging. The best way is the vertical style (detail drawing p. 92), but it requires very straight strips and smooth edges. If your table saw isn't up to that kind of a cut, the horizontal, or flat, built-up style will work better. I avoid the flat technique because it requires more glue, it squishes out of alignment when clamp pressure is applied, and it's more likely to have gaps between layers.

It's easier to adhere the edges with the counter upside down because you can see what's happening, and the glue stays in place. I mix my glue, squeeze a bead along the edge of the outside strip and clamp it in place. The strip should be either flush with the counter or slightly recessed—about 1/32 in. An army of spring clamps on 3-in. centers applies the correct pressure. The second layer gets clamped to the first (top left photo, above). At inside corners, the edging butts into reinforcing blocks (detail drawing p. 92).

After the glue cures, I run my router against my inside corner guide to trim off any squeeze-

Clampfest. Built-up edges, or nosings, are formed out of two strips of Avonite. Here, a vertical strip is clamped to the counter's edge. Then a second strip is glued to its back.

Bullnosing. As he rounds the inside corner, the author supports the router's custom base on edging strips. A dusting of cornstarch greases the track.

Swirling toward the finish. Random-orbit sanding with 60-micron paper followed by 30-micron paper brings out the color and depth of solid-surface materials. A slurry of water with a few drops of liquid detergent speeds cutting and keeps down the dust.

Gluing the sinks. After drilling holes in the counter for pipe clamps, the author runs a bead of fast-set glue along the flange of the sink. The wood strip at its base will align the outer edge of the sink during glue up.

Clamping the sinks. A pipe clamp through each drain hole applies pressure. Wood blocks protect the sinks from the clamps, and the pressure must be light. Assorted other clamps hold down the edges to get even squeeze-out.

Cutting out the sinks. The pipe-clamp hole becomes the starting point for cutting out the sink tops with a bearing-guided straight bit. The little blocks of Avonite were affixed with hot-melt glue to keep the cutouts from falling into the sinks.

out. Then I use the roundover bit to put the bull-nose on the edging. I run the wide Lexan base of my big router on edging strips (lubed with cornstarch) to keep the bit steady and square to the work (top right photo, p. 95).

As I mill the bullnose, I stop the router short of any butt joints that are still to come. This guarantees that I won't have a dip in the nosing caused by an inadvertent back cut. Before I flip the counter right-side up for bullnosing, I smooth the edge with my random-orbit sander running a disk of 60-micron paper.

After rounding over the top side in the same way as the bottom, I'm ready for some serious sanding. Although they are sanded at the factory, the sheets still need to be buffed out. I start with 60-micron paper. I squirt some water and a few drops of liquid detergent onto the surface. This trick lets the paper cut faster, keeps the disk clean and suppresses dust (bottom photo, p. 95).

The sink top—Forget about those stupid little clips that come with some sinks to affix them to their counters. Solid-surface sinks are glued in place and become one with their work surface. I stuck two sinks under this counter.

To make sure the sinks ended up where I wanted them to, I made ¼-in. plywood templates that represented the sinks' outside perimeters and drain holes. I put the templates under the kitchen window and moved them back and forth until I liked the positioning. Then I noted the distance from the wall to the edge of the template.

I put the sink counter upside down on my 2x4 workbench. Then I transferred the sink measurements to the counter and marked the outlines of the templates with a pencil. The sinks are set back 4 in. from the front edge.

I drilled 1-in. holes in the countertop that correspond with the drain holes in the sinks (top left photo, above). Then I mixed another batch of glue for the sinks. Once I had the glue spread and the sinks in place, I ran pipe clamps through the holes to exert some pressure on the assembly. Hand screws and spring clamps provided the rest of the clamping action (top right photo, above).

When the glue on the sinks cured, my colleague, Ed Schairer, and I gingerly flipped the still-tender, but very heavy, assembly and rested it on the 2x4s standing on edge. Then I got out my 2-in. by ½-in. flush-trimmer bit to remove the sink cutouts from the counter. I checked the bit's bearing to make sure it was firmly attached (you don't want it falling off during this operation), and I wrapped some vinyl tape around the bearing to keep it from marring the sink's surface.

From center hole I take the shortest route to the sink edge (bottom photo, left). With the bearing pressed firmly to the side of sink, I cut clockwise. At the 3 o'clock and 9 o'clock positions, I stuck Avonite blocks with hot-melt glue to the sink cutouts. The blocks kept the cutouts from falling into the sinks as I finished the cuts. I used my roundover bit to radius the counter edge where it turns down into the sink, and I smoothed the transition with a random-orbit sander.

Counter support—Solid-surface counters must be mounted on a lattice-type grid of supports 18-

It all comes together. When the top has been sanded and buffed out, the two legs of the counter are joined in place atop the cabinets. Here the author checks the joint for closure.

in. o. c. because plastics are natural insulators. A heat source like a toaster or electric frying pan will cause heat buildup, localized expansion and stress. If the counter sits atop a solid base, such as a sheet of plywood, it won't get enough airflow around it to dissipate the heat. Solid substrates must be cut out to meet warranty requirements.

The old cabinets under this new counter needed a few 1x4s added on the flat to satisfy the warranty requirements. The rule book also calls for continuous support under seams, so I put another 1x4 to the left of the sinks. I put vinyl tape on top of this support because a glued-in-place seam is above it. The glue does not stick to the tape. So the tape ensures that the top is not accidentally glued to the 1x4 support, which could eventually cause a crack to open up.

The supports also serve as anchorage for the counter. Thumb-size dabs of silicone caulk 18-in. o. c. are recommended. The counter squashes the dabs, making flat pads of stickum that can flex a little with the counter. If you've got a one-piece counter, you can put the dabs down before you place the counter. This two-piece job called for a more complicated approach.

Gluing in place—Ed and I wrangled the two counter pieces into position and dry-fit them to make sure the butt joint fit well. There is a ½-in. gap at both ends of the 10-ft. section between the wall and the counter. A backsplash typically hides the gap. For this job the slot in the brick veneer conceals it. The gap gave us enough room to slide the two pieces back a bit, then prop them up like a drawbridge.

I used hot-melt glue to stick clamping strips onto the sections. Then I mixed a batch of fast-set glue while Ed squeezed the silicone dabs onto the 1x4 supports. I dunked the biscuits in the glue, popped them in their slots and spread a bead of glue along the mating edges. Ed and I slowly lowered both counter sections, slipping the biscuits into the second section. I pulled the joint to within ⅛ in. and poured the rest of the glue into the gap. With front edges aligned, I jiggled the two sections together and applied the spring clamps (top photo, this page).

An hour later I skied down the joint to clean up the squeeze-out. Then I went against the manufacturer's recommendations and lightly sanded with the belt sander because the right piece of the countertop was a good deal higher than the left piece at the front edge. Avonite technologists think the unequal heating of belt sanding can cause stress damage to the seam, but two other manufacturers permit belt sanding, and I'm convinced that with a sharp belt and light touch to keep the material cool, there will be no problems. After applying water and detergent, I sanded the surrounding area and then touched it up with a Scotch-Brite pad (photo p. 92).

Manufacturers want to steer fabricator and homeowner to a 60-micron finish followed by a buffing with a Scotch-Brite pad. The resulting flat finish is easy to maintain and doesn't reveal flaws. It also doesn't reveal the beautiful depth in many of the patterns. My compromise is to put a little extra polish on with the 30-micron paper to make a punchier impression at the homeowner's first viewing, then knock it back a bit with a light buzzing with Scotch-Brite on the random-orbit sander.

Faucet cutouts are best done with a jig and a plunge router wearing a collar. But my client hadn't yet selected the faucet by the time I had to install the counter. Because there wasn't room to fit the router behind the sink once the counter was installed, I used a drill with a sharp spade bit to make the hole. Then I sanded out the drill kerfs with a little drill-mounted drum sander.

Backsplash—The client didn't want a backsplash for this job, but many situations will require it. For example, heavy-use areas such as sinks ought to have one. A backsplash keeps water from getting behind the countertop and makes the job look finished. It also offers a bonus to installers by giving them a gap of up to ½ in. along the wall for fitting the counter. Here's how I made a backsplash for another installation.

With a long straightedge as a guide, I use a router to joint enough material for the job, then I rip it to width. I precut it to fit exactly and then mark the butt joints onto their related pieces. Then I round over the top edge, stopping the router at the butt-joint mark.

When I like the fit, I put a fine bead of silicone caulk down the underside and arbitrarily place dabs of silicone on the back (bottom photo, this page). Placed among them, typically at large gaps between the backsplash and the wall, I put globs of hot-melt glue. Within a minute of pressing a backsplash (down and in simultaneously), it is firmly stuck. If temperature changes move the backsplash, it can break the hot-melt glue bond and hang there with the flexible silicone.

If the wall is curved a bit, I place the backsplash piece in the sun. When the piece warms up, I flex it to the desired shape. Let cool. Install. □

Sven Hanson is a woodworker in Albuquerque, New Mexico. Photos by Charles Miller except where noted.

Splash. Counter backsplashes are attached to the wall with silicone caulk and hot-melt glue. The hot-melt glue holds the backsplash in place while the caulk sets up.

Sources of supply

Avonite, Inc.
1945 So. Highway 304
Belen, N. M. 87002
(800) 428-6648

Corian
E. I. DuPont, P. O. Box 80010
Wilmington, Del. 19880-0010
(800) 426-7426

Fountainhead
International Paper, Nevamar Div., 8339
Telegraph Road, Odenton, Md. 21113-1397
(410) 551-5000

Gibralter
Ralph Wilson Plastics Co., 600 General Bruce
Dr., Temple, Texas 76504
(800) 433-3222

Surell
Formica, 10155 Reading Road,
Cincinnati, Ohio 45241
(800) 367-6422

Making Concrete Countertops

Solid, durable and attractive, an uncommon countertop can be cast from common materials

by Thomas Hughes

I was in the last stages of building a house for John and Kathy Buckley when they decided on a concrete countertop for their kitchen (photo facing page). Ordinarily when clients start making last-minute decisions like this, it can drive the builder to the aspirin jar. But I have to admit, my reaction was immediate and not even cautiously optimistic. I liked the idea.

John and Kathy considered marble and granite as a counter surface but felt it was ostentatious. Plastic laminate lacked pizzazz. But concrete had just the right mix of a stark industrial image, weathered outdoor coarseness and coloration, and a sense of solidity and strength.

I've used concrete in many projects, from foundations to flatwork. So I felt comfortable with the task of forming the counters. The part of the project that I wasn't so sure about concerned the finishing of the counter to a surface that would be tough enough to withstand kitchen usage.

First, make test samples—Before beginning the actual counters, I made a series of 10-in. square by 2-in. thick concrete samples, using different finishing techniques on them. I used a magnesium float on some of the samples, which brought more cream to the surface. I steel troweled these samples, and they had a crackled look when they cured.

I let other samples cure without a steel-troweled finish. Then I sanded them with a belt sander and a random-orbit sander to reveal the pattern of sand and aggregate. I applied the finish I had chosen for the counter (more on that later) to the samples and had the Buckleys evaluate them. They chose the most uniformly gray of the steel-troweled batch, with a little aggregate showing from sanding for color and texture.

All three of us liked the somewhat honeycombed edges of the sample blocks. The edges were marked with the typical voids and cavities of poured concrete, where lumpy clusters of cement-coated pebbles reveal the rocky contents.

A two-piece countertop—Where to pour? That's the dilemma facing anybody who's making a concrete countertop. If you cast the top in

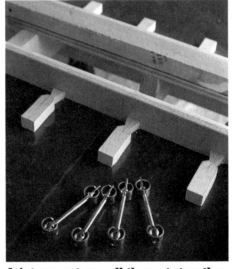

Put handles on the forms. Made of plastic-covered plywood and 2x sides, the forms were affixed to 2x4 handles for transport. In the background, the sink blockout is screwed to the form bottom.

Joint connectors pull the parts together. A quartet of joint connectors was used to pull the two wings of the countertop together. The blocks glued to the form sides were removed after the pour, leaving slots for the connectors.

place, you eliminate the hassle of moving around a heavy, cumbersome slab of concrete. But there are problems with that approach. In addition to dealing with the mess that accompanies any concrete pour, a countertop has to be etched with muriatic acid and then thoroughly rinsed before its finish can be applied. I didn't want to introduce that wild card into the final stages of trimming out the Buckleys' house.

In this case, I made the top in the garage, which meant that I could slop concrete around without worrying about the floors and the walls. Then I could take the top outside to rinse it off.

The kitchen base cabinets were L-shaped, with a 7-ft. wing and a 5-ft. wing. The countertops are 25 in. deep. Even with subtracting the sink cutout, the total weight would be around 500 lb. What's more, the awkwardness of moving such an odd shape out of the garage and up the stairs to the kitchen dictated splitting the top into two pieces.

Building the forms and making the joint—The bottoms of the forms for the countertop slabs were made from ¾-in. plywood. I cut the plywood 3 in. larger than the top in both directions to create flanges that support the form edges. I ran three 2x4s under each form as supports. The 2x4s extended beyond the form to serve as carrying handles (top photo, this page). I attached the plywood base to the 2x4s with drywall screws, making sure the heads were fully countersunk into the plywood. Then I stretched a layer of 6-mil polyethylene over the plywood and stapled it around the edges.

The countertop edges were formed with 2-in. tall strips that I ripped out of 2x stock. I beveled the tops of these strips to minimize the surface where concrete aggregate might collect as I filled the forms. I attached the form sides to the bottom of the form with drywall screws, but in this case I ran the screws from underneath, sandwiching the polyethylene between the plywood and the form sides.

People who make L-shaped counters out of particleboard and plastic laminate often use concealed joint connectors (bottom photo, this page) to draw the two pieces together evenly. I decided to apply the same strategy to this countertop, using Knape and Vogt #516 Tite Joint fasteners (Knape and Vogt Mfg. Co., 2700 Oak Industrial Dr., N. E., Grand Rapids, Mich. 49505; 616-459-3311).

Joint connectors fit into holes that are typically drilled in the underside of the countertop. I avoided drilling by gluing eight ⅝-in. tall keyhole-shaped knockout blocks to the sides of the

A thin, gray line reveals the seam. Cast in two sections, this L-shaped concrete countertop is joined at the inside corner. The two sections are held together by joint connectors (bottom photo, facing page) and epoxy. A tough finish of moisture-cured urethane protects the countertop from spills.

Steel trowel the work surface. After screeding the concrete into the forms and tooling the surface with a magnesium float, the author leans into the final finish of the countertop with a steel trowel. He then wrapped the counter sections in plastic and left them to cure for two weeks.

form. I beveled the blocks and sprayed them with WD-40 for easy removal.

To accommodate the 20-in. by 33-in. sink cutout, I made a block by screwing together two layers of ¾-in. plywood and another layer of ½-in. plywood. Then I screwed the block to the 7-ft. form from underneath (top photo, p. 98).

Reinforce the concrete and strengthen the mix—For strength during not only the life of the countertop but also during transport and installation, I decided to reinforce the countertop pieces with stucco wire. I also added polypropylene fibers to the concrete in the lower two-thirds of the countertop. I didn't use polypropylene for the entire mix because the fibers make it impossible to get a smooth finish on the concrete. Sold under a couple of trade names, these short fibers help reduce microscopic cracks in the concrete. I didn't need enough of the stuff to justify buying a minimum order. Fortunately, my local concrete supplier keeps the fibers on hand and was kind enough to give me a small bag of them.

The narrow bands of concrete in front and behind the sink are potential weak points, so I reinforced them with ⅜-in. rebar.

Preparation for the pour included setting the forms onto leveled pairs of sawhorses so that there was no chance of ending up with a twisted countertop. Because it was handy and not as smelly as form-release oil, I used WD-40 as a release agent on the form sides.

I needed just a small amount of concrete for the countertops, so I used prepackaged concrete mix. Hoe in hand, I mixed the 3½ cu. ft. of concrete ⅔ cu. ft. at a time. As I mixed the batches, I added a handful of the polypropylene fibers. I also added enough extra portland cement to bring the concrete to a six-sack ratio, which increased the concrete's compressive strength.

I screeded the concrete to the tops of the forms, then I smoothed it first with a wood float, then with a magnesium float. After the tops had set up for about three hours, they were ready to be steel troweled (photo above). The concrete should be hard enough that pushing on it with your finger doesn't leave a depression, but you can still compress the top layer of fines (the creamy cement and sand mixture that rises to the surface during troweling) by applying hard pressure with the trowel. You can't be timid about troweling. You really have to lean on it. After troweling, I let the slabs cure for a day.

The next day I removed the form sides, leaving behind the knockout blocks for the joint connectors, and lightly sanded the edges with 100-grit wet-dry paper. That gave me the slightly rounded edges I wanted. Then I wrapped the countertops in plastic and let them cure for two-and-a-half weeks.

Installing the countertops—A few days before I installed the countertop, I wet-dry sanded the entire top to 120 grit. Besides hand sanding, I also found the random-orbit sander, fitted with silicon-carbide paper, to be effective, although not particularly economical with regards to the life of a disk of paper. On the advice of the tile and ma-

sonry contractor, Nikos Maragos—a native of Greece who started out doing terrazzo floors—I mixed up a paste of portland cement and acrylic additive for tile work and squeegeed it over the tops to fill any small voids. Then I sanded the tops again to remove excess filler.

I moved the tops outside, washed them with a diluted solution of muriatic acid and rinsed them with water, as called for in the finish instructions. After the countertops dried, I enlisted the help of my two working buddies, Scott Rekate and Knox Swanson, and we moved the tops to the kitchen for installation.

The maple cabinet bases, 1¼ in. shorter than standard height to accommodate the 2-in. thick countertops, were already installed. I drilled holes in the plywood subcounter to gain access to the joint connectors

By setting up the forms even with the cabinet tops, the countertops could be moved right into place. I slid each top off its form so that I could reach under the ends where I'd placed the knockouts for the joint connectors. I extracted the knockout blocks from below by running a screw into each one, then pulling on the screw.

After sliding the countertops onto their cabinet bases, I test-joined the two tops. Then I loosened the joint, applied epoxy to the joint faces and drew the joint tight again for a permanent bond.

I drilled a half-dozen pilot holes with a masonry bit through the plywood subcounter into the concrete countertops and affixed them with 1¼-in. concrete screws. Finally, I filled the seam gap with a paste of cement and acrylic admixture.

When it set up, I smoothed the joint with my random-orbit sander (top photo, this page), and seeing it was about midnight, called it a day.

The countertop pieces were now united into a monolithic unit and firmly anchored to the base cabinets. The fragile, thin sections of concrete that border the sink were thoroughly supported from below, so with the help of my jigsaw, I removed the block of plywood that located the sink opening (bottom photo, this page).

A tough finish of moisture-cured urethane— The finish recommended to me was a moisture-curing aliphatic urethane called Wasser MC-Clear (Wasser Hi-Tech Coatings, 8041 S. 228th St., Kent, Wash. 98032; 206-850-2967). This is an industrial-strength coating used primarily to protect bridges. It's often applied to concrete structures to protect them from graffiti. Unlike typical finishes, this finish cures faster with higher humidity.

Instructions for a usable surface called for two coats thinned with a proprietary thinner. You can apply the coating with a brush or a roller. I used a brush, and I found that the bristle lines from brushing leveled out quickly, leaving a very smooth, polished surface.

Moisture-cured urethanes contain isocyanates. You can protect yourself while using them by wearing a respirator fitted with an organic-vapor cartridge but only if you're monitoring the vapors to make sure they stay below recommended levels. To be safe, you should wear a supplied-air respirator. Adequate ventilation is therefore an absolute must, and you should make sure there aren't any ignition sources in the area.

There are more user-friendly concrete sealers on the market, but I haven't tried any of them. My concrete supplier recommends waterborne acrylic sealers. They aren't as durable as moisture-cured urethanes, but they can be renewed periodically with minimal effort. The Glaze 'N Seal Company (3700 E. Olympic Blvd., Los Angeles, Calif. 90023; 800-486-1414) sells both water-based and solvent-based concrete sealers that can last eight to 10 years when used indoors.

Framed by a splash of copper—To cap off the elemental feel of the countertops, I ran a 4-in. high backsplash of ⅜-in. thick copper around the edges of the countertop where it meets the wall. Before installing the copper, I washed it a couple of times with a muriatic acid wash. Then I left the copper outside for a week in our salty winter weather. Once the patina looked right, I finished the copper with two coats of D-18 (Ultra Coatings, Inc., 2218 15th Ave. W., Seattle, Wash. 98119; 206-283-4120) to preserve the coloration.

Countersunk brass screws affix the splash to the wall. Where the copper meets the concrete, I sealed the joint with clear Polyseamseal caulk (Darworth Co., P. O. Box 639, Simsbury, Conn. 06070-0639; 800-672-3499). The plumber didn't have any problems installing the cast-iron sink, but he did have to fasten the dishwasher to concrete, rather than to the usual wood. □

Thomas Hughes builds houses and makes furniture on the northern Oregon coast. Photos by the author except where noted.

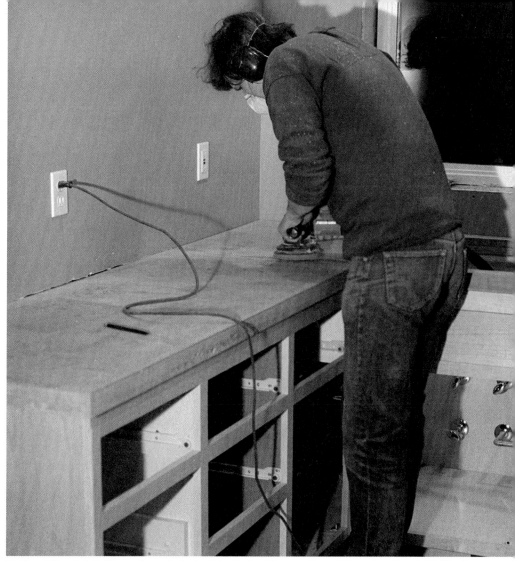

Buff out the joint. The author grinds the joint flush with a random-orbit sander. Next he'll fill what tiny crevices remain with a paste of acrylic admixture and portland cement.

Time to remove the sink blockout. Once the countertop was safely in place atop the base cabinets, the sink blockout could be removed. The author cuts out the bulk of the plywood block by drilling holes near the corners and then connecting them with a jigsaw. The remaining plywood edges are then carefully peeled away from the concrete.

Granite Countertops

An experienced fabricator explains the process from the templating to the final setting of the slabs

Plywood templates minimize guesswork. The location and shape of sinks and other openings are marked directly onto lauan templates. Back at the shop, dimensions from the templates are transferred to the stone slabs.

by Joe Ranzoni

For most of the past 20 years, my company has been taking the rockbound coast of Maine and bringing it into the homes we work on. Our specialty is granite, both rough and refined. We transform thin slabs of the material into beautiful, functional kitchen countertops.

Our shop is located in Orland, an area that once thrived on the granite industry. We're surrounded by such historic quarrying towns as Frankfort, Blue Hill, Franklin, Jonesboro, Mount Desert and Deer Isle, source of one of the most structurally sound granites available. Granite from Deer Isle was used in the memorial to Robert Kennedy at Arlington National Cemetery.

I started working in the masonry division at Freshwater Stone & Brickwork in 1987 as a mason's tender, later moved to the granite side of the business and now work as the company's manager. I have found that there is something sweet in the smell of freshly split granite.

Not just a pretty face—Granite countertops are so breathtakingly beautiful that many people don't realize what a practical choice they are. Granite is one of the hardest naturally occurring materials. It has a compressive strength of 19,000 psi (according to the nonprofit American Society for Testing and Materials). In other words, it takes 19,000 lb. of pressure in 1 sq. in. to break the material. A granite countertop will not scratch under everyday use; it can be used as a cutting board.

Dropping things on granite won't damage the countertop, but I sometimes hear from customers who say I owe them a new coffee cup or dinner plate. Granite also withstands intense heat, so you can take pots right from the stove and set them on the countertop without fear of leaving burn marks.

When submerged in water, granite will absorb only 0.4% of its own weight in water, quite low compared with other building materials. What this means to the homeowner is that granite is naturally resistant to staining. Spilled liquids bead right up. And polished granite doesn't promote bacteria growth. Warm, soapy water is all that's needed for cleaning.

Color indicates composition—Granite is an igneous substance (formed by the solidification of molten rock) that contains mostly feldspar and quartz. The color in a slab of granite comes from minerals and organic matter, such as plant and animal life, present when the material was in the molten state. Shades of white and pink indicate a high proportion of feldspar. Gray stone contains a lot of quartz. High concentrations of biotite are present in black granite.

Granite blocks are cut from quarries with drills and wedges, huge cutting torches, wire saws and water-jet cutters. The quarried blocks are typically 5 ft. by 5 ft. by 10 ft. Blocks are trucked or shipped to processing plants where gang saws, a series of carbide-tipped blades spaced 1¼ in. apart, often work 24 hours a day, seven days a week, slicing the blocks into slabs. The slabs are then polished on one side and put into a huge inventory.

Granite varies in grain and texture as well as color. Deer Isle is a large-grained granite, and Barre Gray is tight-grained. The texture can be consistent, as in Dakota Mahogany, or it can be wild and irregular, as in Blue Fantasy. Each granite slab has its own character, something that distinguishes it from the next slab in the rack.

Material accounts for about half of the cost—You can expect to pay at least $65 per sq. ft. and as much as $125 per sq. ft. for the finished product, installed. The slabs that we and other fabricators use to make countertops are roughly 5 ft. by 10 ft. and are sold by the square foot of surface area. The cost of raw granite slab stock ranges from about $30 to about $100 per sq. ft. Field measurements, templating, fabrication and installation charges will increase the cost by approximately 50%.

I often get requests for ballpark estimates for countertop jobs, which I refuse to give. I need a layout of the project in my hands, with all specifications noted, before I can begin an estimate.

The cost of granite can be influenced by the location of the quarry, the thickness of the slab stock and the finish on the slab surface. For instance, domestic granites quarried in North America cost $20 to $50 per sq. ft. Imported granite from Africa is almost twice as much, due to shipping costs. The industry's standard thicknesses for granite slabs are ¾ in. and 1¼ in. Thinner slabs are less expensive than thicker ones.

Templates made from plywood—When the base cabinets have been installed and the granite slabs have been approved by the homeowner, it's time for the contractor to call us for field

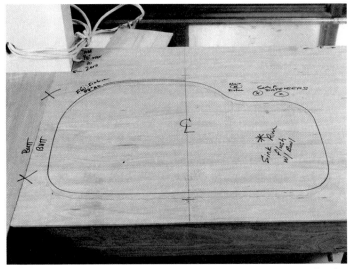

Templates are cut with a jigsaw. Scribing templates to match existing wall conditions is more accurate than relying on a list of measurements. Template sections begin and end in the same location where slabs of granite later will be butt-jointed.

Granite is hard but not unworkable. Granite countertops can be made to accommodate any kitchen sink or appliance. This sink opening was roughed out with a water-cooled circular saw and then rounded and polished with hand-held grinders.

A material that combines beauty and practicality. Granite is well-known for the complexity and depth of its color and its glasslike finish. But it's also highly suitable for the demanding environment of a kitchen. It can't be damaged by moisture and is nearly impossible to stain, scratch or burn.

A diamond-tipped, water-cooled blade cuts the stone. Granite typically is supplied in slabs measuring 5 ft. by 10 ft. Freshwater Stone & Brickwork uses an Italian-made bridge saw to cut the slabs into workable pieces. The sawblade's 48 teeth are embedded with industrial-grade diamonds.

measurements and templating. This point is critical in a granite-countertop project. When we're working in stone, there is little room for error.

We make templates from the installed base cabinets using 4x8 sheets of ¼-in. lauan plywood (photo p. 102; top photos p. 103). The templates are cut on site with a jigsaw to the actual finished dimensions. Notes written on the plywood signify overhangs, rough openings, centerlines, etc.

We usually have the granite hang 1 in. past the farthest point protruding from the face of the cabinets (photo bottom right, p. 103). This point may be a knob or a raised panel. Ultimately, the size of the overhang is up to the homeowner. I advise that extra support, such as knee braces, be installed by the cabinetmaker under overhangs of more than 12 in.

Fabricators take their own measurements—Our on-site measurements are taken by the same workers who make the countertops. This procedure ensures the workers have a complete understanding of each kitchen project.

More often than not, sinks and cooktops are centered on the underlying base cabinet, but sometimes the centerline must be adjusted to account for a kitchen window or an oddly placed upper cabinet. We discuss options with homeowners and contractors before granite fabrication begins.

We ask contractors to make sure that all appliances, including cooktops, sinks and faucet fixtures, are on site the day field measurements and templates are made. Contractors also should tell us about any special requirements, such as polished sink rims for undermounted sinks, centerlines for fixtures, etc. The templates are then taken back to the shop where the measurements are transferred to the granite slabs.

No limits on size and shape—Granite countertops can be fabricated to practically any specification. Any cutting, milling or shaping that can be done in wood or solid-surface material can be done in granite. It just takes more time.

First, the granite slabs are cut to length and width by our bridge saw (photo above). Made in Italy, our Achille MS stone saw (VIC International Corp., P. O. Drawer 12610, Knoxville, Tenn. 37912; 615-947-2882) cuts a granite slab as it lies flat on a stationary table. The saw's 16-in. dia. blade has industrial-grade diamonds embedded into each of its 48 teeth. The blade cuts through the stock as the drive motor and cut motor, both suspended from above, travel along a 4-in. by 4-in., 10-ft. long iron channel.

Grinders smooth the edges—Next, the edge of the stone is milled with a profile selected by the homeowner from samples at the showroom. All of our edge profiles are done by hand.

Router bits that cut granite are available, but they're costly, and the edge they create still has to be hand-polished. We mill the countertop edges with electric grinders and pneumatic grinders, made specifically for the stone industry, that spin at 4,000 rpm. For rough-stock removal, we use a 4-in. dia. cup-shaped wheel faced with 60-grit, industrial-grade diamonds. Then the edges are shaped and polished with a 4-in. dia. diamond polishing pad mounted to a flexible-rubber disk. The polishing pads come in a series of seven grits.

The diamond fragments on the surface of the pads are bonded in a resin-based matrix. The resin holds the diamond particles in place something the way grapes are held in Jell-O. At 4,000 rpm, the resin wears down and exposes the cutting edges of the diamonds.

Rough-opening holes for cooktops and sinks are cut either with a semiautomated router and a stone-cutting bit, or with a worm-drive circular saw with a water-cooled diamond blade (photos top left and center, facing page). The router bit in the semiautomated machine is similar to an edge-profiling pad in that it cuts with industrial-grade diamonds embedded in a silicon-carbide matrix. The machine allows us to cut any circular or oval rough opening in minutes.

Installing a sink with a 22-in. rough opening in a 25-in. deep granite countertop can be tricky. Sometimes we're able to reinforce weak areas

Water keeps the blade cool. Countertop openings can be cut with a 7¼-in. worm-drive circular saw with a diamond-tipped blade. Cloth tape is applied to the stone so that layout lines will remain visible while the cut is made.

Easy does it. Once the cuts have been made, pieces of granite are carefully lifted out of the new openings. The tape is removed from the loose section to allow the suction-cup-based tool to grip the stone.

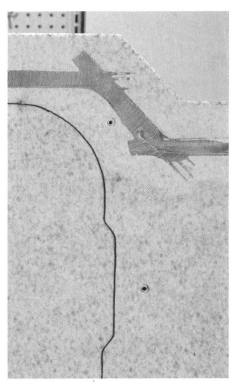

Steel supports vulnerable spots. To reinforce narrow sections of countertop, such as around a sink, strips of steel are glued into grooves cut in the back of the granite.

by kerfing the bottom of the granite and epoxying in a length of ¼-in. by ¾-in. cold-rolled steel (photo above right). In other cases, we have to cut the countertop off at the sink or cooktop opening. Then we fill in the space in front of and behind the opening with strips of granite, butt-jointed where they meet the main top.

Depending on the complexity of the project, the countertops usually are fabricated within three weeks from the day we make the template. Once fabricated and double-checked, the granite countertops are loaded onto an A-frame for transportation to the site. The sections of countertop are carried on edge, wrapped in padded blankets, strapped to the A-frame, then strapped to the bed of the truck. Transport of finished granite countertops is a skill in itself.

Silicone holds the counters in place—At the site, the granite pieces are unstrapped and carried on edge into the house, where they are tentatively set in place. If necessary, the countertops are leveled with hardwood or plastic shims. For the occasional on-site alteration, we bring along portable electric polishers, saws and drills. On-site cutting and polishing is loud and dusty. If possible, alterations are made outside.

The countertops are adhered to the cabinets with construction-grade clear silicone (photo right). The same silicone is used at granite-to-granite butt joints, if there are any. The use of silicone allows some expansion and contraction of the house, the cabinets and the stone to occur without the joint's cracking. Backsplashes are adhered to the countertop and the wall using the same adhesive. The freshly adhered countertops should be allowed to set at least 48 hours before plumbing and electrical appliances are installed.

At the stock thickness of 1¼ in., granite slabs weigh 17 lb. per sq. ft. Yet this weight is distributed evenly over the base cabinets, eliminating the need for reinforcement in most cases.

Sealing provides added protection—After the countertops have been installed, they should be sealed with a silicone stone impregnator. This sealer soaks into the pores of the stone, bonding to the mica, quartz and feldspar, and filling the pores. The sealer should be applied with a clean cloth and allowed to set for 15 minutes before the excess is wiped off. Because granite is extremely stain resistant, the sealer basically is a precautionary measure. One application should last forever.

If a granite countertop is cracked or chipped, a stone epoxy tinted to match the stone can be injected into the crack and buffed smooth. □

Joe Ranzoni is manager of Freshwater Stone & Brickwork Inc. in Orland, Maine. Photos by Roe A. Osborn.

Silicone keeps the top from moving. Sections of countertop are adhered to the cabinets with silicone caulk. The same adhesive is used to glue backsplashes to the walls.

Making Plastic-Laminate Countertops

Cutting shears and spray adhesive are among the tricks that make the job easier

by Herrick Kimball

As a carpenter's helper I learned the basics of working with plastic laminate 12 years ago. Since then I've fabricated more countertops than I can remember. Over the years I've witnessed a lot of mistakes and have made a few of my own. But there was a lesson in every error, and I've learned my lessons well. The tools and the techniques I'll describe in this article make it easier and less frustrating to fabricate professional-quality countertops.

It's not all Formica—Among the general public, all plastic laminate is commonly referred to by the brand name Formica. In fact, many customers don't understand what I'm talking about unless I use the phrase "Formica countertop." The confusion is understandable considering that the first plastic laminate was, indeed, Formica, but now there are other manufacturers.

Although most of my tops are done using Wilsonart laminate, because it happens to be the most readily available brand in my area, there is no difference between working with one brand or another.

Plastic laminate is made by bonding multiple layers of resin-impregnated kraft paper under heat and high pressure. The sandwich is topped off with a colorful layer of melamine.

Several manufacturers also produce a solid-color, or solid-core, laminate. This product is uniformly colored throughout its composition, so the dark band that shows up on the edge seams of standard laminate is eliminated. Another solid-core selling point is its ability to hide scratches that would show up on standard laminate.

I seldom use solid-core laminate, though. It's more expensive, comes in fewer styles and, frankly, my customers don't find the dark seam line unsightly; they expect it on a laminate counter. If you use solid-core laminate, you should know that it's worked like regular laminate, but it's more brittle. Use extra care when handling it, especially while cutting and routing.

Aside from the myriad choices of colors and patterns available, there are also different types of laminate, such as fire rated and chemical resistant. But if you go to your local lumberyard and order a sheet of, say, Erin Glenn #4627-8, the salespeople are going to assume you want the standard, general-purpose laminate, which is what I use on virtually every residential and light-commercial countertop I make.

Sheets of plastic laminate come in nominal widths of 30 in., 36 in., 48 in. and 60 in. Nominal

Low-tech, but effective. To cut laminate with a scoring tool, draw the tool across the laminate several times. Then, holding down one side, lift up on the other, and the laminate will snap cleanly along the score.

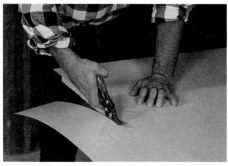

Shear force. Laminate shears, made by Klenk, have three blades—one above, two below—that remove a ⅛-in. strip of laminate. Cutting laminate with shears is faster and more convenient than cutting with a scoring tool.

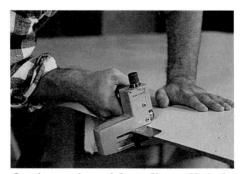

Cutting strips with a slitter. Made by Virutex, this laminate slitter can either be pushed or pulled along a sheet. Its adjustable guide allows you to cut strips anywhere from ¼-in. to 3¼-in. wide.

lengths are 72 in., 96 in., 120 in. and 144 in. The actual sheets measure 1 in. larger in width and length. Some manufacturers also offer 1¾-in. by 12-ft. strips of laminate for edgebanding.

Don't scrimp when estimating—On a small, straight-run countertop, figuring what size laminate you need is simple. But when you get into larger L- or U-shaped tops requiring one or more seams, estimating can be a challenge. Unfortunately, I don't know an easy way of doing this short of sketching out some laminate sizes and figuring each component of the countertop onto the sketched piece of laminate. There are things to keep in mind, though, when you do this.

First of all, even the best surface seams are unsightly, so avoid them whenever possible. If I had a 25-in. wide, L-shaped counter with an 11-ft. leg on one end and a 5-ft. leg on the other, I'd order a 5-ft. by 12-ft. sheet of laminate to do the job. That means I'll have some waste, but it's worth it to avoid a seam.

When a surface seam can't be avoided, I try to position the joint through a sink or a cooktop where it will be visible for only a couple inches in the front and the back. Never seam through a peninsula or other high-visibility spot unless it can't be helped. Keep in mind also that any butt joints in the substrate should be placed as far away as possible from laminate seams.

When estimating laminate, allow at least ½ in. extra all the way around for finish trimming. Also, don't figure too close. If a 5-ft. by 8-ft. sheet will give you more breathing room than a 4-ft. by 8-ft. sheet when cutting out several pieces, get the extra, especially if you're new to the craft.

Tools for cutting and trimming—For years I roughed out all my laminate pieces with an inexpensive, carbide-tipped scoring tool. Using a straightedge to guide the cut, you draw the scoring tool over the top of the laminate (photo top left). This tool actually scrapes a groove through the surface. After a couple passes, hold the sheet down on one side of the line, lift up on the other, and the laminate will snap cleanly along the score. On long cuts, you start the snap at one end and work down the line.

Score-and-snap is an effective cutting technique, but it does have a couple drawbacks. It requires a large, smooth surface to lay the sheet on when cutting, and it's time-consuming.

Fortunately, I've discovered two tools that make cutting laminate sheets more of a snap than score-and-snap. The first is a pair of hand-held laminate shears (middle photo, facing page) (Klenk Industries, Inc., 20 Germay Dr., Wilmington, Del. 19804; 800-327-5619). Similar in appearance to aviator tin snips, these shears have three blades, and together they remove a ⅛-in. strip of laminate. If you're going to make more than a couple of tops, spring for a pair of laminate shears. You'll never regret it.

But using shears can be tiring and time-consuming when you're cutting the long, thin strips needed for edging countertops and backsplashes. For these cuts, a table saw does a nice job—use a 60-tooth, carbide-tipped blade, and make sure the sheet doesn't slip under the fence. A laminate slitter will do the same job without the noise, the dust and the helper that the table saw requires. My slitter (made by Virutex, dist. by Rudolf Bass, Inc., 45 Halladay St., Jersey City, N. J. 07304; 201-433-3800) is hand-held and has two cutting wheels that shear a perfectly smooth line. The slitter is operated by pushing or pulling it along the sheet (bottom photo, facing page), and an adjustable guide allows cuts from ¼ in. to 3¼ in. wide.

To round off this review of cutting tools, I should note that Porter-Cable makes a hand-held motorized laminate slitter that employs a ¼-in. carbide-tipped router bit to cut strips up to 4¼ in. wide. I have one of these, and it does a nice job. But I find the tool awkward to use, so I have relegated it to the obsolete pile along with my carbide-tipped scoring tool.

In addition to cutting laminate sheets to rough size, you also need to trim laminate after it's been glued to the substrate. Basically, trimming tools amount to a router and a bit, but there are choices here, too.

Any router can be used to trim laminate, but a 3-hp plunge router would be overkill. If you're going to deal with much plastic, it behooves you to get a small, lightweight laminate router (or trimmer). I like the Porter-Cable #7310 standard trimmer. At 5.6 amps, it's a powerful unit that I can hold in one hand and maneuver easily. It also has a rectangular base that comes in handy when cutting seams (more on this later).

Laminate-trimming router bits are made to do one of two things: trim excess laminate flush and square to the surface it overhangs, or flush with a bevel at the top. Flush-and-bevel cutters come separately or as a combination bit. Laminate bits have carbide cutters and are guided by either a ball-bearing collar or a self-pilot bit.

When new, ball-bearing pilots work nicely. But after some hard use they can be a problem. I've had bearings stop rolling after being gummed up with contact cement. If the bearing seizes, it will spin with the cutter and burn a mark on the laminate. I'm ashamed to admit that I've burned more than one edge. And in every instance, I knew the bearing was old and not working smoothly, but I used it anyway.

Bearing troubles led me to try a self-pilot bit. These cutters are milled out of a ¼-in. shank of solid carbide, and the pilot is an integral part of the bit; it spins with the cutter and rubs along the guide surface. You avoid burning by lubricating any laminate guide surfaces with a thin coating

Beefing up the substrate. With its flat, uniform surface, high-density particleboard works best as a substrate for laminate. But gluing and stapling strips of plywood under the edges (and the seams) of the particleboard makes a stronger countertop.

Cutting a seam. Although you should avoid seams in laminate whenever possible, sometimes you can't. Mirror-cutting is the way to get the best possible fit between two pieces. To do it, butt the pieces together temporarily and make a router cut through the middle of the seam.

Seize the spray. Although slightly more expensive than brushable-grade contact cement, spray cans offer advantages that make them worth the cost. Spraying means easier, faster application, quicker drying and less fumes.

Yes, those are Venetian-blind slats. As the name implies, contact cement sticks on contact, so you don't want two mating surfaces to touch until they're properly positioned. Venetian-blind slats work well to keep the laminate off the substrate until you're ready to start gluing.

of petroleum jelly before trimming. Because self-pilot bits have less bulk than the bearing pilots, they work particularly well in small trimmers. I tried a self pilot two years ago and haven't used a bearing guide or burned an edge since.

It's also possible to trim the laminate flush with a ¼-in. straight-cutting router bit if you have an auxiliary guide attachment for your router. Such attachments are usually standard issue with laminate trimmers. They work pretty well, but I don't use mine because I can chuck in a self pilot and have half my trimming done in the time it takes to set up and adjust the guide attachment.

The 48-hour rule—With kraft paper as the raw material, plastic laminate is actually a wood product. In fact, a sheet of laminate is very similar to wood in that it has a grain direction, and it expands and contracts according to its moisture content.

Standards for dimensional stability of plastic laminate are set by the National Electrical Manufacturer's Association (NEMA), and they allow for 0.5% dimensional change with the grain and 0.9% across the grain. On a humidity range from 0% to 100%, that means a 5-ft. by 10-ft. sheet of laminate may vary in size by roughly ½ in. in each direction.

Dimensional instability will cause problems if the laminate and the substrate are not allowed to acclimate in the same environment where they'll be assembled. Forty-eight hours, with free air flow around all sides of the pieces, is the recommended conditioning period. An air temperature of 75° F with a relative humidity of 45% is ideal for conditioning, but this is not nearly as critical as the 48-hour rule.

When properly acclimated laminate and substrate are glued together, the two will expand and contract together without incident. What happens if the components aren't properly conditioned? Nothing, if you're lucky. I've found you can bend the 48-hour rule and get away with it, but bending too far makes unhappy faces all around. One common result of insufficient conditioning is that perfectly fitted surface seams will soon separate, and in some cases, edge seams will come apart.

I once had a job that involved redoing a vanity top in the men's executive washroom of a nearby industrial complex. The existing top had two drop-in sink bowls, and water had leaked under the rims, caused the particleboard to swell and started to crack the laminate. I decided that I could do a good job for a good price by removing the sinks, chipping down the swelled spots, attaching a new layer of ½-in. particleboard to the top and the edges and gluing down new laminate. Everything would be done on site without removing the original top.

With the rule in mind, I delivered my materials to the job 48 hours ahead of time, but my plans were thwarted when the clients told me they didn't want the stuff parked in their washroom for two days. I was assured that temperature and humidity were the same throughout the building, and the downstairs maintenance shop would be as good as anywhere else. I had a bad feeling about it, but I left the pieces downstairs.

When I made the top, everything went well; the job was perfect. An hour after I was done, the edges started to separate. I felt sick and wanted to hide, but instead I grabbed my clamps and torqued down on the front edge. I managed to salvage the job, but it isn't perfect anymore. The top pulled back from the edge and is still slightly gapped. The backsplash did the same thing; gone are my once-crisp edge lines. Live and learn? I hope so.

Preparing the substrate—Many of the old site-built countertops I tear out have a ¾-in. plywood underlayment, and there are still a few people around who think plywood makes a better substrate for laminate. But this is one instance where cheaper is actually better. I always glue my laminate to high-density particleboard. Sometimes called core board, this material is inexpensive and well suited for laminate work. Particleboard has a very uniform, flat surface and bonds to the laminate much better than plywood, which has an uneven, wavy grain pattern.

High-density particleboard comes in ½-in. and ¾-in. thicknesses and is sized for laminate work in 25-in. and 30-in. widths and in 8-ft., 10-ft. and 12-ft. lengths. It's also available in 4x8 sheets.

When possible, I take measurements on site, make complete countertops in my shop and then install the finished product. Not only is it easier and more convenient this way, but it also makes for less mess in the customer's home (which is no small matter). Sometimes, factors like size and shape or placement of a counter layout dictate that I make the top on site. If this is the case, and especially if the counter is particularly large, I can often fabricate the substrate in modular sections in my shop, then take them to the job site and finish the assembly.

My method of assembling the countertop underlayment is not the only way, but it's the best way I've found to make a durable substrate quickly and precisely. I use the double-layer approach: ¾-in., high-density particleboard on top and strips of ¾-in. underlayment plywood on the bottom (top photo, p. 107). I use plywood on the bottom because it holds fasteners better, it makes for considerably stronger overhangs and seam cleats, and if water spills over the front edge of the finished counter, plywood won't soak it up and swell like particleboard does—a common problem in front of some kitchen sinks.

I rough out my particleboard top sheets approximately ½-in. oversize each way. After fastening the bottom strips, I'll cut the top to exact size. Because my standard countertops have a finished depth of 25 in. (which gives a 1-in. overhang over 24-in. deep cabinets), I buy 30-in. wide particleboard, rip off a 4-in. strip for the backsplash and have 26 in. left for the rough top.

I cut the plywood bottom strips 3-in. to 4-in. wide and fasten them around the perimeter of the underside with a liberal coating of yellow glue and 1¼-in. long, narrow crown staples in my pneumatic stapler. If you don't own a pneumatic stapler, use 1¼-in. coarse-thread drywall or particleboard screws. Using a Phillips bit in an electric drill, the screws will pull right through and below the surface of the plywood without a pilot

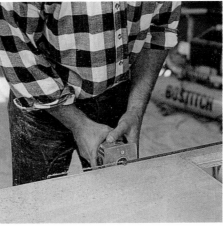

Trimming the edges flush. A laminate trimmer is just a router that's been downsized to make it more maneuverable. Here, the edge strip on the front of the countertop is being trimmed flush with the top of the substrate.

It's not a ball-bearing bit. A ball-bearing bit can can seize and burn the laminate. That's why the author prefers a self-pilot bit. To avoid burning, he lubricates the guide surfaces with petroleum jelly before routing.

Flush-trimming bits don't trim flush. You have to file the laminate top flush by holding the file almost flat to the front edge and stroking downward. You know you're done when the excess glue at the seam shaves off, revealing a crisp, clean edge.

hole or countersink. Whatever fastener you use, keep in mind that the rough top must soon be trimmed to exact size, and fasteners should be kept out of the anticipated cut line.

When fastening the plywood strips, I'm not concerned if they don't align exactly with the particleboard edges because I'll cut them flush later. It is important, though, that adjoining pieces fit tightly together. If there is a gap between abutting plywood pieces, the pilot on my laminate-trimmer bit will ride into the void and mess up the finished edge. When butting two pieces of particleboard together, I'll fasten a cleat underneath that spans the seam a minimum of 12 in. on each side. Peninsulas and islands often have eating areas that cantilever 12-in. to 16-in., and I always beef up these overhangs with a solid piece of plywood extended at least 12 in. back over the top of the cabinets. If a heavy sink is to be installed, I'll be sure to get extra plywood support there, too.

When the rough top is assembled, I cut it to finish size with a carbide-tipped blade in my circular saw and use a clamped straightedge as a guide. For long stretches, I have a 6-in. by 12-ft. length of particleboard that I use for a guide. If I can't get a regular clamp on this type of straightedge, I fasten it temporarily with screws.

When cutting underlayment with the saw, watch out for screws used in assembly. Occasional staples aren't much of a problem, but hardened drywall screws will easily ruin your sawblade. Back the screws out if they're in your cut line.

It's essential that underlayment edges be cut perfectly square. If an edge is beveled in at the bottom, the guide bearing on the laminate bit will cut too close and shave the face of the laminate edge strip.

I cut the front edge and the back edge of the substrate first. Then before I cut the piece to length, I clamp the backsplash and the countertop together, edge-to-edge, and cut both at the same time.

I prefer to have sinks and cooktops in my shop and make all cutouts in the underlayment before I glue on the laminate. After the opening is cut, I'll drop the fixture in to check the fit. There is little hope for salvaging a botched cutout if the laminate is in place. This became crystal clear to me after absentmindedly marking out and square-cutting an opening that should have had radiused corners.

After the underlayment is trimmed to size, and just before gluing, I sweep the surface off with my hands. Fingertips will detect residual grit and surface imperfections the eye can't readily see. Surface imperfections need to be filled before gluing the laminate. Plastic auto-body filler dries quickly and works well. Instead of sandpaper, I use a block plane to knock off gobs of filler, dried glue or uneven seam butts. I also double-check the edges and make a light cleanup pass or two there, if necessary.

Mirror-cutting a seam—If there is a surface seam to contend with, now is the time to match it up. Unfortunately, it's impossible to achieve an invisible seam in plastic laminate, but if done properly, you can make a very tight seam that's not obvious.

The easiest way to make a tight seam is to mirror-cut the two abutting pieces of laminate with a router and a straightedge. To do this, I position laminate sheets on the substrate right where they will be glued down, with the two edges butted. Then I clamp the pieces so that they don't shift around and slide a scrap strip of laminate under the seam (bottom photo, p. 107).

Next I clamp a straightedge guide to one side so that it allows the router bit to cut down the center of the seam. With a ⅛-in. straight-cutting bit in my router, I set the depth to cut completely through the top layer of plastic and into but not through the scrap. I feed the router down the edge in one smooth, even stroke. Before unclamping the guide, I slide a square against it and pencil two index marks across the cut line. I unclamp the pieces of laminate, align the index marks, and I've got a no-sweat, perfect seam.

Before gluing, I scrape or file any burrs off the backside of the seam cuts, but I don't take any material off the face of the seam. If the edges don't meet as well as I'd like, I reset the straightedge and try again, provided, of course, that I can do so without making my pieces too short.

What a difference a spray makes—Contact cement is the adhesive used to glue down plastic laminate. Until recently, small-time fabricators like myself have had to use brushable-grade cement that comes in quart or gallon cans. If you've

ever glued a top using this stuff, you know all too well how noxious the fumes are. And if you've brushed, rolled or squeegeed on as many gallons as I have, you've no doubt wished there was an easier, faster, cleaner way to get the job done. Well, there is.

Without a doubt, the best recommendation I can give on the subject of contact cement is this: spray it on (top photo, p. 108). Production fabricators have used spray equipment for years to glue their tops, but only in the past couple years have the advantages of spray been available to everyone in the form of aerosol cans.

I use Wilsonart's Lockweld 1055, which I get from my laminate supplier. It comes in 17-oz. spray cans, and by my calculations, one container at 100% coverage will glue approximately 5 ft. of standard-depth counter, edge and backsplash. Spray adhesive costs slightly more than brushable grade, but it's worth it. Compared to prespray days, I've found my application time is less than half, drying time is quicker, fumes are considerably less, and except for some minor overspray, there is no mess involved. The spray is flammable, however, and while there are less fumes, they're still harmful, so be sure to have plenty of cross-ventilation when spraying.

To use contact cement, spray an even coating on both mating surfaces, allow the adhesive to dry, then bring the pieces together. When the glued surfaces touch, they stick. When they stick, they're stuck; there is no longer any chance for adjustment. A more permanent bond is made by

applying pressure with a rubber laminate roller, or pounding a cloth-covered block of wood over the surface.

Laminate meets substrate—Edge strips go on first, and I always spray two coats of contact cement on the porous underlayment edges to ensure good coverage. Once the cement is dry on both the laminate and the substrate, bring them together. I start at one end and move across, centering the laminate on the substrate edge and pressing firmly as I go. With longer pieces, it's helpful to have someone support the other end of the strip while you work. On edges, I forego the cloth-covered block and apply pressure directly with a 16-oz. dead-blow mallet. Then I use a router with a flush-cutting trim bit to trim the ends and the top and bottom edges of the laminate flush with the substrate (top photo, p. 109). It's important here to rout in the direction opposite the rotation of the router bit. If I'm standing in front of the counter, for instance, and trimming the top piece of laminate where it overhangs the front edge, I rout from left to right.

After all edges are glued and trimmed flush, I use a laminate file to remove minor milling marks left by the router bit. A laminate file is made specifically for plastic laminate and should be available from any supplier. Other files don't do the job. I hold the file *flat* against the countertop and make a couple sweeps over the freshly routed edges, always filing *toward* the substrate. Don't file too much. Where edge strips

Routing out for the sink. The author cuts sink and stove openings in the substrate before he glues on the laminate, which allows him to test the opening and make adjustments if it fits wrong. Afterward, it's a simple matter to knock a hole in the laminate and run the router around the opening.

meet at an outside corner, I first file the overlapping piece square, then bevel it slightly. I also run the file at a slight angle along the bottom to take off the sharp edge.

With the edges glued, routed and filed, I spray the tops—substrate and laminate. To keep the laminate and the substrate from touching one another while I move the laminate into position, I lay salvaged Venetian-blind slats on the underlayment as temporary spacers (bottom photo, p. 108). After final positioning, I slide the strips out and press the laminate down as I go.

Always make contact from the center out or from one end to another. I once glued up a circular tabletop and made the mistake of pulling all my spacers out and pressing down the edges first. When I got to the middle I had a bubble, and the laminate didn't want to go down. Slightly panicked, I commenced to place extreme pressure on the trouble spot with block and hammer, and it stuck. I won the battle but not the war; a few days later the center popped loose.

In retrospect, I should have removed the laminate and glued it down again. This isn't something you want to make a habit of, but in a real jam it's nice to know it can be done. The only way to break the adhesive bond and separate two pieces is with glue solvent. Use acetone or lacquer thinner. Mineral spirits will do the job, but it leaves a residue that will interfere with glue up next time around. Work a wide-blade putty knife under a spot on one edge and separate it just enough to spray a little solvent in the crack. Keep feeding the solvent in and pry upward as the bond dissolves. Be patient, let the solvent do the work, and you'll succeed.

When gluing two pieces that meet at a surface seam, stick one side down first, align the index marks, glue down the next piece starting at the seam and work away from there.

With the top piece glued into position and rolled or hammered down, it's time to trim the top flush (middle photo, p. 109). Because I use a self-pilot bit, I spread a thin layer of petroleum jelly with my finger onto the laminate edge first. When cutting, always keep the router in motion when the self pilot is riding against the edge. If you have to stop, pull away from the countertop, or you may burn the edge.

To rout any openings in the top, I punch a hole just big enough for the trim bit to fit into, then I run the router around the opening with the self pilot riding against the opening cut in the substrate (photo facing page). Quick and easy.

Most stainless-steel sinks are held down with clips that fasten under the counter and require a ¾-in. thickness to grab onto. If my substrate is 1½ in. (double thickness) and is going to get a stainless-steel sink, I'll rout recesses for the clips at this time. Essentially, I just remove a section of the plywood layer in the spots where the sink clips will be positioned.

More filing—Despite their name, flush-trim bits really don't cut perfectly flush. If you slide your fingernails up the front edge, they'll catch on the slight overhang. I remove this excess and finish off the edges by hand filing.

Some fabricators prefer to use a bevel-cutting bit, which can be adjusted to trim off the overhang and reduce filing time. I don't use a bevel bit anymore because it's a pain to adjust the height, and a bevel cut produces a wider, dark seam line that I find less desirable.

Filing isn't difficult, but it does require a careful touch. A sharp, fine- or medium-cut laminate file is essential. I first remove the overhang by filing almost flat against the front edge (bottom photo, p. 109) Most of the cutting is done on the back half of the file in a forward-sawing stroke. You'll know you've gone exactly far enough when excess glue at the seam shaves off, revealing a crisp, clean edge. If in doubt, double-check with the fingernail test. After all the edges are finished in this manner, I ease the razor-sharp top corner down with a couple of light passes of the file (or sanding block), held at a slight angle. One thing you don't want to do is file inside corners square. The ¼-in. dia. radius left by the trim bit looks very nice and substantially reduces the possibility of stress-cracking in that area. Once you get the hang of it, filing can be done quickly and precisely.

I clean excess glue off the countertop with mineral spirits and a soft cloth. If I run into a difficult stain, I don't hesitate to use a little bit of mild abrasive cleanser (unless, of course, I'm working with a high-gloss laminate).

Attaching backsplashes—Fastening countertops down is a straightforward job. The standard procedure is to drive screws up through cabinet corner braces and into the counter underlayment. This usually works best if a clearance hole is first drilled through the brace, and obviously, you want to make doubly sure the screws you use are long enough to grab well but not so long that they go through the top.

Backsplashes are glued up just like countertops. I make up backsplashes as separate pieces and attach them after installing the countertop. Many fabricators do this by gluing their splashes in place with a bead of silicone on the bottom edge and backside, and they use no mechanical fasteners. I've used this approach too, but I've never felt right about it because I've seen backsplashes that have been installed this way separate from the counter.

I recently noticed some backsplash-attachment devices, called Smart Clips, in the Woodworker's Supply catalog (Woodworker's Supply, Inc., 1108 N. Glenn Road, Casper, Wy. 82601; 800-645-9292) and decided to try them. I wasn't disappointed; Smart Clips allow for quick, tight backsplash attachment. They're also relatively easy to use. The plastic clips are screwed down at least every 12 in. along the back of the counter. Aligned with the clips, drywall screws are driven into routed recesses in the backsplash (photos below).

I run a bead of silicone along the bottom of the splash before snapping it into the clips. The clips have tapered slots that engage the drywall screws in the backsplash and pull the backsplash tightly to the counter. The only drawback to Smart Clips is their price: they're about 60¢ each, and the $50 installation kit is practically a necessity.

Fabricating a countertop is not difficult, but it does require a good measure of concentration and attention to detail. Mistakes can happen all too easily, and they are seldom as easy to correct. This fine line between success and failure is something that I find particularly appealing. Because of the challenges involved, nothing can beat the satisfaction that comes with a well-executed countertop. ☐

Herrick Kimball is a remodeling contractor in Moravia, N. Y. Photos by Kevin Ireton.

The backsplash. Clips hold a backsplash tightly to the countertop. Screwed to the back edge of the counter (photo below left), the clips engage a screw on the back of the backsplash. Once the counter is installed, the backsplash is snapped into place (photo below right).

Tiling a Mortar-Bed Counter

How one tile setter builds the classic kitchen work surface

by Michael Byrne

I think the best part of being a tile setter is that my work doesn't get covered up by someone else's labors. On the other hand, setting tile is tough, physical work—especially large floors, where my knees cry out for a desk job and my back creaks from all the bending. So it's no wonder that I enjoy tiling countertops.

Ceramic tile offers many advantages as a finish material in the kitchen. A hot pot won't damage a tile surface, and a properly waterproofed installation can stand up to all of the splashes and spills that cooks can dish out.

The best tile countertops are done on a thick bed of mortar called a *float*. The float is usually ¾ in. to 1 in. thick, and the solid base it provides for the tile isn't affected by moisture. I'll be describing the most common type of counter that I do. It has V-cap face trim and a single row of tiles for the backsplash. To make cleanup easier for the cook, the sink is recessed beneath the surface of the counter and is trimmed with quarter-round tiles (drawing, facing page).

Choosing the tile—Kitchen-counter tiles should be either impervious or fully vitrified (see *FHB* #17, p. 73). These ratings mean that the tile will absorb almost no water, a property that increases the life expectancy of the installation.

Many tiles are designed to decorate rather than protect. You should be able to find a tile that does both. But you need to be careful even with heavy glazes since some of these are easily marked by metal cooking utensils. I urge my customers to get samples of their favorite tiles, and to rub them with a stainless-steel pan, an aluminum pot and a copper penny. Some tiles can be cleaned up after this kind of abuse—others can't. The surface is important in another way, too. Because most appliances need a flat surface to work efficiently, tiles with irregular faces, such as Mexican pavers, make beautiful backsplashes but lousy work surfaces.

Layout—The goal here is to keep tile cuts to a minimum, to locate them in the least conspicuous places, and to eliminate tiles that are less than half-size. On a straight-run counter, this usually means beginning the layout halfway

Tile layout. **Byrne has used a ³⁄₁₆-in. trowel to spread thinset mortar over the float, and he now aligns the rows of tile with a straightedge. The chalklines at the inside corner of the counter mark the position of the V-cap trim, and the starting point for the first full sheet of tile.**

along its length or at the centerline of the sink. If you take a close look at sink installations, you'll find that there is often a trimmed tile in the center of the front edge, in line with the spout. This trimmed tile keeps things symmetrical, and it allows full tiles along the edges of the sink. I begin the layout on an L-shaped counter at the intersection of the two wings (photo facing page).

Once I have the tiles in hand, I use the direct method of measurement to help lay out the job. I unpack some of the tiles and move them around the cabinet top. Sometimes, shifting the tiles an inch this way or that can make a substantial improvement in the finished appearance. Small tiles are more forgiving, allowing you to adjust the width of the grout lines to make things fit. But unless the counter has been meticulously designed with the tiles as modules, cuts are inevitable.

The substrate—The substrate should be at least ¾-in. plywood rated for exterior use. Particleboard won't do. The waterproofing on most counters consists of a layer of 15-lb. asphalt-saturated felt or a similar protective paper. I take this a step further and laminate the felt to the plywood with wet-patch fibered roofing cement.

Tiling a counter is a messy, gritty project. To keep the asphalt (and later the mortar and grout) from soiling the cabinets, I first drape kraft paper or plastic film over the face of the cabinets, and staple it to the counter plywood. I also protect the floors with canvas dropcloths.

I use a ⅛-in. V-notched trowel to spread a thin layer of roofing cement onto the plywood around the sink and about 3 ft. to each side. This helps to protect the vulnerable areas under the dish drainers. Ideally, the asphalt should cover the exposed plywood end grain in the sink cutout (drawing, below). If the sink is already in place, I squeeze the asphalt into the junction between the sink and the plywood. At the backsplash I make a tight crease in the felt and lap it up the wall about 3 in. Later this flap will be trimmed to about ¾ in. above the finished counter. Combined with the backsplash tiles, it makes an effective water barrier, keeping moisture out of the rear of the cabinets.

Screeds and rails—Once the waterproofing is completed, I set the sink rail. This rigid galvanized sheet-metal channel reinforces the mortar bed down the entire front edge of the counter and makes it easier to level the bed. The rail has narrow vertical slots every 3 in. for nails or screws (photo below left). Along its top edge are ⅝-in. dia. holes. Mortar will ooze through these holes, linking the mortar that faces the counter edge with the countertop float. This helps to anchor the V-cap finish on the edge.

I start screwing the rail in front of the sink, adjusting it to suit the height of the quarter-round trim in relation to the top of the sink. Once all the rail is in place, I use ½-in. thick pine to box in any openings in the substrate that have been cut for the cooktop, chopping block or other built-ins. These are installed at the exact height of the finished float. Attaching the sink rail and boxing the openings is a lot like setting up the forms for a slab floor.

Metal reinforcing—My experience has taught me that metal reinforcing in a counter float reduces or eliminates cracked tiles and grout. Consequently, I use plenty of it. First, I cut 20-ga. 1-in. wire mesh (chicken wire) and secure it to the plywood substrate with ½-in. staples, overlapping neighboring pieces at least 4 in. The mesh (photo below right) extends from the sink rail to the back wall and covers the entire substrate. Rather than cut the mesh a little short to make an easy fit between the sink rail and the wall, I cut it a bit long and bend the excess back over itself.

Finally, I use 9-ga. galvanized wire like rebar to strengthen those parts of the mortar bed that will be narrow in cross section. This prevents the cracks that often appear in the tiles close to the front or back corners of sinks and cooktops. I center the wire and run it parallel to these narrow sections, and I anchor it with ¼-in. or ⅜-in. furring nails. Then I bend it at about a 45° angle where the counter broadens, and extend it at least 6 in. toward the center of the field. At first, I used the wire rather sparingly. But now I use it all over the countertop—at inside and outside corners and across peninsulas—and I've found cracking problems a thing of the past. When all the reinforcing is in place, I check to make sure none of it protrudes above the top level of the sink rail. This can be done either with a 2-ft. level or by sighting the top of the sink rail.

Deck mud—Most of my jobs are in the San Francisco Bay Area, where the adobe soil swells during the winter rains and shrinks in the long

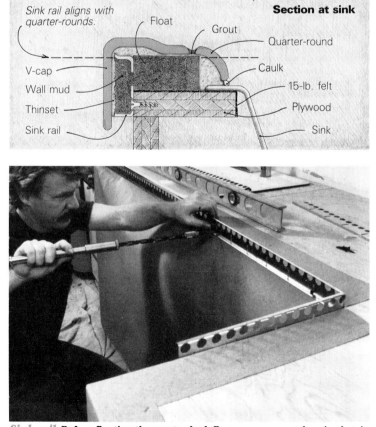

Sink rail. **Before floating the mortar bed, Byrne screws a galvanized strip called a sink rail to the edge of the plywood substrate. It serves as a screed, edge reinforcement and a framework to anchor the thin layer of mortar that will face the edge of the countertop.**

Section at sink

Sink rail aligns with quarter-rounds.
Float
Grout
Quarter-round
V-cap
Caulk
Wall mud
15-lb. felt
Thinset
Plywood
Sink rail
Sink

Reinforcement. **Chicken wire stapled to the plywood substrate covers the area to be tiled. If a mortar counter cracks, it usually does so in the narrows around the sink, or at inside corners. These areas are reinforced with 9-ga. galvanized wire held in place by furring nails.**

A. *Float strips* are the key to controlling the thickness of the mortar countertop. Here the author beds a float strip in a mortar pad, getting the strip's relationship to the sink rail right with a level. The float strips will guide the screed board while the mortar is leveled. Later, the strips will be removed and the resulting voids filled with mortar.

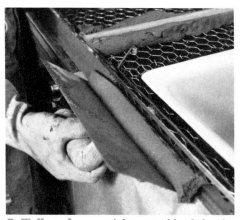

B. *Wall mud*—a special mortar blend that includes masonry lime and latex additive, which help the mortar to cling to vertical surfaces—fills the sink rail before the counter is floated. Some of this wall mud squeezes through the holes in the rail, keying it into the deck mortar.

C. *Deck mud* is loosely spread across the counter with a wood float after the sink rail is filled with mortar. Because the mortar in the rail is still fragile, it has to be supported by a steel trowel so it won't break away.

D. *Leveling the deck mud.* Byrne uses an aluminum straightedge as a screed board, and he moves it in a side-to-side motion as he gradually pulls it forward. Here both ends of the screed are resting on float strips. Note the difference in texture between the crumbly deck mud and the smoother wall mud used on the rail and around the sink.

E. *Edging.* Before it hardens, any mortar that overlaps the sink rim is trimmed away. This allows the sink to be removed later if necessary, without damaging the mortar bed. The open edge will be trimmed with quarter-round tiles.

hot summer. Add to this the occasional earthquake tremors, and you have mortar beds that tend to move around quite a bit. I use 3701, a mortar-and-grout admix made by Laticrete International (1 Laticrete Park North, Bethany, Conn. 06525) that allows my floats to flex a little without cracking. Other companies, like Custom Building Materials (6511 Salt Lake Ave., Bell, Calif. 90201) and Upco (3101 Euclid Ave., Cleveland, Ohio 44115), make similar products.

The amount of admix I need depends on the weather and how wet the sand is (see the sidebar, facing page). This deck mud, as it is called, is considerably drier than brick-type mortars—it has just enough moisture to bind the ingredients and no more. This means that the mix can be compacted into a uniformly dense slab.

Floating the counter—Before I can start spreading the mortar around the countertop, I have to install float strips along any edges that aren't boxed or that don't have a sink rail. Float strips are ¼ in. thick and 1¼ in. wide pine or fir rippings that will sit temporarily atop a layer of mud as I level the mortar. Each float strip begins on a mound of loose deck mud piled slightly higher (about 1 in.) than the height of the finished float. Then I take a level and, placing one end of it on the sink rail for a reference and the rest of it on the float strip, I tap the strip with a hammer until the strip is leveled, as shown in photo A, top left.

Floating begins with filling the front edge of the counter. The channel formed by the sink rail must be filled with what's called wall mud. To make the wall mud, I take a small portion of deck mud (for this job about 2½ gallons), add about a quart (dry measure) of masonry lime, and enough Laticrete 3701 to make a thick, heavy paste. Then, using a flat trowel, I press the mix onto the face of the sink rail until the mud is forced through the ⅝-in. holes (photo B). The resulting extruded lumps of mortar will key into the deck mud.

Once the sink-rail face is filled, I use the remaining wall mud to surround the sink. Then I dump the deck mud onto the countertop and spread it around with a wooden float while I keep the rail and its wall mud steady with my steel trowel (photo C). By this time, the mud in the sink rail has begun to harden, but if it is not supported, it will be pushed off the rail when the nearby deck mud is compacted.

To level the deck mud, I use a straightedge as a screed board (photo D). Using a side-to-side motion, I pull it toward me, gradually removing the excess mud until the straightedge makes contact with the float strips or sink rail. I apply a horizontal rather than vertical pressure on the straightedge to avoid mashing the strips out of position. Smoothing out one area at a time, I gradually work my way around the countertop until the screeding is done. The surface is now flat, but not all the mud is compacted. The float strips also have to be removed, and the resulting voids have to be filled.

I take a lot of pride in my finished floats— they are my pieces of sculpture, and the wood float is my finishing tool. First, I scoop some deck mud onto the flattened top and ram it into the voids where the strips sat with the float. Then with the edge of the tool, I gradually slice off the excess. Experience allows me to "feel" my way across the surface by the way the float sits in my hand. I scour the top until it feels right. With all the voids filled, the top is an unbroken expanse of grey.

The last two areas of mortar to clean up are the sink rail and the sink perimeter. The top and bottom edges of the metal sink rail provide a good surface for the float to trim off the excess mud. Around the sink, I square up the mortar with a trowel, trimming it back far enough to expose the edges of the sink (photo E, facing page). Although it is no picnic, this makes it possible to remove the sink without having to rip up the field tiles. These edges are covered later with quarter-rounds.

Inevitably, some mud will fall away from the rail, or the screed will knock a float strip out of position. Fortunately, the material is very forgiving, and problems are easy to fix. I skip over these minor accidents until the initial work is done, then I go back and fill in dings with fresh mortar before everything sets up.

Setting the tiles—Instead of laying the tiles as soon as I finish the float, I let it harden overnight. This way most of the shrinkage likely to occur will happen before the tiles are in place and grouted, and I can be less concerned about deforming the float as I set the tiles.

The next day, the first order of business is to vacuum loose sand and cement particles from the top to increase the grip of the thinset mortar that bonds the tiles to the float. Then I snap chalklines along the edges to mark the layout for the V-cap trim. I usually spread a few sheets of tile around to confirm my earlier layout; then I mix up enough thinset mortar to last through a couple of hours of setting.

Thinset is a portland-cement based mortar that contains very fine sand. The bond it forms is unaffected by moisture, and it is ideal for applying ceramic tiles to a mortar base. On this job I used Bon-Don (Garland-White & Co., P.O. Box 365, Union City, Calif. 94587). I mix the stuff with water to the consistency of toothpaste, using a drill and a mixing paddle.

The sheet-mounted tiles going on this counter are a little less than ¼ in. thick, so I used a ³⁄₁₆-in. V-notched trowel to comb out the thinset. Spreading too thick a layer will cause the adhesive to ooze up between the tiles. On the other hand, the backs of the tiles must be completely covered. These 12-in. by 12-in. sheets covered the top quickly. I used a short straightedge to help align them.

Everything went smoothly on this job until I reached the open side of the L. There I realized that the tiles were falling short of the V-cap layout line by about ⁷⁄₁₆ in. Checking back, I found that the sheets in one box were all undersized. Adding a narrow row of tiles that have been trimmed to make up for a mistake like this never looks right, so before the thinset dried I quickly widened the grout lines between the rows of tile. The string backing prevents the tiles from being spread apart, so I cut through it with a utility knife, and used a long straightedge to

Mixing the mortar

Of all the skills necessary to produce durable tile installations, none is more perplexing to the novice than mixing mud. There is no substitute for experience, but having a good recipe, the right tools, and knowing a few good mixing techniques can produce workable deck mud. The recipe I use comes from instructions printed on the bucket of latex admix (when using various mortar additives, always follow the manufacturer's recommendations). With Laticrete 3701, the mix is 1 part portland cement, 3 parts mason's sand, and about 4½ to 5 gal. of the admix per sack of cement. To help keep the batches consistent, I measure the dry ingredients in 3-gal. or 5-gal. buckets instead of counting shovelfuls. A full 5-gal. bucket holds ¾ cu. ft. of sand, and when I calculate the volume of mortar for a job, I disregard the cement. It fills the spaces between the sand particles. The sand I use comes damp from the yard, although occasionally I use dry sand shipped in paper sacks. With the dry sand, I measure out the amount I need and mix it with just enough water to dampen it.

I use a steel mixing box and a slotted mason's hoe rather than a rotary mixer, which can cause the mix to form marble-sized lumps. I layer the sand and water evenly in the box and chop them three times back and forth with the hoe. Each time, I take lots of small bites with the hoe, and I pull the ingredients toward me to form a pile at one end of the box. Before any liquid can be added, the sand and cement must be thoroughly blended to prevent lumps from forming.

Next I level the dry ingredients and use the handle of my hoe to punch holes in the mix (photo above right). This allows the liquid to distribute itself more evenly instead of just sitting on top. Then I repeat the mixing procedure, chopping back and forth three times. At this point, I pick up a handful and squeeze it. If the moisture content is right, the deck mud will form a tight ball that sticks together without cracking apart (photo below right). If it oozes through my fingers, the mix is too wet and must be adjusted by adding some dry sand with the right proportions of cement. If the ball falls apart, I need to add more liquid.

The direct rays of the sun can ruin the mud at this point, so I pack it into buckets and get it inside the house. If it's above 90°F, I'll have only about a half-hour to work the mortar. If it's 65°F to 75°F, I may have as long as two hours. —*M. B.*

A steel mixing box (top) is the place to prepare a batch of deck mud. Byrne blends the dry ingredients with his hoe, then pokes holes in the mix with its handle to help spread the latex admix. Properly blended mud is fairly dry, but it will cling together in a ball when you squeeze a handful of it (above).

open up the joints, as shown in the photo at left. For getting out of a jam, nothing beats a good set of straightedges.

Cutting the tiles—The narrow tiles in front of and behind the sink can be cut with a snap cutter (see *FHB* #17, pp. 70-72), but I prefer to use a diamond-bladed wet saw for the accuracy and smoothness of cut I get in one step. The saw is set up outside the house, and running back and forth for each cut eats up time, so I accumulate a stack of tiles to be cut for each trip. You can use a ruler to take measurements and then set the saw fence to these, but that leaves a lot more room for error than just marking the tile directly. The water jet on the saw can sometimes blast away a pencil mark while cutting, so I cover the tile with masking tape and make my mark on the tape.

V-cap, backsplash and quarter-rounds—After all the field tiles are positioned, I set the V-cap. Complicated trim tiles like these often distort a bit in the kiln, so they must be set with extra care. I usually butter each piece with thinset and then tap it into place, controlling the amount of thinset I use to suit the alignment (photo facing page, top left). At inside and outside corners, the V-cap tiles are mitered, and I cut them a bit short to allow for a grout line.

Before I can set the single row of backsplash tiles, I trim the excess tar paper down to about ½ in. to ¾ in. above the deck tiles (drawing, facing page). The joint between the backsplash and the deck must allow for free movement, so later, when the grout is dry, I seal it with a bead of silicone caulk. I allow a full-width joint here rather than have the splash tiles rest directly on the deck tiles. Bon-Don is especially sticky thinset, allowing me to hang these relatively light tiles on the wall without any support from below. Heavier tiles usually require wood or plastic shims between the last course of deck tiles and the bottom edge of the backsplash tiles.

The last tiles to go down are the small radiused tiles that trim the sink. Unlike the other tiles, these quarter-round trim pieces are set on a bed of grout. This grout is the same used to pack the joints, only it is mixed stiffer. To make sure that the quarter-rounds adhere to the float mud around the sink, I coat both the float and the back of each quarter-round with thinset for a stronger bond between the tile and the grout.

Factory-made inside corner pieces look and feel better than the miter cuts you can make on a tile saw. They are set before the straight sections of quarter-round. With quarter-rounds, it's important to apply more grout than is actually needed to set each piece. As the tile is slowly pushed home (photo facing page, below left), the excess grout is squeezed out of the joint. Once the piece is in the right position, I support it with my fingers for a few seconds to prevent it from moving. When all the pieces are set, I

Adjusting the courses. **Instead of adding an unsightly row of narrow tiles, the distance between courses can be slightly increased. This strategy can spread out a discrepancy so it can't be seen, and save tedious tile-trimming.**

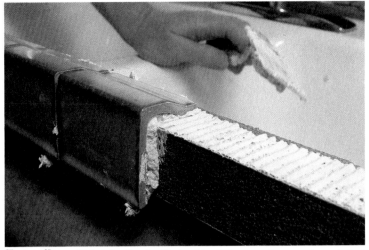

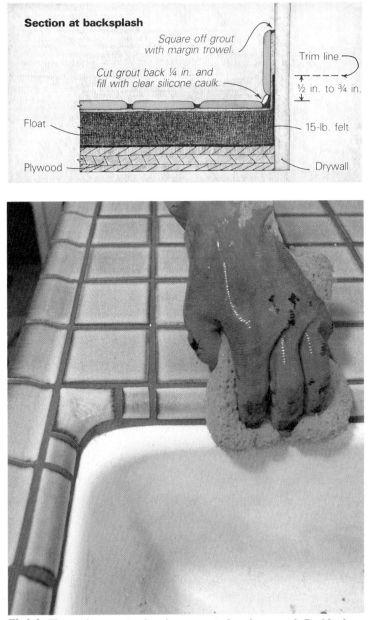

Section at backsplash

Square off grout with margin trowel.

Cut grout back ¼ in. and fill with clear silicone caulk.

Trim line

½ in. to ¾ in.

Float

15-lb. felt

Plywood

Drywall

V-cap tiles, which trim the leading edge of the counter, receive a lot of contact. It's important that they be securely anchored to the mortar bed—any voids between them are unacceptable. Byrne butters the back of each trim piece with a generous helping of thinset, and presses it in place until it's in the same plane as its neighbor.

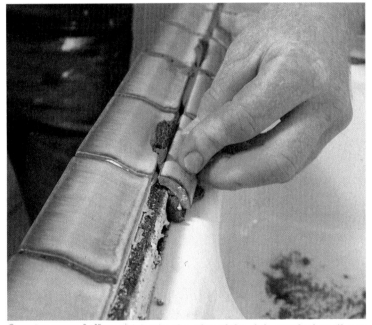

Quarter-round tiles, which trim the edge of the sink, are the last tiles to be placed. They are set on a bed of stiff grout. Before bedding them, Byrne applies a thin layer of thinset mortar to the tiles and to the float. The thinset mortar helps to strengthen the bond between the two.

Finish. The entire counter has been grouted and sponged. Residual cement is cleaned up with a damp sponge. The corner of the sink is trimmed with a factory-made inside-corner piece. Next to it, the quarter-rounds have been trimmed to align with the V-cap edge trim and the field tiles. The last step will be to undercut the grout around the sink, and fill it with silicone caulk once the grout dries.

leave them alone for about a half hour or so to allow the grout to set up. Meanwhile, I prepare another batch of grout.

Grouting—I prefer a grout made with a latex admix because it is a lot stickier than regular grout. This allows it to adhere tenaciously to the slick edges of glazed tiles—an important advantage on a tile work surface that gets constant use. Also, grout with admix is far more resistant to liquids, and to the erosion they can cause.

To prepare the grout, I follow the directions on the sack, which usually recommend combining the dry ingredients with water or a latex admix to the proper consistency, and then allowing the mix to sit for five or ten minutes. The grout is then mixed again and it's ready for use. During this wait, I trim the excess grout from the sink quarter-rounds.

There is no single method for grouting, and the techniques for grouting floor tiles (*FHB* #17, p. 75)

can also be applied to a counter. The porosity of the tiles, the moisture content of the setting bed, the addition of admixes, temperature and humidity levels are all factors that determine how much grout can be spread before it's time to clean off the excess. Usually, I begin by spreading about 8 to 10 square feet. I hold the rubber trowel at an angle between 30° to 40° as I force the grout into the joints. I work the grout from different directions until I'm satisfied that the joints are packed solid.

I start the cleaning by scraping away loose grout with the edge of my rubber trowel. Then I take a wet sponge and wring out as much water as possible. This is important because any excess moisture will weaken the grout. I work the sponge across the counter, gradually lowering the level of the grout until it is slightly below the plane of the tile, with a concave surface. During this process, the pores of the sponge quickly fill with grout and must be flushed constantly. Once

the entire counter has undergone this step, I go back over it with a clean sponge to remove most of the cement haze (photo above right).

The last step is to trim the grout in a few places. At the sink, I undercut the grout below the quarter-rounds about ⅛ in. so the joint can be caulked with clear silicone. This allows the sink to move a little, without breaking the waterproof seal, and lets the color of the grout show through the caulk. Because the counter and the wall will move slightly in relation to one another, I use the same technique to seal the joint between the deck tiles and the backsplash. At the top of the backsplash, I square up the grout line with my margin trowel. This makes it easier to paint or paper the wall.

Finally, I remove any grout haze with cheesecloth or fine steel wool, followed by a thorough vacuuming to take away the loose particles. □

Michael Byrne lives in Walnut Creek, Calif.

Tiling a Backsplash
Decorative tiles liven up a kitchen

by Tom Meehan

Years ago, ceramic tile served as a basic material for wall and floor covering. Decorative tiles—handmade, handpainted European tiles, for instance—were rare. Today our basic needs are met with vinyl flooring, fiberglass tub surrounds and other synthetic materials that are less expensive and easier to install than tile. But there's been a strong revival of interest in ceramics, and I think this is because tile offers decorative possibilities that other materials just can't match.

One of the biggest trends seems to be toward the use of tile in the kitchen (chiefly for floors and backsplashes). It has become common to have a plastic laminate or synthetic solid countertop set off by a fully tiled backsplash. In a recent project I did for Lane DeCamp and Alice Korach, I installed a Dutch tile backsplash in the remodeled kitchen of their 200-year-old Connecticut home (photo below). It was a job that combined basic setting techniques with advanced layout techniques.

Dutch tiles—Lane and Alice chose Royal Makkum Dutch tile (imported to the U. S. by Country Floors, 15 East 16th St., New York, N. Y. 10003-3104; 212-627-8300). This tile is packed by hand into wooden frames before firing, which creates a unique tile whose unevenness enhances its old-world look. Local artists paint many of the tiles with scenes of the countryside, children playing, flowers, ships and windmills.

The body of this tile is relatively soft and easy to cut. Still, I used a wet saw: the tile has a tendency to break unevenly if cut on a snap cutter. Because it's expensive, we ordered very close to what we actually needed, rather than the normal 5% to 7% extra.

Surface preparation and layout—This job was part of a remodel, so we glued and screwed new drywall over plaster walls that

Backsplash art. The completed kitchen (photo above) features imported Dutch tiles. A backsplash isn't subjected much to water, so it's fairly simple to tile. Meehan used an all-purpose mastic, applied with a ¼-in. notched trowel, to install the tiles (photo left). The setting time of the mastic was slow enough that he was able to spread an entire section before placing any tiles. Shortly after finishing this section of backsplash (photo right), the owner announced that he wanted the border tiles to turn up along the window casing. Fortunately, Meehan was able to make the change.

had been cut up to update the electrical wiring. We taped the joints and applied one coat of joint compound. The wall was intact above the window over the kitchen sink, so we simply scraped off the loose paint to establish a solid bonding surface.

Before we could start installing the tile, we had to consider the layout of the three walls that were to be tiled (drawings below). On a complicated job like this, careful layout would be the key to success. We were using plain, off-white 5-in. field tile surrounded by 2½-in. by 5-in. border tiles painted with acanthus leaves. There were also seven individual decorative tiles—painted with scenes—to be spaced evenly about the kitchen, as well as two 4-tile murals of flower vases. Over the stove, there was to be an even larger mural—12 tiles—of flowers in a vase. Finally, there was a tile plaque of a birdcage, roughly 8 in. by 10 in., to be scribed into the field tiles above the window at the sink.

The layout of the first wall (top drawing) was determined by the placement of the 2½-in. square corner piece. This tile makes the transition between the horizontal row of border tiles running along the countertop and border tiles running vertically up to the wall cabinets. When it came time to tile this wall, I'd already used up the corner tiles I had, so I mitered two border pieces to serve as a place holder (top left photo, next page).

The sections of backsplash on either side of the sink window (middle drawing) were easy to lay out. Because the window is the visual center of the kitchen, I wanted a full tile on either side; any necessary cutting would end up in the corners. Three individual decorative tiles would go to the left of the sink, and one more would go on the right along with one of the 4-tile murals.

Over the window, I centered the birdcage right to left, but top to bottom was a different story. For aesthetic reasons, I wanted a full tile on top of the window casing to present the birdcage as cleanly as possible. This left two thirds of a tile cut into the ceiling, which happened to match the side pieces, anyway.

On the wall behind the stove (bottom drawing), I made a judgment call. The stove and the cabinet above it were off center from each other by about 1 in., so I had to decide whether to center the 12-tile mural on the cabinet or on the stove. I centered it over the stove (bottom left photo, next page) because I felt it had a stronger visual connection to the tilework.

As we planned the location of the decorative tiles, we kept in mind what would be seen first upon entering the kitchen, and then what would be seen most frequently. It was also important to know where the small appliances (blender, toaster, etc.) would be located to avoid blocking the decorative tiles from view.

Installation basics—Because these tiles were handmolded, they were uneven in thickness. That's why I used a ¼-in. notched trowel to spread the mastic on the walls. (I used mastic rather than thinset because it's easier to work

with and is perfectly adequate for installations that aren't subjected to water.) This trowel delivered enough mastic to fill out the irregularities of the tile. The relatively thick layer of mastic also set up more slowly, so I was able to move the tiles around freely. I used an all-purpose mastic called Elastiment Multi-21 (Boiardi Products Corp., 453 Main St., Little Falls, N. J. 07424; 800-352-8668). There is very little slippage with this product, which enabled me to set the tiles without using spacers to hold them in place. It set slowly enough that I was able to spread mastic over a whole section of backsplash before setting any tile (bottom left photo, facing page). In general, I spread only as much mastic as I can cover in 25 or 30 minutes.

The Dutch tiles also vary considerably in dimension, which means it's impossible to keep a uniform grout joint—but then again, that's the beauty of the tile. I gauged the grout joints totally by eye, maintaining roughly a ¼-in. joint with ⅛-in. variance either way.

I started by laying border tiles just along the counter, and then continued with full field

tiles above that until I reached the bottom of the cabinets (bottom right photo, facing page). As with most backsplashes, I did not use a level because my tile was only four or five courses high. Regardless of whether or not the cabinets and counter are perfectly level, the job looks best if the tiles follow them.

I really hit only one snag on this job. After I had just finished laying the field tiles on both sides of the window at the sink, Lane came in and decided that he wanted the border tiles, which I had run only along the bottom, to turn up along both sides of the window trim. Thanks to the help from my associate Rick Filep, and to the slow setting time of the mastic, we were able to slide over all the field tiles 2½ in. without any major problems. We then cleaned off the excess mastic before it had a chance to set up on the tiles.

Setting the fancy tiles—Installing the murals and the individual decorative tiles was basically the same as installing the field tile. The only challenge was in determining exactly where to place them. Because the mastic I use

Drawings: Karen Negri

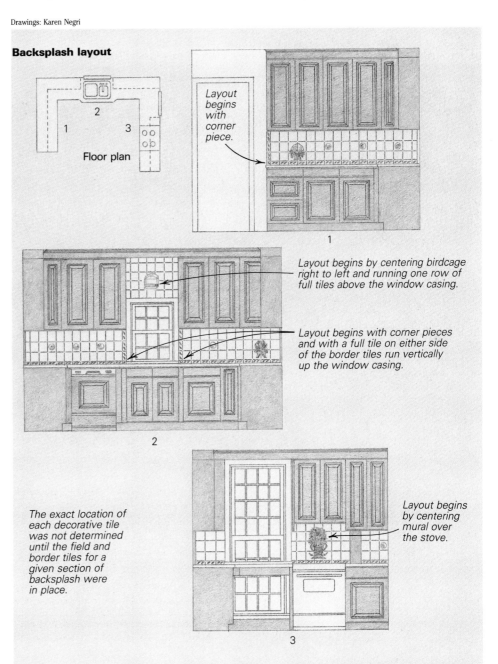

Backsplash layout

Floor plan

Layout begins with corner piece.

1

Layout begins by centering birdcage right to left and running one row of full tiles above the window casing.

Layout begins with corner pieces and with a full tile on either side of the border tiles run vertically up the window casing.

2

The exact location of each decorative tile was not determined until the field and border tiles for a given section of backsplash were in place.

Layout begins by centering mural over the stove.

3

is slow to set, I set all the field tiles in a given section of the backsplash. Then I stood back with Lane, and we considered where the decorative tiles should go. Once we'd made a decision, I removed the necessary field tile by prying it out with the trowel and replaced it with the decorative tile.

The birdcage plaque, on the other hand, required skill and patience. The first thing I did was to lay out on the counter all the field tiles necessary to fill the space above the window. Then I positioned the plaque on top of the tiles and traced its outline onto the field tile below (top right photo). I held the pen at an angle to allow for the grout joint around the tile.

At first I tried to cut all the ins, outs and curves with the wet saw. But the spray from the machine washed off the ink marks, and the machine was not accurate enough on the curves. I remembered a similar project I'd done using tile nippers and decided to employ that tool here. Having a soft clay body, the tile offered little resistance as I whittled away at it with the nippers (bottom right photo). I cleaned up the cut edges with a Carborundum stone.

With all the cutting complete, I installed the field tiles, leaving a birdcage-shaped hole in the middle of them. Then I buttered the back of the plaque with extra mastic to allow the plaque to protrude about an 1/8 in. beyond the field tile. This protrusion made the birdcage (which had a beveled edge) look real. Because of its size and weight, this was the only tile that required spacers—two pieces of folded cardboard—to hold it in place until the mastic set.

Grouting—I went back the next day to grout the job. I wanted the color of the grout to blend well with the field tile. This way the uneven grout lines, while still contributing to the old-world charm, would be less obtrusive. There wasn't a premixed grout that would give me the color I wanted so I had to mix my own.

With the grout joints being as wide as they were, I had to use a floor grout. Any grout joint over 1/8 in. wide, should have a sand base (which makes it a floor grout). I mixed one part light portland cement to ten parts white floor grout to get the color I wanted. Although

I don't believe it's called for in every situation, a liquid latex grout additive was useful in this case. Because these were porous tiles, they could draw moisture out of the grout and weaken it. The latex additive reduced this.

The grouting itself was slow, but not too complicated. The tile still absorbed the moisture of the grout fairly quickly, which meant that I had to grout small sections at a time. When cleaning the grout from the tile, it was important to move the sponge diagonally across the tiles so as not to rake grout from the joints. Ten minutes later, I wiped the tile down with an old towel to polish it up, and the job was done…almost.

Keeping in mind that lighter grouts will stain, especially where the tile backs up to a cooktop, I went back two weeks later to apply a coat of grout sealer to the joints of all the tiled areas. It may not be 100% insurance against staining, but it will be a considerable help. □

Tom Meehan is a second-generation tilesetter and owner of Westport Tile & Design in Westport, Connecticut. Photos by Kevin Ireton.

Meehan made the mitered corner tile in the lower lefthand corner because he didn't have enough manufactured corner tiles. The mitered pieces served for layout purposes and were later replaced.

After laying out the necessary field tiles on the counter, Meehan centered the birdcage and traced around it, holding the pen at a slight angle to allow space for a grout joint.

The stove and the cabinet above it were off center from each other by 1 inch, so Meehan elected to center the 12-tile mural on the stove because it seemed to have a stronger visual connection to the tilework.

Meehan tried to cut out the intricate shapes on his wet saw, but the water kept washing off his cut lines. Then he discovered that the relatively soft tiles were easy to cut with his nippers.

Installing a Dishwasher

How one plumber hooks up the common grease-gobbler

by Peter Hemp

Installing a dishwasher is a snap. Well, it can be if you've got the right tools, the cabinet space is big enough, the supply and waste lines are readily accessible and you do things in the right order. While this article focuses on how I install a new dishwasher in a new kitchen, there are a couple of conditions that can bedevil the person faced with taking out an old one. Let's look at these first.

Extracting a defunct dishwasher—Before removing any dishwasher, be sure to turn off the water and power prior to disconnecting the water supply and electrical hookups under the machine. In addition, the machine will probably be screwed to the underside of the counter, and perhaps the floor, through metal flanges attached to its chassis.

Some dishwasher installations go back 30 years, and there are still quite a few surviving appliances of this vintage. Two major obstacles commonly prevent their removal. The first obstacle can be a new floor. If somebody put down a layer of underlayment in front of the dishwasher, it's trapped, and either the floor goes or the countertop goes.

The second obstacle is a water supply that emerges from the floor under the dishwasher. The pipe stub prevents the machine from being slid out from beneath the counter. You can tell if yours falls into this category by looking under the kitchen sink. If there is *not* a rigid copper pipe running from the dishwasher to the hot-water supply for the sink faucet, you've probably got a pipe stub under the dishwasher. To make absolutely certain, remove the panel at the bottom front of the appliance. Use a nut driver or a 4-in. crescent wrench for hexhead screws; for the nearly inaccessible Phillips head screws you'll need an offset screwdriver. Panel off, use a flashlight to spot the supply stub. If you've got one, you'll have to sever it with a reciprocating saw or a mini hack saw. If the water heater is above the level of the dishwasher, drain it first.

Dishwasher removed, use an Ace EX-7 pipe nipple back-out (available at Ace Hardware Stores) to take out the remainder of the pipe stub, and cap the line with a plug. To prevent leaks, wrap the plug's threads with Teflon tape. As you look at its threaded end, wrap it clockwise with four layers of tape. Now cram the square end of the plug (along with some well-chewed bubble gum) into a 12-point $^{11}/_{16}$-in. ratchet wrench socket. The gum will keep the plug from falling out as you feel around for the old fitting.

Angle stops and air-gap inlets—I work in the Bay Area in northern California, where the code requires that a new dishwasher have its own shut-off valve and an air-gap inlet. The shut-off is called an angle stop. The kind I use has two shut-off handles and two branches (photo 1), and it attaches to one stub-out (a capped pipe or tube).

An air-gap inlet is a "break" in the waste line that prevents waste water from back-siphoning into the dishwasher. The air-gap inlet is located on the edge of the sink, near the faucet. When I install an air-gap inlet, I use only one brand and model—the Eastman CD-4 (U. S. Brass, 901 10th St., Plano, Tex. 75074; see photo 2). It works better than any of the other air-gaps I've tried.

Installing a new dishwasher—Let's imagine that we have a nice, clean opening for our new appliance, and that it is properly sized for the new machine. The width of the space should be ¼ in. to ⅜ in. wider than the dishwasher, which is usually 24 in. wide. A dishwasher space needs to be at least 34 in. tall.

Taking care not to mar the kitchen floor, maneuver the machine in its carton to within 3 ft. of the cabinet opening. I slide the box on a 3-ft. by 2-ft. piece of carpeting, fuzzy side down. Cut the banding, remove the top of the carton and use a utility knife to cut carefully down each corner of the carton and across the bottom on all four sides.

Because most people are right-handed, the dishwasher will usually be to the right of the sink. Regardless of which side it's on, now look at the side of the dishwasher that will be next to the sink cabinet (photo 3). You're looking for gaps between the dishwasher components and chassis that will afford a route for the drain, power and water lines. Make measurements to ascertain where you can route the lines through the chassis to a 1½-in. hole that you will bore in the cabinet wall.

Next, look to see whether your drain hose is already attached to the pump under the ap-

Connections under the sink. An angle stop is a valve that connects the domestic water supply with individual fixtures (photo 1). The one in the lower left corner has two outlets— one for the sink and one for the dishwasher. In the upper right corner of the photo, a ⅝-in. drain line from the dishwasher is connected to the air-gap inlet. A ⅞-in. drain line connects the air-gap to an inlet in the tailpiece draining the sink. Most of an air-gap inlet is hidden below the sink (photo 2). The portion above it is covered with the chrome cap to the left of the hole. If the air-gap clogs, water will escape through the holes in the cap. So it's important to place the air-gap below the sink's flood rim. The author used a chassis punch to cut this hole in a stainless-steel sink.

pliance (photo 4). Some manufacturers route this hose up the side, over the top and back down the other side of the machine, and they affix it permanently to the chassis with straps or clips. This is a precautionary measure that prevents the water used in washing cycles from being siphoned out of the machine. With this configuration you'll be connecting an additional piece of standard ⅝-in. dishwasher hose (hardware and plumbing supplies have it), and routing it to the air-gap inlet.

Other manufacturers reason that the air-gap inlet will prevent back-siphoning, and forego the wrap-over drain hose. If your new machine has no such hose already installed, and you see a naked pipe stub (called a "barb") projecting from the pump housing, then you need to provide a length (usually 5 ft.) of ⅝-in. rubber-hose waste line.

In any case, the hose must be able to pass from the machine (and sometimes all the way around it) to the bottom of the air-gap inlet. The route should be direct, with gentle bends and no kinks. Hose is cheap. It's better to use 8 ft. of it than to settle for a kinked or spliced hose.

Most dishwashers are bolted to a wooden skid. Remove the bolts (sometimes these will be the threaded height adjusters—they'll need to be rethreaded into the bottom of the appliance), latch the door and carefully tilt the machine onto its back. Now you can remove the skid and tilt the machine back onto the carpet. Taking it very slowly, slide the ap-

Drain hose and supply line. After cutting away the packing carton, the author unbolts the machine from its wooden skid (photo 3). At the lower right corner of the machine is a plastic blower housing. The drain line will pass through the notch to its left on its way through the sink cabinet. The drain hose (photo 4) is attached to the pump in the center of the photo. On the left, the brass inlet of the solenoid valve is ready for the elbow that will attach it to the water supply. Below the valve are the machine's adjustable feet. The author threads ⅜-in. tubing through a 1½-in. dia. hole in the side of the sink cabinet toward the supply el in the lower left corner of the dishwasher (photo 5).

pliance into the cabinet. Check to see if your hose can reach the hole in the side of the cabinet. If not, slide the machine back out and drill a new hole.

Waste and power lines—If the waste hose must be extended to reach the air-gap inlet, begin a splice with a piece of ½-in. rigid copper tube (type L or M) about 3½ in. long. This copper pipe will have a ⅝-in. outside di-

ameter. Use a reamer or ultra-sharp pocket knife to remove any burrs. Then slide 1¼-in. to 1⅜-in. stainless-steel, worm-drive hose clamps onto each piece of hose. Shove the copper tube an equal distance into each hose and tighten the clamps to complete the splice.

Now crawl far enough into the enclosure so that you can shove the end of the drain hose through the hole in the cabinet wall and make sure the hose is almost taut. If the pow-

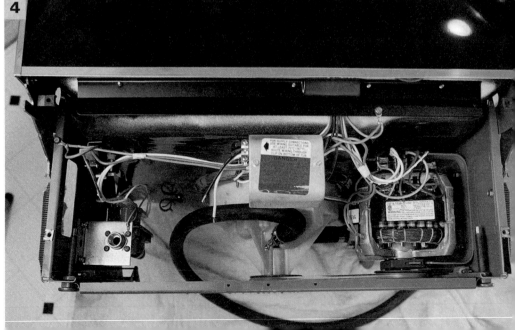

er supply is going to be a line cord with a plug, it is awfully nice to have enough cord to plug into the outlet and still have your machine totally out of the enclosure. Because you have to provide this cord, you can select its length. Now is the time to thread the cord through the hole in the cabinet.

With the machine still atop its carpet and the drain and power lines started through the hole in the cabinet, inch the machine into its space while pulling on the lines through the hole in the cabinet. Once you get four or five inches into the enclosure, pull the carpet pad out from under the rear feet.

Side to side, up and down—Now that the little brute is all the way in, you should check for side clearance. It is very important that the door not strike any portion of the cabinet or counter edging before closing. If it does, eventually it will become permanently sprung, and leaks will appear at the door bottom. Try to get the dishwasher door flush with the cabinets.

Most machines have adjustable feet that screw up or down, with a nut that allows you to lock the feet at the desired setting. They're easy to reach in front, but excruciatingly difficult to reach in back. That is, unless you're installing a Maytag dishwasher. Their rear adjusters are operated by turning hex bolts at the *front* of the appliance. This can save you both aggravation and sliced fingers (sheet-metal chassis have sharp edges, so be careful in there). Shim shingles may also be used to adjust the rear feet.

Crank on the front feet until the two mounting tabs at the top of the machine touch the underside of the countertop. Drive a screw through each tab, securing the machine.

Supply line—Before you can hook up the water supply, you need to install a "dishwasher el" at the front of the appliance. This elbow attaches to the solenoid valve that regulates water intake. The elbow can be of two sizes. The most common is a ⅜-in. IPS (iron pipe size) by ⅜-in. compression. Or it could be ½-in. IPS by ½-in. compression. In both cases, the compression dimensions refer to the inside diameter of refrigeration tubing (not pipe), and you might find a printed, nasty threat amongst the installation papers stating that the machine with the ½-in. FIP (female iron pipe) solenoid valve connection should be plumbed only with ½-in. refrigeration tubing, or your warranty is void. The statement is true, but the facts are baloney. Any under-counter residential dishwasher can perform just beautifully on ⅜-in. tubing, provided you've got enough water pressure. Most dishwashers require a minimum of 35 psi to function properly, and excessive pressure (above 80 psi) is your dishwasher's greatest enemy. I have installed many machines that called for ½-in. tubing, but I substituted ⅜-in. tubing by using a ⅜-in. by ½-in. el at the solenoid. I've *never* had any call backs or performance problems. Of course, the water pressure is adequate

where I do my work. If it was below 50 psi, I'd go with the ½-in. tubing. Regardless of which diameter you choose, you need to supply the el fitting.

It is a good idea to purchase 6 ft. to 7 ft. of copper tubing for the water supply even though you will probably only use 5 ft. of it. The extra length allows you the leverage you need to put a bend in the tubing near its end, while still leaving a portion with a perfectly round cross-section. And you won't get a watertight seal without a round cross section.

I thread the supply tube through the hole in the cabinet, forming a gentle bend that leaves the end of the tube pointing straight out from the front of the machine (photo 5).

Use a tubing bender to make the 90° bend needed to align the supply tube with the el. As you cut the tubing end that will fit into the el, make sure to leave at least 1 in. of straight tubing so that the brass ferrule in the compression fitting will make a tight seal. Wrap the el's threads with a couple of layers of Teflon tape before you put on the compression nut. Follow this same procedure to hook up the supply line to the angle stop under the sink.

Under the sink—The air-gap inlet has two legs. One is ¾ in. in dia., the other is ½ in. The ⅝-in. drain line from the dishwasher slips over the ½-in. leg, where it is held fast by a pipe clamp (photo 1). The other leg is attached either to the side inlet of the sink tailpiece (buy a chromed, all brass strainer, and a 17-ga. tailpiece), or the side inlet of a garbage disposal. In either case, the ⅞-in. hose (usually 3 ft. long) should be routed in the most direct, downhill path. This hose evacuates by gravity, so no bends are allowed in it.

I will sometimes put the air-gap inlet on the side of the sink farthest from the dishwasher if it allows me to have a better path for the ⅞-in. hose to the waste inlet. Picking the side for the air-gap inlet is easy with stainless-steel sinks because I can punch my own 1¼-in. hole. I use a Greenlee #5004003 chassis punch, a device made for cutting large-diameter holes in sheet metal (Greenlee Tool Co., 4455 Boeing Dr., Rockford, Il. 61109). Don't be tempted to put an air-gap inlet on a counter. Sooner or later it will clog, and water will pour out of the vent holes.

If you attach the ⅞-in. hose to the side inlet of a garbage disposal, make sure to remove the little plug inside the inlet, which will allow the drain water from the dishwasher to enter the disposal.

Testing—The lower panel is still off. We can see our ⅜-in. copper supply and dishwasher el connections and also our drain hose connections. Now, slowly crack open the hot water for the dishwasher. Turn on the valve just far enough to hear the water start to flow and then leave it on at this low setting until all the noise stops. Look at your water connec-

tions under the machine. If you have a drip or little squirt, shut the valve off and slightly tighten the connections. *Do not overtighten* the compression nuts on the angle stop and dishwasher el. These nuts must be really snug, but you can ruin them with too much torque. Now look at the packing nuts behind the handle on the double angle stop. If you have a drip, tighten the nut just one-quarter turn at a time, until the drip stops. Open the valve all the way.

If the power is connected, and all the freebies and styrofoam are out of the dishwasher, run the machine on the "rinse-and-hold" cycle. The front panel should be in place to prevent shock during these tests. If all goes well on that cycle, run it on the longest cycle. Sometimes a leak will appear only after the vibration of operation sets in. Occasionally the water-inlet solenoid valve will leak, even on a brand-new dishwasher. This valve usually has a green or orange plastic housing on its top. Give it a good visual inspection. You want to know right now if it is faulty, so you can let the factory rep deal with it.

Dishwasher addenda—Dishwashers have three main enemies. The first is water pressure above 80 psi, which can be alleviated with a pressure-reducing valve installed on the main water line. The next two enemies can never really ever be eliminated: large dinner parties and olive pits. After a large party and many helping hands moving too fast, an olive pit can find its way into the dishwasher. It goes through the machine and lodges in the top of the air-gap inlet. Now no water can get through, so it escapes past the door seal and floods the kitchen. Cheap air-gap inlets are particularly prone to this situation. The CD-4 might choke up a bit and drool into the sink, but usually most of the drainage gets into the disposal, not onto the floor. To rectify the problem, pop off the chrome top of the air-gap inlet and dislodge the pit.

In closing I'd like to say a couple of words about dishwasher pans—the kind that resemble big cookie sheets. Dishwashers sometimes develop slow, continuous drips that can damage floors. If you've got an expensive floor, you ought to get a pan.

To my knowledge, no one markets a ready-made dishwasher pan such as the kind available for water heaters. But your local sheet-metal shop can fabricate one for you out of economical galvanized-steel flat stock. If the dishwasher is over a crawl space, you can add a drain to your pan. If you are in a multi-unit building and have living space below you, even a holding-pan can save you some headaches. □

Peter Hemp is a plumber and writer from Albany, California, and author of The Straight Poop *(Ten Speed Press, P. O. Box 7123, Berkeley, Calif., 94707, 1986. $9.95, softcover; 176 pp.), a book on plumbing maintenance and repair.*

Choosing a Kitchen Sink

There are lots of shapes, sizes, materials and accessories available today, but it's still a good idea to get what suits your needs

by Steve Culpepper

When there's room, small extra sinks add convenience. In larger kitchens with more than one cook, a smaller second—or even third—sink makes sense. One of these stainless-steel under-mounted sinks has a disposal. Both can be used for preparing food while the main sink is occupied.

When I was 6 years old, my family moved into a brand-new, state-of-the-art ranch house in a treeless subdivision freshly scraped out of a cotton field. By state of the art, I mean the house had built-in kitchen appliances that matched the kitchen sink, which was a gleaming copper-tone brown unit set into a gold-flecked, turquoise Formica countertop.

Actually, that sink wasn't anything special. In those days, almost every new sink in every new subdivision was either copper-tone brown, avocado green or snowdrop white; had two bowls; and was cast iron or enamel on steel. (I'm sure there probably were lots of stainless-steel sinks, too, but just how much is a 6-year-old expected to notice?)

As ordinary as it was, that copper-tone sink served the family well. My mother washed vegetables, scrubbed pots and pans, soaked dishes and polished silver in that sink. She also delivered the occasional haircut to an uncooperative head held over the sink.

That was a generation ago. Lifestyles, tastes and even the way people cook have changed substantially in that time. Sure, sinks are still used for washing things and filling things and preparing things. They're still required to take a good beating. The kitchen sink remains just as versatile and is still the most frequently used "center of activity" in the home, according to the National Kitchen and Bath Association (NKBA). But much has changed. For one thing, sinks don't just come in two-bowl copper-tone brown, avocado green or snowdrop white anymore; nor are they made only of ferrous metals.

What's important in a sink?—Let's say you're in the market for a sink. And for the sake of argument, let's say you've found a sink you like, one that looks good and that comes in a color to match your collection of Elvis commemorative plates. Besides looks, what else should you consider before plunking down hundreds of dollars?

If you're installing the sink yourself, you should consider ease of installation. For example, there's a lot more to installing an underhung, or under-mount, sink than there is to installing a self-rimming sink or drop-in sink, which basically involves laying a bead of caulk and setting the sink into a hole in the counter. And unless you've had the training, I wouldn't recommend even trying to install an integral sink of solid-surface material, such as Wilsonart's Gibralter or DuPont's Corian.

Before you buy, you'll also want to consider the durability of the sink material. Will it chip, dent, stain, rattle, tarnish, scratch, crack, rust, blister or mar? And how quiet is it when water floods into the basin or runs down the drain?

Before you commit yourself to one type of sink, consider how easy is it to clean and otherwise maintain it. Depending on the type and amount of cooking you do, a low-maintenance sink may be what you want. With two boys in my house, the less scrubbing and wiping something needs, the better. However, somebody with no kids and a real compulsion for polishing may take a shine to a brass or copper sink. When it comes to size, depth and shape, sink choices increase as prices

increase. It's like a car. You can buy a lot more bells and whistles on a Lexus than you can on a Geo. And if money is no object, you can buy any sink you like and hire somebody else to install it and keep it clean—you can even hire somebody else to use it, for that matter. If you don't have a fortune, you still can buy a sink and choose from a wide variety of shapes, configurations, materials, sizes and depths.

Sinks of all varieties: as deep, wide or weirdly shaped as you want—People shopping for modern kitchen sinks are looking for bigger, deeper and different choices. Manufacturers appear to be glad to accommodate them.

An important consideration is depth of the sink bowl. While standard sinks are 6 in. to 8 in. deep, more and more sinks are available in depths of 10 in. to 12 in. or more. With solid-surface materials, an almost unlimited bowl depth is possible.

You might wonder why anybody would need their sink to be a foot deep. More things fit into a

Eurodesign sinks feature smooth contours. A high-quality, 18-ga. stainless-steel sink, such as this German-made sink by Franke, looks good and endures years of use. Top-of-the-line sinks are available in a variety of shapes and sizes, and can include a range of accessories and combinations of bowls, such as this large basin and a small vegetable sink.

A single-bowl sink is just right for a small kitchen. Kitchen designers recommend using single-bowl sinks like this cast-iron one for small kitchens that are less than 150 sq. ft. This single bowl is only 24 in. by 21 in., so it takes up less counter space.

deeper sink. Also, if the sink bowl is a standard size (about 14 in. by 16 in.), the sink will seem much larger if it's deeper than normal. There are other benefits to a deep sink. Water from the tap and soups or sauces poured into pots or bowls are less likely to splash out of a deeper sink. A tall stockpot fits neatly inside a deep sink. A taller person can operate more efficiently with a deeper sink. And in a neat, efficient use of space, many new sinks come with one large basin and one small basin (top photo).

Sink shape is often simply a matter of preference. However, there are certain shapes that fit certain locations, such as corners or small island countertops. (The NKBA suggests that corner sinks don't sit back more than 2 in. or 3 in. from the edge of the countertop.) Second sinks, popular in larger kitchens, often are round, oval or small rectangles (photo facing page). Designers insist, though, that before buying a sink with an unusual shape or one that's particularly small, deep or shallow, you should try to imagine how it

will work in your kitchen. With the variety of sinks available, homeowners can select the exact shape and size that fits their cookware and their kitchen, designer Charles Olsen says. Before you choose a kitchen sink, first give your cooking style, your lifestyle and your cookware a thorough examination

Designers consider the sink another appliance. That concept almost requires that a good deal of thought go into choosing the size and shape of the sink. While shopping a plumbing-supply showroom, ask yourself these questions: How many cooks will use the sink? What size pots do you use? Who does the cleanup? What bugs you about the sink you have now?

There's something else to consider. Although most homeowners want to maximize the amount of space beneath a sink, it's good to think about the location of the drain as it affects the garbage disposal. Many new sinks have offset drains, which are placed in a rear corner. This placement means the waste pipes are pushed to the

rear, leaving more space under the sink, but it means there's less space for the disposal. An offset drain can make installation of a garbage disposal a real problem for the plumber because there's not much room between the drain and the back of the cabinet.

Finally, a few rules of thumb. According to the NKBA, single-bowl sinks are recommended in small kitchens, which are less than 150 sq. ft. (bottom photo). This single-bowl sink usually is 24 in. by 21 in. and fits into a 27-in. wide cabinet. In kitchens larger than 150 sq. ft., double or even triple bowls, which often include a small disposal bowl, should be specified.

Stainless steel is still the sink standard—For good reasons, stainless-steel sinks continue to be the most popular. They're durable, they're easy to keep clean, and they come in a variety of sizes, shapes and price ranges. They can be undermount, rimless or self-rimming and can have one, two or three bowls, often of different size

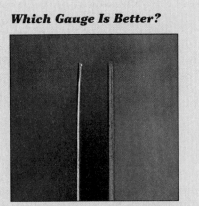

A new cast-iron sink that has an old-fashioned look. Kohler's new cast-iron apron sink comes in a new model with a traditional look. This single-bowl, tile-in model also comes in an undermount version.

and depth. They're also available in a wide range of qualities.

The broad spectrum of qualities means you have to be careful what you buy. However, price is generally a good indication. You can buy a really cheap, single-bowl stainless-steel sink for $25 or less at a home center and expect to get what you paid for. A good, heavy-duty stainless-steel sink with double bowls can run several hundred dollars (top photo, p. 125). If you spend even more money, you can install a stainless-steel sink integrally with a stainless-steel countertop, with no visible seam.

By far, the most important thing to remember about stainless steel is that thickness matters. The thickness of stainless steel is measured in gauges: the lower the gauge, the thicker the steel and, consequently, the better the sink (top photo left). A 22-ga. sink isn't quite paper thin, but it sure will dent more easily than heavier gauge stainless. The best stainless-steel sinks are 18 ga. In the middle are 20-ga. stainless-steel sinks.

For what it's worth, the stated gauge of a sink is slightly misleading. It's like a quarter-pound hamburger. It weighs a quarter-pound before cooking. In the same way, a blank of 18-ga. stainless steel is 18 ga. before it's set into a huge metal press and squeezed into a basin shape. Afterward, it's a bit thinner.

The content of the steel also is important. Nickel and chromium are two of the most critical elements added to the stainless-steel alloy. Steel with higher contents of both nickel and chromium will be more resistant to rusting and pitting than steel that contains less of the two metals. Typically, stainless steel contains 18% to 20% chromium and 8% to 10.5% nickel. A top-of-the-line, 18-ga. stainless-steel sink would have a chromium-nickel content of 18:8, which means 18% chromium and 8% nickel. Carbon is another key ingredient. Good stainless contains from 0.08% to 0.15% carbon.

Most stainless-steel sinks come with a sprayed-on undercoating, although really cheap models don't. The coating helps insulate and soundproof the metal, which is important when water is running in the basin or when dishes and pots bang against the side. The coating also prevents condensation on the underside of the sink.

Peter Hemp, a plumber in Berkeley, California, describes thin, cheap stainless steel as having the appearance of pewter. "It contains very little nickel and it's very rough. You could almost sand your nails against the grain. And you don't dare put disposals in cheap stainless-steel sinks because it'll shake the tar out of them."

Joe Carmody, a plumber in Matunuck, Rhode Island, complains that in most inexpensive stainless-steel sinks, "the clips that hold them to the countertop are not stainless, and they'll break free if water gets on them." He likes good stainless, though. "I'm building a new house now, and it's coming with a double-bowl stainless sink. It's very practical and very durable. Stainless also

gives. If you drop a 16-oz. drinking glass in it, chances are it'll bounce off the bottom. If you do that with cast iron, you'd better get your gloves, because the glass is broken."

Lou Hall, a certified kitchen designer in Fresno, California, says stainless sinks are no longer his biggest sellers because of improvements in man-made materials and because of the look stainless gets as it ages. "Stainless steel seasons, and it takes a set. And it's never going to be as pretty as the day it came out of the box," he says.

If you can stand the occasional chipping, cast iron looks great and performs well—In its prime, the two-bowl, cast-iron copper-tone sink that I grew up with had the tone of, well, copper. In later years, however, its luster faded: Iron began showing through in dark, crescent-shaped bruises wherever heavy pots or skillets had slipped through soapy hands. The sink still did the job, but as its finish grew dimmer and hazier from daily applications of Ajax, its splendor waned.

The main drawbacks of cast iron are its weight and its tendency to chip. If you've got a sturdy countertop, the weight of a cast-iron sink should not be a problem—unless you're lifting it. Chipping is a problem. Although the enamel is fairly durable, it will chip off. If it does chip, the black cast iron can show through and could rust. Cast iron's beauty is its rich color, traditional look and substantial feel (photo above right). Lynda

Left photos: Boyd Hagen. Right photo: Kevin Ireton.

Seamless contrast. DuPont, the pioneer in solid-surface sinks, makes this sink and countertop of acrylic Corian, which can be fused so that there are no seams to collect dirt. Also, scratches can be buffed out with a light abrasive.

There's a lot of solid-surface competition. This integral sink and counter are made by Wilsonart of its Gibralter material. Gibralter, which has properties similar to Corian, resists scratching and denting.

Wilhelmus, an Evansville, Indiana, kitchen designer, likes cast iron because of its good looks and because it comes in a great variety of colors. She warns, however, to be aware of the maintenance involved. "There is a little more upkeep in cast-iron sinks because they can chip, and you have to be more careful with them. Sometimes you have to use soft-scrub cleansers because certain kinds of pans leave marks on the sink. But they're beautiful."

"The one I'm using the most of is a unit made by Kohler, called their Executive Chef model," says Lou Hall. "A lot of my clients are heavy users of the kitchen. They cook. One compartment is 10 in. deep. It's oversize, and it allows room for those bigger pots and pans and stockpots to be washed. And the other compartment is still close to the traditional double-bowl sink size."

Chipping is the age-old problem of cast-iron sinks. Kitchen designer Charles Olsen says he

asked Kohler to refinish some old cast-iron sinks, but the company wouldn't do it. Basically, it's as easy to make a whole new sink. Enameling and firing a cast-iron sink takes a long time and involves repeated applications of powdered enamel and intense firing at 1,250°F.

Even in good sinks, though, there can be problems. Hall warns that occasionally a sink will have a run in it where the porcelain hasn't adhered properly. Under the right circumstances, the porcelain can pop off. "It's like a gun going off. I've dug porcelain out of a ceiling, like shrapnel." He suggests first dusting new sinks with graphite to find hairline cracks.

Professionals all suggest that a new cast-iron sink be thoroughly checked for nicks and chips as soon as it arrives, especially around the rim and the drain hole, and especially in self-rimming sinks.

Some cast-iron sinks can be undermounted, which is currently one of the most popular forms of installation. Hemp says he installs a lot of cast iron mounted under solid-surface counters.

Hemp has been a plumber for 23 years and still prefers cast iron to all other materials, despite the fact that he has to lift it. "If somebody asks me what kind of sink to use, I'll still tell them cast iron. But more and more homeowners are separated from this decision. More people are using professional designers, many of whom tend to pick things up from their appearance and not based on their performance record. I have a cast-iron sink, single bowl, that's been in this house since 1957, and it's still in pretty good shape. Every now and then I've got to put a little bleach in there, but it's held up very, very well."

Compared with stainless, cast-iron sinks are a little pricey. You can buy a basic two-bowl model for about $180, or you can spend twice that for an exotic color or combination of bowls—and even more if you add lots of accessories.

Solid-surface sinks are coming into their own—One of the biggest kitchen revolutions since electric refrigeration replaced block ice occurred in 1969 with DuPont's introduction of Corian, a material made of acrylic resin and alu-

Comparing Sink Costs

The price of a kitchen sink can vary tremendously from retailer to retailer. Price also is affected by other variables, such as color. For instance, a cast-iron sink in black costs about $100 more than a cast-iron sink in almond. Accessories, naturally, can add a lot to the price of a sink, as can extra-large sizes or extra-deep bowls.

For the sake of comparing apples to apples, I got price quotes on middle-of-the-road sinks from a half-dozen different Connecticut distributors from cities and towns large and small, and from building-supply stores, home centers, plumbing-supply stores and designer showrooms. Except for the stainless-steel sink, I

specified a white, double-bowl sink, approximately 22 in. by 33 in., with four holes for faucet, handles and sprayer. In stainless steel, I asked for a 20-ga., two-bowl sink with undercoating.

These are Connecticut prices and are among the highest in the country. You could pay less.—*S. C.*

Material	Highest cost	Lowest cost	Average cost
Stainless	$265	$89	$182
Cast iron	$386	$189	$263
Enamel-on-steel	$186*	$49	$123
Solid surface	$265	$205	$235
Composite	$720	$550	$635

*American Standard's Americast

Top photo: Courtesy of Corian. Bottom photo: Courtesy of Gibralter.

Buying an Exotic Sink Isn't Exactly Like Pouring Money Down the Drain

If you think a sink is just a sink, you might be content with the $49 enamel-on-steel model for sale down at the home center. But if your kitchen sink needs to make a statement—and perhaps outlast Western Civilization—there are alternatives to the run-of-the-mill.

Right up there with the more eternal materials available is the German-silver, nickel-silver or vermeil sink, each of which is handmade to the customer's specifications by the German Silver Sink Company (89 Kercheval Ave., Grosse Pointe Farms, Mich. 48236; 313-885-1010).

Maggi Goscicki said her company's German-silver sinks come in any size the customer wants, or in any variation of bowl sizes and shapes. The traditional sink contains an S-curve design partition that runs between the bowls (bottom photo).

Company literature recommends the sinks be "resoldered every 30 to 45 years." And unlike other sink manufacturers, the German Silver Sink Company heartily advises customers to abuse their sinks. "The most charming vermeil sinks have the most dents, large and small. The more dents, the better the appearance." The company even will predent the sink for customers who don't have time to dent it themselves. The S-curve sink retails for about $3,400.

Charles Olsen of Ducci Kitchens in Torrington, Connecticut, said other luxury sinks available are made of slate or soapstone. "We are contemplating putting in a slate sink currently. It's about $900 for a single bowl. But it's very heavy slate that they rabbet out and glue together with a marine glue, just like in a chemistry lab. It's almost impervious."

Kenton Lerch of Structural Slate Company (222 E. Main St., Pen Argyl, Penn. 18072; 610-863-4141) says his company sells three or four slate sinks a year. They make them by rabbeting the pieces and gluing them together using stone epoxy. The average thickness is 1 in., and the average one-bowl slate sink weighs about 125 lb. Compared with other custom-made sinks, slate is fairly cheap. A single-bowl sink sells for about $380.

A number of places make soapstone sinks (top photo), such as Vermont Soapstone Company (P. O. Box 168, Perkinsville, Vt. 05151; 802-263-5404). These sinks are fairly expensive. They average $800, but can be as inexpensive as $450 and as expensive as $2,000, depending on the number of bowls and whether they have a backsplash. They are guaranteed for life.

There's also brass, which is a lot more popular for relatively easy-use bar sinks than for heavily used kitchen sinks. For one thing, there's still no good coating for brass that will make it hold its shine and also stand up to constant use and wear. The alternative is just to keep polishing.—S. C.

Soapstone sinks are guaranteed to last a lifetime. Soapstone sinks can cost as much as $2,000 or as little as $450, depending on the size and extras such as backsplash. Vermont Soapstone Company made this model.

It looks expensive because it is. This German-nickel, or vermeil, sink could be yours for about $3,400, a price that can include predenting. The heavy, hand-soldered sink is quite durable and should last many years.

minum trihydrate. The really radical thing about Corian is that pieces of it can be fused seamlessly together, joining the counter with the sink. Also, its color goes all the way through.

DuPont worked hard to market its new material, and by the end of the 1980s, Corian began showing up everywhere in higher-end kitchens and baths. For countertops, Corian now comes in 41 colors, although sinks are available in only eight colors.

Over the last five or six years, a number of other man-made materials have come on the sink market, each an attempt to break into the niche created by Corian (top photo, p. 127). As a group, these sinks are called solid surface. Besides Corian, the bigger names include Gibralter, which is made of polyester and acrylic resin (bottom photo, p. 127); Swanstone, which is a modified acrylic; and Avonite, made of polyester resins and mineral fillers. Other brands of solid-surface materials continue to enter the market. Despite its higher price per foot, Corian is still the biggest seller.

Cameron Snyder, president of the NKBA, says costs of solid-surface sinks are fairly similar. "By the time they're installed in the counter, for a double-bowl sink you're looking at $700 to $900. I don't see one brand as having a price advantage over the others, and that includes Corian."

Solid-surface sinks have their drawbacks. The material is expensive. Installation is specialized and labor-intensive, and the material doesn't like heat. DuPont suggests that if a pot is too hot to handle, it shouldn't be set on Corian. Manufacturers also recommend against use of harsh chemicals or stove and drain cleaners.

Still, people are buying more and more sinks made of solid-surface material. Kitchen designers like Stephanie Witt of Grand Rapids, Michigan, describe phenomenal sales of Corian. Sinks of the material are produced in 15 to 20 different shapes and configurations, which can be varied even more with the help of a good fabricator. Depth and shape can be determined on site.

Because of the material's flexibility, solid-surface sinks can be made to disappear into the counter. Or with different colors for the counter and the sink, the sink can be made to stand out. Gibralter sinks come in 13 colors, and Swanstone comes in 18 colors. Kitchen designer Wilhelmus sees a continuing interest in solid-surface material because there's no lip to clean around or to get water into.

Solid-surface sinks don't have to be integral with the counter, though. Often, they're under-mounted below a countertop of different material. Some manufacturers (Swanstone and Corian) also make self-rimming sinks out of solid-surface material. But the main high-end use of solid-surface sinks is in an integral application.

Like stainless steel and cast iron, solid-surface sinks come in a variety of bowl shapes. Customers can purchase one-, two- or three-bowl sinks, or they can buy almost any variety of bowl shapes and depths and have them fused into an integral piece. Unlike stainless steel and cast iron, solid-surface sinks can cost up to $600 or more for a two-bowl sink. You can buy a decent, two-bowl solid-surface sink, though, for as little as

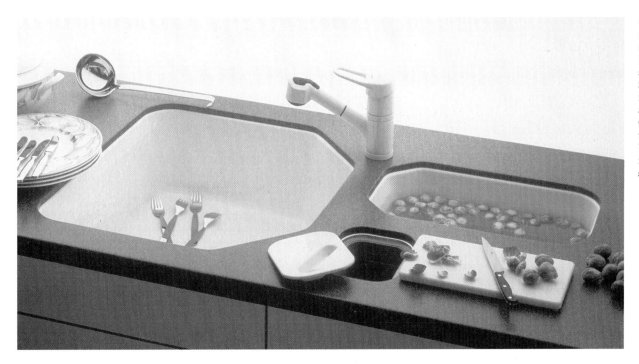

Composite is the newest material for sinks. Blanco's Blancotec composite sink is made of Silacron 2000, which is formed of quartz and acrylic resin. Quartz sinks such as this one take heat better than solid-surface sinks, but they scratch more easily.

$205. Plumber Peter Hemp generally likes solid-surface sinks, although he says the material is so thick around the drain hole that it's difficult to install standard basket strainers and garbage disposals. Unfortunately, bottoms of solid-surface sinks are thick so that they won't break if something heavy is dropped in them. Hemp suggests that manufacturers find some other material to reinforce the drain hole so that they can make it thinner at that point.

Repair of solid-surface material varies. Most manufacturers recommend you use abrasive compounds or pads to take out tiny nicks. Solid-surface sinks actually look better after a good scrubbing. Serious damage, such as burns or cracks, is much harder to repair.

Composite sinks can stand the matches but not the scratches—The newest innovation in sink materials is the composite sink, which generally is molded from acrylic resins and crushed minerals. These sinks stand up to heat a lot better than solid-surface sinks, but they scratch much more easily.

Quartzite, Cristalite, Asterite and Silacron 2000 (photo above) are examples of composite sinks. All are made from quartz bonded in an acrylic resin, which means the color goes through it. Because composite sinks are made with acrylic resins, they can be manufactured in a stunning array of colors. Asterite alone comes in more than 100 colors.

There are drawbacks, however. Composite sinks are expensive (prices range from a few hundred dollars on up). And although they're tough, they're not indestructible. Cameron Snyder says owners of composite sinks should take extra care not to scratch the material. He recommends that owners of composite sinks not use any sort of abrasive on them. Manufacturers recommend cleaning with baking soda, or water and vinegar.

In general, they're a little more finicky than solid-surface sinks. However, they are more durable than solid surface where heat is concerned.

Joe Carmody's only problem with both composite and solid-surface sinks is in securing self-rimming models to the countertop. They're fairly light, compared with cast iron, which is secured to the countertop with caulk. Because man-made materials are much lighter, they have to be clipped to the countertop.

Enamel-on-steel sinks are for the budget-conscious—When price is the only object, a porcelain steel or enamel-on-steel sink often is the first choice. These sinks look like cast iron, but they're much lighter and flimsier. They do suit some needs, though. Lou Hall has an enamel-on-steel sink in his mountain cabin, where it does just fine because it doesn't get a lot of use.

Hemp doesn't mind enamel-on-steel, either. "I think you can buy a good enamel-on-steel kitchen sink. If you're a real handy person and you can install the sink, I would almost rather put one of those in and after five years, when it started to look not so good, pop it out and put another one in there. The problem is if you have to hire a plumber to install it, it's not economical."

Enamel-on-steel sinks don't handle impact well. Also, they're thin and noisy, and they don't take garbage disposals well because the material flexes. But they are reasonably priced.

There are enamel-on-steel sinks on the market that seem to have overcome some of the traditional problems of the material. For instance, Americast, made by American Standard, is porcelain-coated, enamel-grade metal backed with a ⅜-in. thick layer of polyester-resin insulation (photo bottom left, p. 126). Jeannette Long of Americast says the material is half the weight of cast iron but about the same thickness.

"The backing material makes it more forgiving than cast iron, so it absorbs shock better than cast iron," according to Long. The backing makes it quieter to use and prevents flexing that can cause the enamel to pop off.

In general, enamel-on-steel seems to have all of the disadvantages of cast iron with none of the advantages. Its main selling point is price, which ranges from about $50 to about $185.

Accessories increase costs but also make life in the kitchen a little easier—The most recent innovation in kitchen sinks is the advent of custom accessories and varied bowl sizes. Unlike the old days when the only thing you could get with a new sink was a box, sinks today can feature soap dispensers, filtered-water dispensers, cutting boards, dish racks, drain boards, vegetable holders, chilled-water spigots, instant hot water, colanders, baskets, recycling chutes, containers—just about anything that could possibly be fixed to a sink. These gadgets sometimes add hundreds of dollars to the cost of a sink.

NKBA president Cameron Snyder says, "If you pay $400 for a good sink and $300 to $500 for a good faucet—with things like instant hot water and some of the other accessories—you could easily spend $1,200 to $1,500 on the sink and not be out of the ordinary."

Lou Hall says he finds that accessories are becoming an important part of the decision-making process in choosing kitchen sinks. "People tend to go to sinks that offer accessories. Part of the reason is that in a lot of tighter spaces, it allows us to use the sink as a functional part of the kitchen—as a workstation rather than just a cleanup station.

"People need the ability to buy accessories for the sink that makes it function really well," Hall says. "For instance, built-in colanders and strainers and drains and cutting boards that fit the sink exactly, sinks that have the strainers that are off-center, those are good." And unlike Peter Hemp, Hall likes sinks with off-center drains. "I like the units where the drains are way back in the corner. You can mount a disposal out of the way and have most of the sink available to you." □

Steve Culpepper is an associate editor at Fine Homebuilding. *Photos by John Kane except where noted.*

Venting the Kitchen

To expel kitchen moisture and grease efficiently, select an appropriate exhaust system and make the duct run short and straight

by Wendy Talarico

More heat requires more ventilation. Professional-style ranges generate more heat than residential cooktops, up to 15,000 Btus per burner. Larger hoods and more powerful exhaust fans are necessary to pull away heat and cooking effluent. Photo courtesy of Viking.

Concealed dual-purpose hood even offers storage space. The Hideaway system, a range hood mounted into a cabinet, activates the exhaust fan when the cabinet is tilted out over the range top. The hood is located inside the bottom of the cabinet. Photos courtesy of Broan.

My family once lived in a house in Buffalo, New York, that had no kitchen exhaust system. It wasn't much of a problem in summer. A stiff breeze off Lake Erie whisked cooking odors, heat and steam out the window. But in winter, when cooking made the house smell like a crowded apartment building, we cranked open foggy kitchen windows and let the arctic winds draw the odors—and the heat—outside.

If you've ever lived without kitchen ventilation, having it may seem like a luxury. Kitchen exhaust systems go a long way toward improving air quality throughout a house, however. They suck out odors and heat and get rid of the grease and moisture generated by cooking. They also remove noxious by-products of combustion from natural-gas ranges and some types of indoor grilling. Exhaust systems are invaluable in cooking accidents, too.

There are two types of kitchen ventilation: intermittent and continuous. Range hoods and downdraft ventilators—switched on as needed—are examples of intermittent systems. These types of units move a large amount of kitchen air relative to the second type of system, which is a continuously running whole-house exhaust fan, or multipoint system, sometimes referred to as background ventilation. (A multipoint system is not a heat-recovery ventilator, although multipoint HRVs are available.) A multipoint system typically has a kitchen intake and often contains a device that lets the user turn up its exhaust capabilities during cooking.

There's lively debate among indoor-air-quality specialists and manufacturers about the amount of ventilation needed in the kitchen and about the best-working systems. Some professionals prefer intermittent fans because of their location at the range, which is the origin of the problem. But because dishwashers, garbage cans, refrigerators, coffee makers and other appliances generate unpleasant smells, vapors and excess heat, some professionals favor continuous systems. A third group advocates both intermittent and continuous exhaust fans, especially for installation in tightly built homes.

Oddly enough, no state or national code that I know of requires a downdraft ventilator or an exhaust hood in the kitchen. Only two states, Washington and Minnesota, require mechanical ventilation in the house, although neither specifically references the kitchen. The American

Society of Heating, Refrigerating and Air-Conditioning Engineers' (ASHRAE) Standard 62, which provides ventilation guidelines referenced by state and local codes, says an operable kitchen window is plenty of ventilation. If there is no window, however, ASHRAE 62 offers minimal mechanical-exhaust guidelines.

This article focuses on range-hood and downdraft exhaust fans because these fans are the most common forms of kitchen ventilation. Before heading down to the local home center with your checkbook, however, it's first important to understand how these fans work, what their performance characteristics are and how to install them without diminishing performance.

Exhaust fans should match the amount and type of cooking—Air movement is rated in cubic feet per minute (cfm). Range hoods and downdraft systems move anywhere from 100 cfm to 1,800 cfm. The Home Ventilating Institute (HVI), a trade group that works with an independent laboratory to rate ventilation equipment, recommends a minimum of 40 cfm per linear foot of hood. For an average 30-in. wide hood (the same width as most stoves), that means at least 100 cfm. The National Kitchen and Bath Association (NKBA) says this number is skimpy. Its technical manual suggests a minimum of 50 cfm to 70 cfm per linear foot, or 200 cfm for a 30-in. hood.

Special equipment requires special ventilation. The NKBA recommends at least 600 cfm for an open grill or barbecue. Stronger ventilation is necessary for users of commercial ranges (top photo, facing page). Burners on these units generate upward of 15,000 Btu. (A standard household-range element rates only about 6,000 Btu.) The exhaust system must pull excess heat, combustion by-products and vapors out of the kitchen. Fortunately, companies that make professional-style exhaust hoods recognize that homeowners aren't always cooking enough to feed an army of guests, and most of them make their fans adjustable.

Systems that exhaust high volumes of air can create problems. They take a lot of electricity to run, and because they remove so much indoor air, they waste heating and cooling energy. In tightly built houses, exhaust systems, especially those in excess of 600 cfm, can cause backdrafting. This condition occurs when a house is depressurized and toxic combustion gases are sucked from the furnace or water-heater chimney into the living space. For that reason, it's important to think of the entire house as a system and to evaluate all exhaust appliances before settling on a ventilation system for the kitchen.

Size, quality and location of fan determine how noisy it will be—The noise a fan makes is measured in sones. To get an idea how loud 1 sone is, sit in a quiet kitchen and listen to the refrigerator hum. That's about the equivalent of a sone. Most fans generate between 3 sones and 8 sones, depending on how many cfm they're pulling and how well-built they are.

Manufacturers certified by the HVI sometimes provide sone and cfm ratings in their product lit-

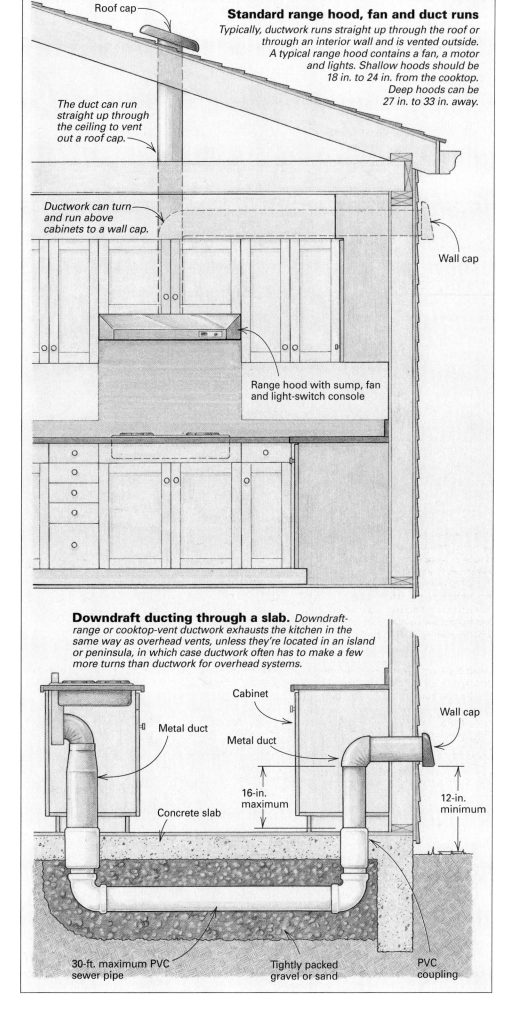

Standard range hood, fan and duct runs
Typically, ductwork runs straight up through the roof or through an interior wall and is vented outside. A typical range hood contains a fan, a motor and lights. Shallow hoods should be 18 in. to 24 in. from the cooktop. Deep hoods can be 27 in. to 33 in. away.

Roof cap

The duct can run straight up through the ceiling to vent out a roof cap.

Ductwork can turn and run above cabinets to a wall cap.

Wall cap

Range hood with sump, fan and light-switch console

Downdraft ducting through a slab. Downdraft-range or cooktop-vent ductwork exhausts the kitchen in the same way as overhead vents, unless they're located in an island or peninsula, in which case ductwork often has to make a few more turns than ductwork for overhead systems.

Cabinet

Metal duct

Metal duct

Wall cap

16-in. maximum

12-in. minimum

Concrete slab

30-ft. maximum PVC sewer pipe

Tightly packed gravel or sand

PVC coupling

The hood is in the shelf. This space-saving range hood is built into the shape of a shelf that holds a microwave oven. The fan and motor are located behind the microwave. Two openings reach well out over the range top to draw cooking vapors away from the kitchen.

Hood slides out to cover most of the range. Slide-out range hoods stay hidden beneath cabinet doors but slide out a foot and half.

erature. Otherwise, the information can be obtained from the company. The ratings can be misleading because the number of cfms varies from kitchen to kitchen, depending particularly on the length and size of the ductwork. The number of sones also varies at the point of installation. Remote systems, including exterior-mounted fans, remove the noise from inside the kitchen.

Measurements also don't take into account the high-pitched whir of air moving through a hood's filter, which to some may be more annoying than the noise of the fan. As a rule, the noisier the system, the less likely people are to use it.

The heart of the system is in the hood— Before examining the various configurations of range hoods and their effectiveness, let's eliminate recirculating hoods from consideration. These units are the least expensive and least effective of all range hoods. They require no ductwork because they merely pull cooking effluent through a filter and then blow the cleaned air back into the room.

The exterior, or shell, of the average hood is light-gauge steel of 20-plus ga., although high-end hoods are 18-ga. to 16-ga. steel. (The lower the gauge number, the stronger the steel). If you tip a hood upside down, you'll notice the shell forms a hollow area, the sump, where cooking by-products collect (top drawing p. 131). The deeper the sump, the more cooking effluent it collects. Sumps in professional hoods are deeper than most, as much as 24 in. Residential hoods are shallower, and slide-out units have sumps of only 1 in. or 2 in.

Under the hood you'll also see a mesh filter that prevents grease from invading the ductwork. Although most filters are flimsy and allow much of the grease to pass, better quality hoods incorporate sturdier, higher quality filters that do a better job and don't bend readily during handling. These filters also fit more tightly so they won't rattle, leak or whistle when the air is drawn through them.

Some range-hood manufacturers, including Vent-A-Hood Ltd. (for address see sidebar, facing page) and Viking Range Corporation (P. O. Drawer 956, Greenwood, Miss. 38930; 601-455-1200), shun the filter altogether because it makes the fan noisier and diminishes pulling power. In place of a filter, their hoods remove grease from the air using a patented process that cools the air by spinning it so grease condenses and sticks to the fan housing. The housing is detachable and washable. (Vent-A-Hood and Viking use filters on exterior-mounted hoods.) Depending on the amount of cooking that is done in a kitchen, the filter or housing should be cleaned at least twice a year.

The fan and motor are tucked behind the filter. Low-end models use propeller fans, but others use one or several squirrel-cage blowers. The latter are both quieter and more efficient. To achieve high cfm ratings, some hoods incorporate two, four or even six blowers, which are sometimes independently switched so a blower can correspond to a specific burner on the stove. Some companies mount the motor on a neoprene base that absorbs vibration. You can mount fans in crawlspaces or attics, on a roof or on an exterior wall, which means they draw air instead of pushing it through the ductwork. These remote-mounted units are more expensive because the fan and motor must be protected from the elements, and they require more power to pull air through the duct run. But for quietness, a remote system can't be beat.

Codes don't always require dampers, though most manufacturers include at least one at the duct connector to keep outside air from blowing into the house through the exhaust unit. A second damper, located at the wall cap or roof jack, is additional insurance against drafts.

Range hoods can blend in or stand out—
There are two approaches to range-hood aesthetics: Make the hood blend with surrounding appliances and cabinetry, or let the hood make its own statement. Judging by what manufacturers offer, most people prefer the first route, although some companies do a brisk business in custom hoods (sidebar right).

A lot of exhaust hoods hide behind other kitchen items, such as cabinetry or microwaves. Here are some examples:

• Pull-out hoods look like another set of cabinets until cooking time (bottom photos, p. 130). When the bottom is tipped out, the light and the blower turn on automatically. The hood is actually inset into the bottom half of the cabinet, and the top of the cabinet remains open for storage.

• Broan (926 W. State St., Hartford, Wis. 53027; 414-673-4340) makes a hood that doubles as a microwave shelf (top photo, facing page). The fan and motor are housed behind the microwave. Two openings beneath the shelf serve as ducts to move effluent into the system.

• Slide-out units, offered by KitchenAid (Sparks Administration Center, 701 Main St., St. Joseph, Mich. 49085; 616-923-4600) and other manufacturers, consist of a sliding panel that's pulled from beneath over-the-range cabinetry to expose the louvered opening (bottom photo, facing page). The fan and the motor are in a sheet-metal housing that's hidden behind the cabinet doors above. The panel slides out about 18 in. and covers most of the range top.

Downdraft systems offer discrete performance—Hoods tend to stick in your face while you cook. So about 30 years ago, manufacturers introduced downdraft ventilators (photos p. 134). These types of systems give the range top a smooth, streamlined look and open more space for cabinetry above the range. If ranges are installed in kitchen islands, downdraft ventilators also allow unobstructed views of and from the island. But their real advantage is they take the exhaust system—and its attendant noise—out of your face.

Downdrafts can be integral to the cooktop, in which case the intake usually sits in the center, or you can add downdrafts to the sides or the back of the range. Rear-mounted exhaust systems are normally flush with the range top but can rise mechanically to a height of 8 in. or 9 in. In some cases, that height is variable so if you're just simmering a short pot on a back burner, you can

Custom Range Hoods: High-End Kitchen Ventilation

Serious cooks, and serious aestheticians, want a serious range hood custom designed to suit their needs. They can get the range hoods that they want from an architectural sheet-metal shop—or from one of several companies that specialize in making custom hoods, including Abbaka (435 23rd St., San Francisco, Calif. 94107; 415-648-7210) and Vent-A-Hood (P. O. Box 830426, Richardson, Texas 75083-0426; 214-235-5201).

Abbaka, which also deals in imported range hoods, got into the custom-hood business about two years ago. Their one-of-a-kind designs, including one that looks like the Millennium Falcon from *Star Wars* and another, a giant cylinder, that looks like a *Star Trek* transporter tube (photo below), start at about $3,000 and climb steeply from there. Most of the company's design ideas come from clients or their architects. The sketches arrive crude and crumpled or fresh off a CAD system and may be interpreted in a variety of metals, ranging from 16-ga. mirror-polished stainless steel to pure copper. To date, the largest hood was 8 ft. across and pulled 2,200 cfm. Below were a range, a deep-fat fryer, a dedicated wok burner and a barbecue.

Vent-A-Hood also will make range hoods in custom size or shapes. Ed Gober, national sales manager for the company, said Vent-A-Hood can make a hood for any custom design.

Gayle Olsen, a kitchen designer with Ducci Kitchens in Torrington, Connecticut, said any good sheet-metal company should be able to fabricate a hood from a customer's design. The design and final product need to meet the local building code and be properly sized for filters and fan, she said.—*W. T.*

High-tech range hood reminiscent of *Star Trek*. Cylindra is a shining example of high-end custom range hoods.

raise the pop-up to just 2 in. or 3 in. A louvered intake protects the top or front of a downdraft ventilator. The fan pulls air down through a mesh filter into a plenum. The squirrel-cage blower (or blowers) and motor are set beneath the range. As with most hoods, there's usually a damper at the connection to the duct run. The duct itself runs beneath the floor or along the cabinet kick space and either up the wall or out at the foundation. You can mount downdraft fans outside the house for quietness.

To understand the differences in how hoods and downdraft units work, you have to remember that hot air, even when it's carrying moisture and grease, is lighter than cool air. It rises. Hoods capitalize on this basic principle. When the plume of cooking effluent rises, the hood holds it until the fan can evacuate it. Downdrafts have to work harder because they have to overcome the physical properties of hot air. Also, because they don't have a hood to hold the cooking by-products, downdrafts must rely on velocity, or higher cfm, to pull air down and out. Because of that reliance and because pop-up units require more moving parts and a motor that raises and lowers the unit, downdrafts are more expensive than comparable range hoods.

Performance depends on the proper sizing and placement of the ducts and hoods—The University of Minnesota's Cold Climate Building Research Center conducts some of the most thorough studies on the performance of various kitchen exhaust systems. Researchers tested the pulling power of exhaust units by using optically dense water-vapor fog and steam so they could photograph airflow and trace capture abilities of different fans.

Among other things, the study found that for a ventilation system to perform well, workers must install it correctly. Galvanized steel ducts should be at least as large as the manufacturer recommends, and runs should be as short and as straight as possible. Leaks, elbows and connectors also compromise performance. It's best not to use flexible duct because it creates back pressure and air turbulence. Also, grease is easily trapped in the spiral ribs.

Properly sized wall-mounted hoods are the most efficient (top photo, p. 130). Side baffles—sheets of metal or glass that extend down from the sides of the hood to the range and project at least 12 in. from the rear wall—help the fan perform even better because they further contain contaminants. These baffles aren't readily available through manufacturers. You can, however, make your own baffles if you're building a home for someone sensitive to gases and odors.

The hood should cover the entire cooking surface and extend 3 in. beyond both sides of the cooktop. According to the research, for instance, a range that's 30 in. wide should have a 36-in. wide hood. The depth of the hood's sump, or holding area, determines its distance from the cooking surface. Shallow hoods should be 18 in. to 24 in. from the surface of the cooktop. If they're any closer, they get in the way of cooking; if they're farther away, their capture ability is compromised. Deep hoods can be 27 in. to 33 in. from the range.

Different types of hoods, including slide-out and tilt-out varieties, generally are most effective when the homeowner does most of the cooking on back burners. Air intakes are at the rear, and the hoods aren't deep enough to cover the entire range. Unfortunately, homeowners are not likely to restrict their cooking to back burners.

Among downdraft ventilators, pop-up units at full height perform well when pulling pollutants from pots and pans, even tall ones, set on back burners. They also pull well from low pans set on front burners. Their capture rate for tall pots on front burners is poor, even with the fan on its highest setting. Flush units successfully remove effluent from pots and pans shorter than 3 in., but even the most powerful units capture little rising from pans more than 3 in. in height, such as woks or Dutch ovens.

Fans mounted on the exterior are less efficient on hoods and downdraft units because they draw air through ductwork and encounter resistance before they even begin to pull away cooking by-products. They also draw air from leaky areas along the run so that well-sealed joints are even more important.

The results of the studies, says Wanda Olson, an associate professor and housing-technology specialist at the University of Minnesota, indicate it's essential that builders work with homeowners to evaluate the amount of cooking they will do and the kind of kitchen equipment that will suit their needs. From that information, builders can determine what type of exhaust system will work best. "A downdraft isn't practical for a family that does a lot of cooking or one that uses lots of tall pots to cook pasta, just as a commercial hood isn't necessary for couples," she says.

Pop-up vent is there when you need it. Rear-mounted downdraft units hide inside the range top until you need them, then pop up at the press of a button. Their pop-up design gives them better capture abilities than the conventional, flush-mounted downdraft ventilators.

Homeowners should discuss these factors long before a house or renovation project is under way, she adds.

Correctly installed ductwork maximizes exhaust and minimizes problems

Ed Gober, national sales manager at Vent-A-Hood, tells a story about a $4,000 range hood his company designed for a $2 million house near Philadelphia. Gober later received a call from the homeowner, who said smoke was backing up into the kitchen. When he visited the site, Gober found the builder had run the ductwork under one beam and over another, reducing the duct from 8 in. to 6 in. in the process. So despite a powerful set of blowers, the exhaust air couldn't make it through the maze of ductwork and instead flowed back into the kitchen.

"The most important advice I can give the builder, the remodeler, the kitchen designer or the architect is to think ahead—during the design stage is best—about where the ducts will run," Gober says. That's particularly true when installing a high-cfm unit that requires extra-large ducts, dual ducts or a downdraft system that's routed through a slab (bottom drawing, p. 131).

In planning the ductwork, it's important to limit the run to 30 ft. or less in length and to minimize twists and turns. Elbows and transitions restrict airflow, which means that each elbow equals about 5 ft. to 10 ft. of duct run while transitions equal about 1 ft. to 5 ft. (sidebar right). You could, for instance, have two elbows and 15 ft. to 20 ft. of duct run without significantly affecting airflow. Anything longer would require advice from manufacturers, most of which maintain technical departments that can give you the help that you need.

It's good to follow manufacturers' recommendations in choosing the correctly sized ductwork. You can use a size 1 in. or 2 in. larger than what's recommended, but never smaller. Exhaust systems as large as about 600 cfm work fine with 3¼-in. by 10-in. or 7-in. round ducts. Higher cfms require larger ducts. Hoods with multiple blowers may require 6½-in. by 8-in. or 12-in. round ducts, or dual 8-in. round or 3¼-in. by 14-in. ducts. You should never downsize ductwork midrun.

Manufacturers recommend wrapping ducts that pass through unconditioned airspace with 1 in. of fiberglass insulation to prevent condensation. The NKBA recommends adding insulation along the 3 ft. of duct adjacent to an outlet because cool air is likely to seep in.

If you're replacing an old system, make certain the existing ductwork is vented to the outside and that the ducts are the correct size. Reseal the joints with tape or silicone sealant, and make sure you've insulated ductwork where necessary.

Use common sense in locating the end cap. If it's on the wall, make sure kitchen fumes aren't blowing over the deck or the patio or into a window (although codes require that caps be a certain distance from windows). If you're venting from the roof, pick a place where the end cap isn't noticeable from the street. ☐

Wendy Talarico is a senior editor with Home Mechanix.

Duct fittings impede airflow

Manufacturers recommend that duct runs be as short and as straight as possible and that the maximum length be kept to around 30 ft. or less. Turns, transitions and connectors create resistance and impede the flow of air through ductwork. The resistance of a duct fitting is measured in terms of equivalent length, so air flowing from a 6-in. duct through a 90° rectangular elbow encounters air resistance equal to about 4½ ft. of straight duct run. Shown below are the equivalent lengths of various standard duct fittings.

90° elbow=5 ft.

45° elbow=2.5 ft.

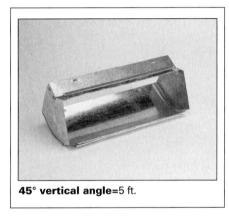

45° vertical angle=5 ft.

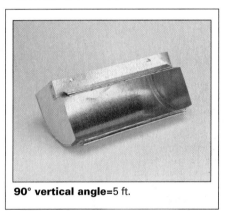

90° vertical angle=5 ft.

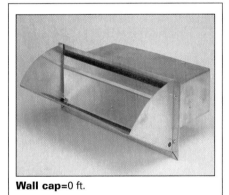

Wall cap=0 ft.

3¼-in. by 10 in. flat elbow=12 ft.

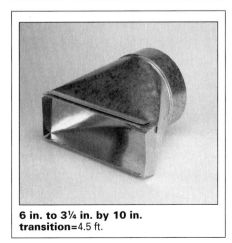

6 in. to 3¼ in. by 10 in. transition=4.5 ft.

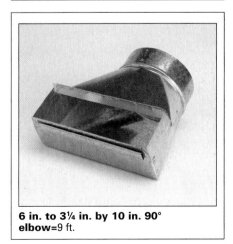

6 in. to 3¼ in. by 10 in. 90° elbow=9 ft.

Two Projects Customize a Kitchen

A spice shelf and a decorative steam-bent
dish rack improve the looks
and the utility of any kitchen

by Rex Alexander

Don't take this the wrong way, but odds are good that your kitchen could use a little spicing up. I'm not talking about anything major like a complete overhaul, or anything as minor as a new set of knobs and pulls. No, I'm thinking of something in the middle. Something that takes a moderate amount of work but that yields a clear improvement both in looks and in function.

As a custom cabinetmaker, I see a lot of kitchens, and most have become monotonous runs of cabinet doors and drawer fronts in order to squeeze out all available space. I grapple with such issues in almost every kitchen I design and build, so I came up with a couple of useful fixtures that would perform a task, add a little bit of dimension to the kitchen and be fun to look at

Photos this page: Tom Kachadurian

This shelf unit is as simple and useful as it looks. *The shelves and drawer divisions are doweled together, the drawers are dovetailed, and the whole works beautifully over a range or cooktop.*

Dowels

Shelves

Cut-out pulls

Dovetails

Drawers

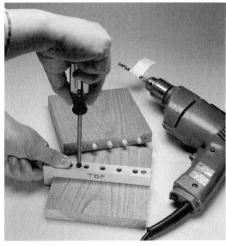

An easy jig aligns dowel holes perfectly. After screwing this simple jig to the end of the shelf and drilling the dowel holes, the author registers the jig to a mark on the side piece and drills again, producing the perfectly aligned dowel holes.

The joint I use to connect the shelves to the sides depends on where the shelf will be installed. For example, if the unit will sit alone, I dovetail the four corners of the carcase and dowel the shelves and vertical divisions for the drawers. If cabinetry will flank the unit, I simply drill holes with a countersink bit and screw it together with drywall screws. Should price be a factor and the sides be exposed, I drill, countersink, screw and then plug the holes.

Regardless of construction technique, building this shelf unit with spice drawers is a simple way to enliven a kitchen.

A simple doweling jig makes construction easy—If I'm going to dowel the sides, I first size the wood for the shelf unit and either handplane, scrape or sand each piece, depending on the species of wood I'm using. Next I make a doweling jig on the drill press. The jig for this unit is a piece of wood that's 6 in. long by $\frac{3}{4}$ in. square (the same size as the end of the shelf), with a $1\frac{1}{2}$-in. long piece of the same dimension screwed at a right angle to the end so that it can swivel. I space dowel holes in the long section of the jig every 1 in. and screw it to the workpiece through two countersunk holes (photo above).

To drill the dowel holes, I place the jig flush with the end of the shelf. After drilling the dowel holes into the shelf end grain, I unscrew the jig and swivel the end of it. I then set the jig against marks I've drawn on the side piece to show where the dowels will be drilled. I screw the jig to the piece, set my depth guide and drill. I use the same jig and the same procedure for the short drawer partitions. I use 2-in. long, $\frac{5}{16}$-in. dia. fluted dowels to attach the shelves.

If I want the shelf also to be able to hold plates or saucers, I chuck a core $\frac{1}{2}$-in. box bit in my router before gluing up and cut a plate groove in the shelving 1 in. from the back edge. Using a smaller-diameter dowel to

Thanks to downdraft range vents and whole-house ventilation systems, range hoods can be eliminated from a lot of kitchens. So to take advantage of that space wherever possible, I eliminate the range hood from my designs to give the kitchen a more open look.

In place of the range hood, I designed a shallow, open shelf unit to display plates or useful cooking items (top photo, facing page; drawing above). Somewhere within the unit I install small dovetailed drawers that not only show a high degree of craftsmanship but also hold spices, recipes, teas or anything else that needs to be convenient to the stove. The shelves are open and decorative, so I build them of solid wood.

I install this unit over 30-in. ranges, which means the width of the unit is 30 in. The height of the unit can vary, rising above or falling below the horizontal lines of the upper cabinetry, or blending with the cabinetry through the use of custom molding. Ordinarily, I use two shelves and make the four equally spaced spice drawers $3\frac{3}{4}$ in. high by $6\frac{9}{16}$ in. wide. I keep the maximum depth of the unit a shallow 6 in. so that the drawers and the shelving don't interfere with the operation of the cooktop.

Photo this page: Scott Phillips. Drawings: Bob La Pointe.

Kitchens 137

Cutting dovetails is finicky but not hard

Start sawing at an angle. Using an English backsaw, the author cuts down the pencil mark at an angle so that he can align the bevel and end-grain cuts.

A sharp chisel takes out the waste. The author registers the flat side of a sharp chisel against a wooden clamp perpendicular to the workpiece; waste wood is between dovetails.

Only a little at a time. After chiseling down into the waste, the author peels away the waste gradually, a few thin chips at a time before he begins cutting down again.

Trace the tails to mark the pins. The author carefully lines up the new dovetails with the end grain of the opposing workpiece and transfers the marks for the pins.

Tap the two pieces together. If they were cut with care, the dovetails and pins should wedge tightly together under mild pressure. Here, the author taps the drawer side in place using a smooth-faced hammer.

spread the glue, I next insert the dowels in the longer holes and glue and clamp up the shorter divisions for the spice drawers. I attach the drawer section and the rest of the shelving to one side and follow by gluing and clamping the other side.

The fun is in the dovetailing—I look for just the right piece of wood to use for the drawer fronts. When the drawers are in their proper positions, it's quite dramatic if the fronts are cut from one plank and the grain runs continuously from one to the next. After I select the wood for the sides and for the bottoms of the drawers, I surface the sides to ½ in. and the bottoms to ¼ in. Finally, I cut the dovetails for front and back.

Dovetailed drawers add a rich, handmade look to any kitchen, and creative layout of tails and pins can take the effect even further. For this shelf unit, I try to keep each drawer symmetrical, and as a rule, I never go over 12° for the angle of the tails. I've used a lot of different varieties of saws to cut dovetails, but the two that I now use exclusively are an English, 20-tooth-per-in. backsaw for hardwoods and a 21-tooth Japanese dovetail saw for softer woods.

To lay out the tails, I lightly mark the depth of the cut on each side of the piece using a cutting gauge. After establishing my 12° angle on a sliding bevel, I mark the angle of the tails and then square the marks across the

end grain. I clamp the piece in a bench vise and cut the tails to the mark (photo above left). After these cuts, I clamp a squared 2x block onto the piece flush with the depth mark at the bottom of the tails. It's important that the 2x has a piece of fine-grit, self-adhesive sandpaper covering the bottom to prevent slippage. Then I chisel halfway through between each tail (photo above center). To avoid tearout, I flip the piece over and repeat the process from the other side (photo above right).

After the tails are cut, I saw along the depth mark to the dovetails at each end, then pare it clean with a sharp chisel. That takes care of the waste at the ends and leaves a row of clean dovetails. Then I lay the freshly cut dovetails over the end grain of the piece that will yield the pins. I trace around the dovetails with a 5mm mechanical pencil (photo bottom left) to transfer the angles. Finally, it's a simple matter of aligning a square with the pencil marks to mark the sides of the pins.

Cutting and chopping out pins are done the same way as tails. I then take a sliver off the inside edge of each tail using a thin, sharp knife to ensure a smooth, tight fit. Finally, I tap the two pieces together (photo bottom right).

If a hole is to be cut out of the drawer front for a pull, now's the time. I've had luck cutting out this pull with a Forstner bit in the drill press and a ⅛-in. blade on a bandsaw. Before assembly, I cut rabbets in each drawer side to accept the ¼-in. bottom.

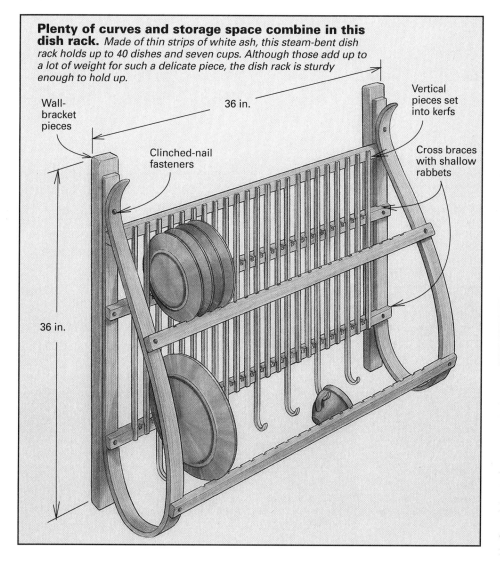

Plenty of curves and storage space combine in this dish rack. *Made of thin strips of white ash, this steam-bent dish rack holds up to 40 dishes and seven cups. Although those add up to a lot of weight for such a delicate piece, the dish rack is sturdy enough to hold up.*

Wall-bracket pieces

36 in.

Clinched-nail fasteners

36 in.

Vertical pieces set into kerfs

Cross braces with shallow rabbets

Soft as leather after 20 minutes of steaming. This strip of white ash bends easily after steaming, but it needs to be quickly shaped around the form before it loses its pliability.

One day as local craftsman Tim Joseph worked in his shop steam-bending white ash for the toboggans he makes, I approached him about designing and building a dish rack for me. A few days later, we sat down at his kitchen table, and he began doodling a rough sketch for a rack that would hold small and large plates and a row of cups (drawing above).

Toboggan building must have been at work on his imagination because the dish rack (bottom photo, p. 136) began to take on the shape of one of his small sleds. After a discussion of structural engineering and dimensions, I developed a scale drawing, and Tim built it. Tim has made only one more dish rack since then, but we're planning on building another for my own kitchen.

Choosing the right wood takes some thought—The weight of 40 dishes and seven cups can be substantial, so the choice of wood and the cut of the wood are important. For this design, the wood had to be steam-bent the same way Tim makes his toboggans. Oak, ash, birch and walnut all bend well. But Tim had already quartersawn and air-dried a log of white-ash pieces for his toboggans, so he had plenty of wood left for a dish rack.

Quartersawn or straight-grain cuts (wood that is cut perpendicular to the annual rings) is best for steam-bending. But even with quartersawn

wood, you have to inspect the pieces carefully because small wormholes, knots or other imperfections can cause cracks or breaks.

Air-dried wood is more elastic and bends more easily than kiln-dried wood, so it's a better bet for steam-bending. But if you have to use kiln-dried wood, soak the pieces in water several hours before steaming and bending.

Tim made a basic steam box for steaming the ash. To form the long, narrow box, he nailed four 1x4s together, closing off one end with a 3½-in. by 5-in. square piece of 1x. He also tacked a small piece across the other end, leaving just enough of an opening to slide in the wood. For steam, he puts a few quarts of water in a large pressure cooker and sets it on a small butane burner. A plastic hose connects the box to the pressure cooker. After he slides the ash into the box, he closes it off by wrapping a wet cloth around the open end.

Frames are bent around a form—Tim made several forms to shape the teardrop main frames and the cup hooks. The main frames were sized to hold the weight of a row of plates as large as 11 in. dia. and several smaller plates down to 6¾ in. dia.

Tim cut the form for the teardrop-shaped frames from a 2x12. He cut holes in the face of the form so that a clamp can gain purchase to hold the main frame while it dries on the form.

To prevent splintering of wood, Tim chamfers and lightly sands the edges of an ¹¹⁄₃₂-in. by 1⅝-in. by 7-ft. piece and then puts it into the steam box. Once the wood is pliable, usually after 10 minutes to 20 minutes of steaming, he removes it and very quickly bends (photo above) and clamps the

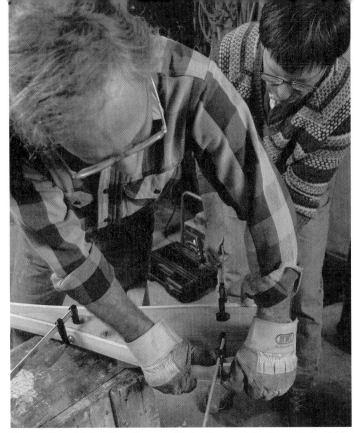

Clamp it quickly. Once the wood is bent around the form, it should be clamped in a hurry to avoid splitting the wood. The clamping is best done as a two-man job: One holds the workpiece and the other clamps.

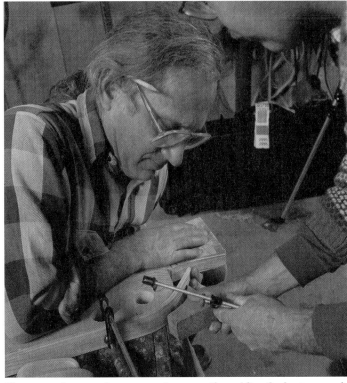

The second curve is a separate operation. After the large curve is clamped and dried, the other end is steamed and bent to create the slight reverse curve at the top of the main frame.

main frame around the form (photo above). After two or three hours, he removes the frame from the form and ties the ends together. Until the wood is completely dry, tying helps maintain the teardrop shape and frees the form for bending the other frame piece.

The top ends of the main frame also have a slight bend to them, and these ends have to be steam-bent. Tim has another form to create that slight curve at the end. He steams just the last 12 in. near the tip of the main-frame piece. Again, he quickly clamps the main frame to the form, fitting a smaller piece that follows the shape of the form over the end to reinforce the curve (photo top right). Because the bend is so sharp and because the piece is so small, the tip of the piece will spring back slightly once the clamp is removed.

The cup hooks are slender pieces—⅜ in. square by 27½ in. long—which makes it difficult to bend them without breaking them. So to prevent splits or breaks, Tim runs the end to be curved through a bandsaw to split the last 6 in., which then will be steamed, bent and later glued back together.

A pipe-and-steel form bends the cup hooks—Tim uses three different forms to shape the hook. First he screws a 2-in. stainless-steel strap to a piece of 1½-in. galvanized pipe (bottom photo) to make a sort of T-shape. The hooked end of the workpiece fits under the steel strap and is held between the screws that hold the strap to the piece of pipe.

So just before the slender hooked piece is pulled from the steam box, Tim mounts the galvanized pipe in a bench vise and heats both pipe and strap with a propane torch to slow the release of heat from the workpiece. He pulls the pliable piece from the steam box and, wearing heavy gloves, quickly slips the piece under the steel strap and through the two screws that hold the strap to the pipe.

Then Tim bends the end of the piece around the pipe and tightens the bench vise to hold it in place. Once the piece is bent, he cuts a C-shape out

This clamp shapes the cup hooks. After steaming, the slender cup hook is bent around a 1½-in. galvanized pipe and held in place by a 2-in. stainless-steel strap that's screwed to the pipe. The pipe and the strap are heated ahead of time with a torch so that the workpiece won't lose its heat too quickly.

of a piece of 1x and inserts the hooked piece into it. The C-shape works like a clamp to hold the hook tightly until it dries.

Later, when the hook is dry, Tim makes a form that fits the inside of the hook. He waxes both forms to prevent sticking, then glues the sawn ends of the hook back together and clamps the piece into place (top photo). Once the glue is cured, he removes the piece, and scrapes and sands it to get a smooth finish. For an added touch, he carves the tip to a dull point.

Preparing the other parts—Twenty-one other vertical parts are needed, including fourteen ⅜-in. by ⅜-in. by 22-in. vertical dividers and seven ⅜-in. by ⅜-in. by 27½-in. cup hooks that will hold the plates.

Also, three cross braces—¾ in. by 1 in. by 35⅛ in.—fit across the back of the main frame. And two cross braces—⅞ in. by 1¼ in. by 35⅛ in.—fit across the front of the main frame. These front pieces are kerfed every 1⅛ in. with a ¼-in. dado blade. Tim cuts these pieces using a radial arm saw. The kerf follows the shape of the dado blade, making a natural, rounded resting place for the plates (bottom photo).

Using a sharp chisel, Tim lightly chamfers all of the openings, then lightly sands. This work allows the plates to nestle, and it keeps the edges free from chipping.

The three rear cross braces have the same ¼-in. kerf and chamfer as the front braces. Also, all three will need dadoed slots ³⁄₃₂ in. by ⅜ in., spaced every 1 in. to house vertical dividers and occasional cup-hook pieces. All five cross braces now will have rabbets cut into each end ⅛ in. deep and 1⅝ in. across so that they fit neatly over the main frames.

The two remaining parts of the dish rack are ⅞-in. by 2⅝-in. by 35-in. strips that create a flat surface for attaching the frame to the wall. All of the parts of the dish rack need to be scraped and lightly sanded before they are assembled.

Assembling and finishing the dish rack—After laying the assembled pieces on a flat surface, we dry-fit all of the parts. Using the different-size plates that will perch in the rack, Tim and I establish the location of the front and rear cross braces.

When we built the first dish rack, we both felt that a clinched nail with a decorative head would hold the front cross braces to the frame better than screws and would add to the visual appeal of the rack. We used nails from the Tremont Nail Company (800-842-0560), which makes some interesting and traditional cut nails using old patterns. Tim ended up using an 8d clinch nail with a rose head after first drilling a hole slightly smaller than the nail through the cross brace and main frame.

After applying glue to the cross brace, Tim nails through the predrilled hole, takes a pair of pliers and hooks the end of the nail. This hook will act as an added fastener once the nail is clinched. He then sets the piece on a hard surface and clinches the nail with a hammer.

Tim spring-clamps the main frame to the wall-bracket pieces and predrills a hole for a nail through both frame members and wall brackets close to the tip. He squirts a little glue between the frame members and nails and clinches together the main frames at the top of the wall bracket.

Laying the assembled frame flat on a bench, he spot-glues the slender cup hooks and other verticals to their dadoed homes. After the glue cures, Tim removes any exposed glue with a chisel or scraper and lightly sands any rough surface.

Using a rag, Tim applies three thinned coats of polyurethane. Then he lightly sands with 400-grit wet/dry sandpaper between coats. After I install the dish rack, I put a thin coat of beeswax over the surface and rub it off for a dull sheen. ☐

Rex Alexander is a custom woodworker who specializes in cabinets and staircases. He lives in Brethren, Michigan. Photos by Steve Culpepper except where noted.

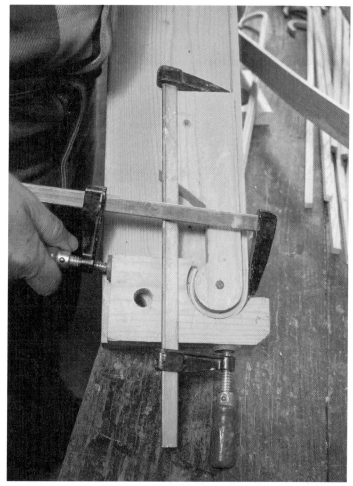

The sawn hooks have to be glued. To bend the tight curve in the cup hooks, a 6-in. long bandsaw kerf was made in the end of each piece. The jig shown above was used to glue the kerfed ends back together.

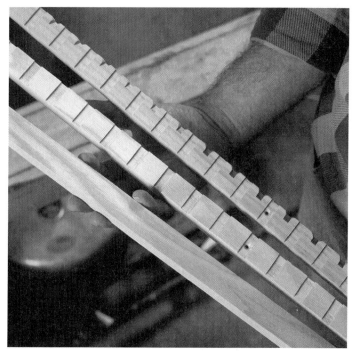

Finally, the cross braces are sized and kerfed. Shown here are the three stages of the cross braces used on the dish rack. These pieces will go on the back of the rack. The dadoed slots between the curved kerfs hold the vertical dividers and the cup hooks.

INDEX

The articles in this book originally appeared in *Fine Homebuilding* magazine. The title, date of first publication, issue number, and page numbers for each article are given below.